The Financial Times

Guide to Strategy

The Financial Times Guide to Strategy

HOW TO CREATE AND DELIVER A WINNING STRATEGY

Third edition

Richard Koch

London · New York · San Francisco · Toronto · Sydney
Tokyo · Singapore · Hong Kong · Cape Town · Madrid
Paris · Milan · Munich · Amsterdam

PEARSON EDUCATION LIMITED

Edinburgh Gate
Harlow CM20 2JE
Tel: +44 (0)1279 623623
Fax: +44 (0)1279 431059

Website: www.pearsoned.co.uk

First published 1995
Second edition 2000
Third edition published in Great Britain in 2006

ISBN-13: 978-0-273-70877-3
ISBN-10: 0-273-70877-5

British Library Cataloguing in Publication Data
A CIP catalogue record of this book can be obtained from the British Library.

Library of Congress Cataloging in Publication Data
A catalog record for this book is available from the Library of Congress.

10 9 8 7 6 5 4 3 2 1
10 09 08 07 06

Typeset in Plantin 10pt/14pt by 30
Printed and bound in Great Britain by Bell & Bain Ltd., Glasgow

The Publisher's policy is to use paper manufactured from sustainable forests.

About the author

Richard Koch is the author of 18 acclaimed books, including the best-selling 80/20 trilogy – *The 80/20 Principle* (over 700,000 copies sold), *The 80/20 Individual*, and most recently *Living the 80/20 Way*.

As well as lecturing and broadcasting, he is an extremely successful entrepreneur and investor. His ventures have included Filofax, Belgo, Plymouth Gin, Capstone, and currently Betfair, the world's largest betting exchange.

Formerly Richard Koch was a consultant with the Boston Consulting Group, a partner of Bain & Company, and a founder of LEK Consulting. He was educated at the University of Pennsylvania and at Oxford University.

He is now an outside director of several companies, including listed venture capital houses in Luxembourg and the UK.

He has homes in London, Cape Town and the south of Spain.

Other books authored or co-authored by Richard Koch

Wake Up and Shake Up Your Company (Pitman, 1993)
The Successful Boss's First 100 Days (Pitman, 1994, 1998)
The Investor's Guide to Selecting Shares that Perform (FT Prentice Hall, 1994, 1997, 2000)
The Financial Times Guide to Management and Finance (FT/Pitman, 1994)
The A–Z of Management and Finance (FT/Pitman, 1995)
Managing without Management (Nicholas Brealey, 1996)
Breakup! (Capstone, 1997)
The 80/20 Principle (Nicholas Brealey, 1997, 1998)
The Third Revolution (Capstone, 1998)
Moses on Leadership (Capstone, 1999)
Smart Things to Know about Strategy (Capstone, 1999)
The Power Laws of Business (Nicholas Brealey, 2000)
The 80/20 Individual (Nicholas Brealey, 2002, 2003)
Smart Things to Know About Leadership (Capstone, 2002)
Living the 80/20 Way (Nicholas Brealey, 2005)
The Breakthrough Principle of 16X (Pritchett, 2006)
Suicide of the West (Continuum, 2006)
Simply Strategy (FT Prentice Hall, 2006)

Contents

Part 2

Part 3

Part 4

Part 5

Foreword to the third edition

I'm delighted that this very simple guide to one of the most important forces in the universe – the strategy of *individual* businesses, the creation of new wealth from raw materials that nobody else thought to use that way before – has made it to a third edition. And I'm even more pleased that the strategy area is alive and well, with more exciting new thinking in the past five or ten years than in the previous twenty – far more than I ever expected, with no signs of drying up.

What is different?

Since the last edition in 2000, I've dramatically changed my view of *Corporate Strategy* – that is, the strategy for whole companies, over and above the strategy in existing business units. To be frank, I used to regard Corporate Strategy as largely a snare and a delusion, something that the head office bosses played around with to justify their existence, and which reliably did much more harm than good. So, whereas I was really excited when writing Part One of this book on *Business Unit* Strategy, I was at best ambivalent about the virtues of *Corporate* Strategy. Perhaps it is no surprise that friends and critics alike told me that Part One of the book (Business Unit Strategy) was very much better than Part Two (Corporate Strategy).

But now I have seen the light. I have torn up my previous work on Corporate Strategy and written a completely new Part Two. Largely because of the work of two giants of strategic thinking, Andrew Campbell and Peter Johnson, I now realise that it is companies rather than markets that are mainly responsible for creating new products and services and for supplying them in unexpected, cheaper, better and fresh ways. It is individual genius but also human collaboration that makes it possible to boldly go where no person and no market has gone before. And the job of crafting companies so that they can create new space and can supply customers in that space with something that no other company can do, or do so well is what continually swells the wealth of the world. It is also the job of Corporate Strategy. I find this exhilarating.

What I have also realised is that Corporate Strategy is not just the province of fat and happy behemoths, the bloated and over-complex mega-corporations that have long been my pet hate. Corporate Strategy is also the province of entrepreneurs and managers in any firm, small, medium or large, newly founded or venerable, complex or simple, single-business or multi-divisional, local or global. Business Unit Strategy explains what happens in particular business positions, and is generally confined to the position at one time or over a relatively short period of time. To make any substantial progress in business requires innovation and the creation of new market segments – what I now call *ecosystems*, because they involve the satisfaction of human needs by other human beings and the organisation of a separate and distinctive way of doing so. Creating white space in business and delivering a new product or service in that space is sometimes the work of a loose network of individuals, but more than 99 per cent of the time it is the product of inspiration and co-operation within a firm. In short, it is Corporate Strategy.

I have also realised that economists have exaggerated the importance of markets and almost wholly neglected the work of diverse companies, in short, the work of human agency. Do not misunderstand. I love markets and in the large majority of cases I am in favour of the freest possible markets. But markets cannot of themselves supply new products, different services, or dramatically better or cheaper products. Only people can do that. Only companies can do that. Only Corporate Strategy can do that. And companies can only do that when and because they are quite different from other companies. So Corporate Strategy is all about diversity, differentiation, surprises, peculiarity, change, creativity, and the fascinating, very difficult and very rewarding process of crafting a multi-human organism – to which we give the dry, desiccated and offputting name of *firm*, *company* or *corporation* – that is uniquely able to deliver better and better things that people want. If that isn't a fun subject, I don't know what is. Vital for human progress too.

To make it even more fun, the darkness hasn't gone away. Most Corporate Strategy is bungled. This is not because the people doing the bungling are stupid or malevolent – far from it. It is largely because the tools of strategy have only recently explained why the odds favour bungling, and because most people – even those in charge of the bungling – haven't yet caught up with the state of the art theory. Meanwhile, there is all sorts of money to be made – by understanding the sources of bungling, by identifying bungling before other people do, and, if you absolutely have to, by doing something other than bungling, something even vaguely sensible in the area of Corporate Strategy, which is still pretty rare. Making money is fun too. So Corporate Strategy should be even more fun than online poker. It's even more fun and it tells you how to make money reliably, which only a very few poker players can do. Somehow I can't see Corporate Strategy replacing poker as the hottest new leisure pursuit, but there you are. If everyone were keen on Corporate Strategy, it would be much harder to make money at it.

I hope you will be as thrilled as I am by the new thinking. I also draw together extremely practical advice on when and how to enter new markets – and, just as important, when not to. For the right thing for large and mature companies may be – and usually is – to find growth in sales, profits and cash in the base business.

Beyond specific advice on the trappy art of devising successful Corporate Strategy, I've tried to grope my way towards a new 'ecological' theory of Corporate Strategy. In this view, markets are where people meet – customers, people from firms, and other interested parties such as intermediaries, suppliers and technologists. The market is usually created in the first place by innovation on the part of firms. But firms can only innovate successfully if they have a unique formula, based on the insight, knowledge, skills and ability to collaborate of their people, and also based on the firm's residual character, flowing from its history, the oddities of its founders, and the impact that competitors and the struggle for survival have had on the firm. In the 'ecological' view, each new marketplace has its own 'ecology', its own rules for survival and thriving, derived from the tangle of messy interactions between all the people involved, and above all from the actions of people in firms, customers and competitors. Each firm has its unique 'genetic code' which will be more or less suited to each 'ecosystem' (unique marketplace) than the genetic code of other firms. In this view, the art of Corporate Strategy is deciding where to deploy the genetic code of the firm and how to adapt that code to match existing ecosystems and to create new ones, as far as possible, in its own image.

What else is new in this edition? I'm tempted to say, what more do you want? The exciting new Part Two on Corporate Strategy is about 80 per cent of the change. The rest is updating throughout and especially new thinkers and concepts in Parts Three and Four.

A guide to this guide

One friendly reviewer has said that in previous editions of this book 'the whole is less than the sum of the parts' because it is not clear how the parts relate to one another or what the reader should think about each part. I accept the criticism. Let me try to put it right.

The core of the book is the short Introduction, Part One on Business Unit Strategy, and Part Two on Corporate Strategy. These probably comprise 80–90 per cent of the value of the book for most readers, and for this edition I did consider just stopping at the end of Part Two. What this means is that even the most dedicated strategist can at least take a breather having reached the end of Part Two, and consider his or her work very largely done. If you are interested in just one of the two subjects, read that part first. But I recommend you at least skim through the other part, because there is almost no duplication between the parts and some of Part One is relevant to Corporate Strategy and some of Part Two will give you a deeper context and perspective from which to contrive Business Unit Strategy.

What, then, is the point of Parts Three, Four and Five, and how do they relate to the first two 'core' parts? First, these parts are 'optional'. You can get an excellent idea of strategy and how to devise a strategy without reading them. Why then have I included them again? Mainly because they are, I hope, easy to dip into and read when you have a spare moment or want to consult a particular topic, and because in their different ways they reinforce and perhaps deepen the understanding you'll have gained from the first two parts.

Part Three is a series of short essays about Strategic Thinkers, the people from whom I think strategists have the most to learn. Nearly all of the insights from the thinkers are already present – if I have done my job properly – in the earlier parts of the book, but seeing the points emphasised in the words and thought patterns of the thinkers should drive home particular ideas. This section is also for students and others who want a quick introduction to a guru, to see whether or not they're likely to be worth reading properly, and – why not be honest? – for crib purposes. Life is too short to do without some cribs.

Part Four serves identical purposes, but from a different slant. Here I look at strategic concepts, tools and techniques. The essays here give a quick summary of the buzzwords and methods used in strategy formulation. Usually also I give my own gloss on the value or otherwise of the ideas, and when they are most useful. Cross-referencing to names and terms discussed in Parts Three and Four is indicated by the use of SMALL CAPITALS.

Part Five is different. Writing in 2000, I attempted to sketch some differences in strategy that were likely as a result of the Internet and theories of networks and increasing returns. As I write five or so years later, I believe that nothing in this section invalidates anything earlier in the book. I also think that the changes described in Part Five are perhaps not quite as important – or pervasive – as I thought before. The changes described relate to competition not in all businesses, but in certain types of businesses – not just information technology-sensitive businesses, but also ones where vertical integration is widespread and where integrated firms may be sitting ducks. Perhaps 20–30 per cent of all business activity currently falls into these areas, and although this percentage may rise, that will probably be quite a slow and inconclusive process.

Having made those points, I think the essay in Part Five stands the test of time well, and is just as true now – in those industries and competitive systems where it is true – as it ever was. I hope you enjoy reading the piece and that it makes you think. But it almost certainly won't change your view derived from the rest of the book.

Richard Koch
Cape Town
January 2006

Acknowledgements

I would like to thank everyone whom I thanked before in the first and second editions of the book. I trust they all have a copy of it and so I don't need to bore other readers here with a long list of names. But if you were one of those people, I'm just as grateful now as ever!

I'd like to thank particularly two people who have changed my view of strategy, especially Corporate Strategy, over the past few years. One is Andrew Campbell, founder and director of the Ashridge Strategic Management Centre in London, who features quite large in this book, and quite rightly so. I regard Andrew as the best corporate strategist in the world. Certainly the most honest and uncompromising!

Most of you have probably heard of Andrew, but perhaps few of you have heard of my second view-changer, Dr Peter Johnson of Exeter College, Oxford. Peter has been substantially responsible for my moving from the '*positioning*' view of strategy to what I call the '*ecological*' view. I explain what I mean by this in Part Two, but I'll just say here that it's just a bit like a religious or at least ideological conversion. I still believe that market position is terribly important, but I now think that people – and the way they relate to one another – are even more vital to success. A weak market opportunity with a great team trumps a great market opportunity with a weak team. Thank you, Peter, for taking the scales from my eyes. Peter is not yet well known to the broader public interested in business strategy, but the strength of his ideas means that he soon will be.

Introduction

CHAPTER 1

The use and abuse of strategy

Strategy can be valuable both at the Business Unit level, and at the Corporate Level, that of the whole firm

Business Unit Strategy

The most neglected use of strategy insights is for managers who are running clearly defined businesses. If you are one of them, strategy can:

- help you define the different parts of your business, where you need to do different things to be successful
- show in detail where you make the most profits and cash, and why
- understand the customers' perspective and why they buy from you or from competitors
- indicate where you should concentrate most effort and cash
- work out the extent of likely profit improvement opportunity, from changing product/customer mix, prices and/or cutting costs
- help you to understand why you have been successful or unsuccessful in particular areas and initiatives
- show up any missing skills
- identify businesses or product lines which should be discontinued or sold
- show which customers should be cultivated most and how to build their loyalty.

Corporate Strategy

Corporate Strategy, the strategy for the entire firm, is about guiding the evolution of a firm, about how it grows and develops over time. Firms are social groupings that collaborate internally in order to create and satisfy customers. Each firm has its own unique character – what in Part Two I call its GENETIC CODE – that will determine how successful or unsuccessful it will be in each of its markets. Successful firms are well adapted to their most important markets. To continue being successful, they must remain better adapted to those markets than any competitor.

Part Two presents an 'ecological' account of Corporate Strategy. Some animals can only cope with one very specific environment, and live on one particular type of food. Other animals can thrive in several environments and eat lots of different food. Corporations are similar. Some can only work effectively in one market (ECOSYSTEM). Others have capabilities that can stretch across many ecosystems. The art of Corporate Strategy is to operate only in ecosystems for which the corporation is well adapted, but to operate in many such ecosystems. Corporate Strategy adds the greatest value when a firm either creates a new ecosystem, to which it is well adapted, or when the firm changes its character so that it can flourish in an attractive ecosystem where it has not previously operated. Such mutations, however, are fraught with danger. Aggressive growth strategies usually end in tears. Part Two describes how to beat the odds.

Who should develop strategy?

It is no use one set of people drawing up a plan, making recommendations and monitoring their implementation by another set of people. The world does not work like that.

A new strategy has to be adapted to real-life relationships between people (employees, customers, suppliers and so forth), gradually introduced and crafted and re-crafted as circumstances change and the validity of the underlying assumptions is tested, proved or disproved. This is only likely to work if those pursuing the new strategy not only understand and believe in it, but also have the authority and confidence to develop and/or dump parts of it as commercial life evolves. The sad fact is that strategy development is rarely done by the right people. This book is an attempt to put that right.

Business Unit Strategy should be developed by operating managers in each Strategic Business Unit (SBU). Corporate Strategy should be developed by the chairman, chief executive, and a few close colleagues, but should be influenced, checked and approved by a cross-section of the best business unit managers.

The second-best solution, which often does work, is for the firm to have a long term relationship with a strategy consultancy. The firm's consultants develop a new strategy and are actively involved in its implementation, gradually fading out (sometimes, very gradually) as the operating managers feel more and more comfortable with their control of the strategy and ability to adapt it.

This method is very expensive, but can be justified by the consultants because the profit benefits are normally a high multiple of their fees (typically the annual profit increases are 5–20 times the total fee). What the consultants do not say is that all of these benefits, and more, could often be obtained if the operating managers were able to develop the strategy themselves. Almost everyone assumes this is impossible. They are wrong.

CHAPTER 2

A brief history of strategy

The study of strategy and the development of the micro-economic intellectual foundations of strategic thinking can be traced back at least to Alfred CHANDLER (b. 1918), who was active and influential from the late 1950s. His 1962 book, *Strategy and Structure*, said that corporations should develop their strategy before deciding their structure. He defined strategy as the setting of long-term goals and objectives, the determination of courses of action, and the allocation of resources to achieve the objectives. Arguably, the roots of strategy go back much further, for example to Alfred SLOAN's reorganisation of General Motors in 1921 (though this was documented only in *My Years With General Motors*, not published until 1963).

A case can also be made that Peter DRUCKER set the strategy ball rolling much earlier. His 1946 book, *Concepts of the Corporation*, looked at General Motors, as well as General Electric, IBM and Sears Roebuck, and concluded that the most successful companies were centralised and good at goal-setting. Drucker was also the first to see that the purpose of a business was external, that is, in creating and satisfying customer needs.

Whether strategy began in 1921, 1946 or later, it definitely grew to powerful adolescence in the 1960s. The first half of the decade saw a new focus on strategy in academic quarters. In 1960 Theodore LEVITT published 'Marketing Myopia' in the *Harvard Business Review*, one of the first attempts to look at Corporate Strategy from a radical and broad perspective; the article has since sold more than half a million reprinted copies. In 1965 came the Bible of strategic planning, H. Igor ANSOFF'S monumental

Corporate Strategy, a thoughtful and incredibly detailed blueprint for planning a firm's objectives, expansion plan, product-market positions and resource allocation.

But perhaps the most important development in the history of strategy was the founding in 1964 of the Boston Consulting Group (BCG) by Bruce HENDERSON. Starting with 'one room, one person, one desk, and no secretary', by the end of the decade Henderson had built a powerful machine combining intellectual innovation and boardroom consulting, and had invented both the EXPERIENCE CURVE and the GROWTH/SHARE MATRIX, probably the two most powerful tools in the history of strategy. More generally, BCG blended market analysis and research together with financial theory to produce the micro-economic analysis of competitors and their relative costs that is the bedrock of all subsequent strategy. BCG's period of maximum intellectual creativity and invention can be traced fairly precisely to the years 1967–1973.

In terms of invention, then, the 'golden years' of strategy were approximately 1960–1973.

Further intellectual development has continued since. In terms of books, the most important in the 1970s were *The Nature of Managerial Work* (1973) by Henry MINTZBERG, and *Strategic Management* (1979) by H. Igor ANSOFF. The 1980s saw the emergence of two other writers who have influenced and deepened our view of Strategy: Michael PORTER and Kenichi OHMAE. Porter, a Harvard academic, shot to prominence as a result of his very important 1980 book, *Competitive Advantage: Techniques for Analysing Industries and Competitors*. Porter argued that the profitability of corporations was determined not only by a firm's relative competitive position (as Henderson had proved), but also by the structural characteristics of the firm's industry, which could be described in clear, micro-economic terms.

Ohmae, a cosmopolitan Japanese, described quite brilliantly how Japanese companies had benefited by using strategy (though largely without strategy consultants or Western academics). His 1982 book, *The Mind of the Strategist: The Art of Japanese Business*, is compulsive reading, and still one of the best explanations available of how strategy is most effective when it combines analysis, intuition and willpower in the pursuit of global dominance.

Over the past decade or so, important new contributions to strategic thinking have been made by Gary HAMEL and C. K. PRAHALAD, by John

KAY, and by a trio of writers from the Ashridge Strategic Management Centre – Andrew CAMPBELL, Michael GOOLD and Marcus ALEXANDER.

In 1989, Gary Hamel of London Business School and C.K. Prahalad wrote a ground-breaking article entitled 'Strategic Intent'. They argued that successful companies had ambitions out of all proportion to their positions and had a commitment to change the rules of the game. The following year, Prahalad and Hamel argued in another article, 'The Core Competence of the Corporation', that the real key to strategy was a firm's distinctive skills, technologies and assets, and its collective learning ability. Professor Kay and others have elaborated this 'resource-based' view of strategy.

The area of Corporate Strategy received a fresh approach with the publication in 1994 of *Corporate-Level Strategy* by Goold, Campbell and Alexander, which argued that the corporate Centre should be seen as a 'parent' and develop 'parenting skills' to help its operating companies, and that unless the Centre comprised the best possible parent for each business, they should be divested.

The best estimate is that the number of strategy consultants employed by the leading, recognised strategy consulting firms grew by an astonishing 15–20 per cent per annum compound between 1965 and 1991, and at a remarkably consistent rate. The strategy consulting industry stopped growing between 1991 and 1993, but has since resumed steady expansion.

It would have been impossible to sustain this growth, which has few parallels in other professional services, without delivering great value. If the customers are right, the value of strategy has increased, is increasing, and shows no sign of diminishing.

CHAPTER 3

Swings in strategic thinking: six phases

The *first* focus, at the end of the 1950s and in the 1960s, was on the best way to plan the development of large, multi-product firms. This was the province of *classic strategic planning* at the Centre, although the dominant prescription was to decentralise into largely autonomous divisions, and to diversify by making acquisitions in attractive but often unrelated businesses.

The *second* and most fruitful period, roughly from 1965 to 1975, was that dominated by BCG and its concept of *portfolio management*. BCG's micro-economic approach was highly prescriptive, telling firms to:

- focus on business positions where the firm had, or could realistically obtain, market leadership
- divest other businesses
- focus on cash rather than profit
- aim for cost advantage over competitors (i.e. have lower costs than them)
- manage competitors so they would withdraw from the firm's key profit segments
- use debt aggressively to finance growth, reinforce market leadership and raise returns for stockholders
- avoid over-extending the product line or building in too much complexity or overhead
- use excess cash flow to diversify and apply the precepts of portfolio management to a new set of businesses.

BCG's ideas encouraged two already established and related trends: towards building up large central planning departments in conglomerates and towards further diversification. Neither of these was central to BCG's view of the world, yet both came back to haunt strategists later.

The *third* phase, the mid to late 1970s, was one of intellectual exhaustion, corporate disillusion, and a retreat into pragmatism on the part of the strategists. By now it was clear that the micro-economic techniques for analysing competitive advantage were very powerful. They were increasingly used, however, not at the level of central, Corporate Strategy, but for developing *Business Unit Strategy*. This was partly because the earlier promise of central portfolio management became increasingly discredited. After the oil price shock of 1973 and the stock market crash of 1974, which hit go-go conglomerates particularly hard, the virtues of both central planning and conglomerate diversification became seriously tarnished. Furthermore, firms like GE and Siemens that had established huge central strategic planning departments soon found the results from these bureaucratic behemoths profoundly disappointing. Intellectually, the GROWTH/SHARE MATRIX, the icon of portfolio management, came under sustained attack. The assault was largely misconceived, but BCG chose discretion rather than valour. The BCG MATRIX went largely undefended and became unfairly neglected.

The *fourth* strand in strategic thinking, stretching from 1973 to the present, was a mild dose of heresy, a wave of reaction to the excessively analytical orientation of the Boston school. It involved a realisation that firms generally did not derive their strategies scientifically and rigorously, and a celebration of the intuitive, adaptive and creative aspects of strategy.

In 1973, Henry MINTZBERG challenged accepted thinking about *The Nature of Managerial Work*, pointing out that successful chief executives were intuitive action men, not reflective planners, that they cherished soft information and anecdotes rather than hard facts and figures, and that they read and wrote little, preferring face-to-face communication and decision-making. Mintzberg has since developed the idea of 'crafting strategy' using the creative, right-hand side of the brain, rather than the logical left side.

The 1980s also brought to prominence Kenichi OHMAE's celebration of successful Japanese strategists: intuitive, creative leaders of Honda, Toyota, Matsushita and other firms, who were totally obsessed with establishing market leadership, beating competitors, and satisfying customers. The period from 1980 to 1994 has further consolidated the ranks of the *soft strategists*, influential writers like Charles HANDY, Rosabeth Moss KANTER, Tom PETERS, Richard SCHONBERGER and Robert WATERMAN.

The 1980s also saw the *fifth* development: the strengthening of the rigorous micro-economics school of strategy, with the emergence of the Michael PORTER phenomenon. Porter extended the BCG framework of competitive advantage to include structural industry factors like the threat from new entrants, the bargaining power of customers and suppliers, and the threat from substitutes. His message, though based on additional data and analyses, was similar to that of BCG from the start: the firm should try to find markets and niches where it could dominate and erect barriers against competition, either by low cost or by product/service differentiation. Porter also built on early work by economists and strategy consultants and developed a theory of national competitive advantage to overlay or underpin the micro-economic analysis of individual firms' competitive advantage.

The *sixth* trend has been a new focus on a firm's skills and capabilities (generally called its 'CORE COMPETENCIES'), its ambitions and commitment ('STRATEGIC INTENT'), its ability to learn, its sense of MISSION or VISION, and on the role of the Centre as the 'PARENT' of its operating businesses. Corporate Strategy is therefore seen less as overseeing the allocation of resources, and more as the definition, creation, stimulation and reinforcement of ambitious skills and capabilities that can then be applied across several market segments. The most important writers here include Gary HAMEL and C.K. PRAHALAD, John KAY, and the Ashridge trio Marcus ALEXANDER, Andrew CAMPBELL and Michael GOOLD, all of whom are profiled in Part Three.

These trends represent more a progressive enriching of strategic insight than a set of contradictions. At the level of the strategy consultant there have been other influences, notably the renewed integration of strategic analysis and focus with cost reduction (especially in BUSINESS PROCESS RE-ENGINEERING); the application of competitive data-gathering and analysis in order to value acquisition candidates; the emphasis on quality and responsiveness to customers; the importance of TIME-BASED COMPETITION, that is, getting the product to the customer as quickly as possible; a renewed focus on limiting the product-line, on outsourcing and on the part of the VALUE CHAIN where the firm can have an advantage, in order to reduce the COSTS OF COMPLEXITY; and a new emphasis on organisation structure as determining the ability of an organisation to get close to the customer and respond appropriately.

At the same time, however, the work of strategists at the start of the twenty-first century is recognisably the same as that of their counterparts 50 years ago. The key is establishing difference from competitors and having skills and positions that no competitor can match or approach, by specialising in areas where you have a better technology, product or service, or a lower cost position. Today, in many business, it may be more important to have a dominant technology or standard, and to be central to unlocking value for customers, than it is to have a cost advantage based purely on scale and market share. Yet the basic idea is the same as it ever was: to establish and maintain a dominant position based on specialisation and the ability to create value, in the area of focus, to a much higher degree than anyone else. The primitive concepts developed by BCG in the late 1960s are as relevant as ever.

CHAPTER 4

Towards a synthesis

Originality in strategic thinking is of much less importance than synthesising what is already available, being clear about where it is most useful and about the trade-offs between different approaches, and putting the heart of strategy back where it belongs, in the messy entrails of business unit reality.

My charter for making strategy more useful stresses the following five points:

1 *Business success requires a differentiated strategy.* You must be different to competitors, and able to do things that they cannot do, or can't do as well. This requires selectivity, and also careful attention not just to the positions you have in any market, but also the skills that underpin success.

2 *Operating managers are the people to craft, execute, re-craft and re-execute strategy for their business unit.* It is the most interesting part of any line executive's job, and it must not be filched by anybody else.

3 *In companies that have more than one important business, the role of executives at the Centre is extremely challenging.* On the one hand, devising and directing the Corporate Strategy – for the whole company, not for one business – is the most creative and important task in the whole of business. On the other hand, there are inbuilt reasons, as we'll see in Part Two, why most intelligent and well-meaning executives at the Centre do far more harm than good than good to their firms. They do too much. They do the wrong things. They tend to be far too optimistic. So there is a paradox. Corporate Strategy is enormously important.

Lasting value cannot be build by markets alone. It can only be built by building the character and abilities of a firm, by innovation in the creation of new products and markets, and by matching a firm's 'genetic code' to that of its customers and the operations necessary to serve them best. Yet, just as good Corporate Strategy can create fantastic value and make the world a richer place in all senses, so too bad Corporate Strategy can quickly destroy value that has taken generations to build. And, in large and complex firms, bad Corporate Strategy is much more common than good Corporate Strategy.

4 *You should be pragmatic about the amount of effort required in formulating strategy.* Be willing to gather insight and improve decision-making, without trying to prove beyond any reasonable doubt that any particular strategy is correct. This method of 'progressive approximation' is discussed below.

5 *Strategy should not be over-planned.* Ideally, it should emerge as part of an iterative process of thought, hypothesis, experimentation, success, and renewed experimentation. The process should combine analysis and intuition, and should be open-ended. There should never be a 'final solution'; the strategy should always evolve, and continually deepen.

CHAPTER 5

Progressive approximation in developing strategy

A great deal of time can be wasted on trying to get precise and definite answers to strategic issues. Very often the worst result is not the waste of time, but exhaustion or impatience on the part of the participants, leading them to throw out strategic thinking as being too academic, wearisome or anti-action. The answer to this syndrome is *Progressive Approximation.*

The basic point is that you should come up with your best initial answer very quickly, and then decide whether it is worth the time and effort to improve on it by data-gathering and analysis. This is actually the way nearly all managers and others generally behave as they go about their daily lives, and I see no reason why strategy development should be an exception.

The procedure is:

- State as clearly and crisply as you can the questions you want to answer: the Critical Issues. The idea is that if you knew the answers to the Critical Issues you would know exactly what to do. Do this on one sheet of paper: you should have no more than seven Critical Issues (ideally between four and six).
- Then construct, on another clean, single sheet of paper or screen page, your Hypotheses on the Critical Issues. Your hypothesis on each Critical Issue is your best guess at what the answer might be. At this stage it matters not a hoot whether you are right or wrong; the key thing is to imagine the shape of a possible answer, so that you can then reframe the hypothesis later in the light of new information or insight.

- Now list on a third sheet the information you would ideally like to help you resolve each Critical Issue. When you have finished, take another page and compile two columns, labelled Most Important Data on the left and Easiest-to-Find Data on the right, and rank the information you want under both headings. Decide as a first cut which bits of information you would think about acquiring: in other words, some combination of the most important and most accessible. Italicise the data you aim to collect in this first round.
- Decide who among your fellow managers to involve in the strategy development process. This should include anyone who will be important in actually carrying out the new strategy. Then ask each of them to go through the steps above.
- You and your colleagues should then meet or use e-mail to compare notes and come up with a consensus three pages of Critical Issues, Hypotheses and Data. Decide how the data are to be acquired, who is to do this, and when you will all meet again to review the results.
- Review the new data, and see whether it is pretty clear what the new strategy should be. If you are still in serious doubt, or there is lack of consensus, agree what the most important points still at issue are, and decide what data should be gathered in the second round to help settle the issue. Then decide who will collect the data and when you will review the results collectively.
- Continue the process until you are agreed either on the answer, or there is a consensus that the answer is likely to be X, and that the cost and delay involved in further investigation is not merited, so that everyone agrees that X should be pursued.

This process of progressive approximation will give you a quicker, cheaper and probably better answer than conventional methods, but the key benefit is that the new strategy will be implemented more quickly and effectively. On some complex and important issues you may still need to use consultants, but do it under the control of the working managers and do not allow them to usurp the process. The operating managers must remain in charge, and must do the main thinking.

It is now time to start – with a strategy for your own business.

PART 1

Business Unit Strategy

A do-it-yourself guide

CHAPTER 1

Overview

Business Unit Strategy is the process of developing strategy for a single, largely self-contained business. The business unit could be a whole firm in a small or medium-sized company (or even in a large firm focused on a single line of business), or a separate, largely autonomous part of a larger firm, comprising a profit centre that has its own set of external customers and competitors (often called an 'SBU', Strategic Business Unit).

This Part will take you through a step-by-step guide to developing strategy for your Business Unit. It assumes you have a real-life business for which you wish to develop or validate strategy. If you don't, it will be easier and more rewarding for you to think of a business you know fairly well – perhaps that of a friend or relative or one you have worked in – and imagine that you are developing its strategy.

The first thing to appreciate is that developing a strategy is not difficult. It is only made to seem difficult by the strategy 'professionals': academics, corporate planners and consultants. Anyone with a reasonable degree of intelligence and knowledge about business can develop a strategy. The first barrier to overcome is the sense of intimidation or fear of stepping over the threshold.

The second barrier is the jargon. The language of strategy is often peculiar. As with most fields of study, the jargon is actually quite useful as a form of shorthand once you have mastered it. I try to explain exactly what I mean by any unfamiliar term, but if you run into difficulties, refer to the A–Z definitions in Part Four. A bit of patience and perseverance should soon make the meaning clear.

Apart from this overview, a short conclusion, and an additional note on theory, there are nine sections in this Part, each taking a particular question or topic that will together make up the total picture of Business Unit Strategy. Each section explains the basic idea before providing displays and checklists illustrating the points. Wherever possible you should try to reproduce similar displays for your own business. Do not worry initially if you feel you don't have the information to sketch out your own display: just take your best guess, and then see what insight would follow if your guess were right.

Later you may want to go back and collect whatever data are necessary to compile a more correct display. It is very important, however, to get the total picture of Business Unit Strategy by imagining what it could be in the round. If you stop every time you don't have the answer to a question you will never complete the exercise and will lose interest. If you carry on and see the power of the total process, you will want to go back and make sure your assumptions were probably correct. So the rule is: first time round, if you don't know the answer, *guess*!

To illustrate the voyage of strategy development and discovery I will use the example of one particular American company, which I shall call the United Tea Corporation (UTC). This is a real-life case history but disguised to protect the guilty. We will show how strategy development changed the views of UTC's top executives and see whether its CEO, Randy Mayhew, manages to hang on to his job.

I have nine questions to ask both you (as you think about your firm) and Randy. The first question looks easier than it is. It is also the beginning of wisdom and the foundation of all later strategy.

United Tea Corporation: can strategy save Randy?

Randy called me up one warm and sunny November day and asked me to visit UTC's Pasadena head office. UTC is one of America's largest suppliers of branded tea, mainly in tagged bags, and part of a large conglomerate in branded goods generally.

When I arrived, Randy, an old friend, came straight to the point. 'I can't figure out what's wrong,' he told me. 'We keep growing our sales but our profits hardly go up at all and our ROI [Return on Investment] keeps slipping. We've missed our budgets in the last two quarters and if I can't explain to Chicago [the conglomerate's head office] what's wrong and how I'm gonna fix it, I'm history.'

Randy explained that he was a hands-on manager who'd never had much time for 'all that strategy stuff', but he wanted me to sit down with him (why do Americans always use that expression?) over a weekend and work out what was going wrong, and whether it could be fixed. As Randy had done me a favour in the past, I agreed to see if I could help.

CHAPTER 2

What businesses are you in?

Within your total Business Unit, there are almost certainly a lot of different businesses, or BUSINESS SEGMENTS: far more than you realise. The first step is to define what these different Business Segments (or 'segments' for short) are.

Let me explain why this is important. One of the most glorious insights about life, the Universe and everything, is the EIGHTY/TWENTY (80/20) RULE. This states that 80 per cent of the value of any activity is likely to come from 20 per cent of the inputs. Thus, 80 per cent of the value you generate in your work, or come to that, in your home life, is likely to come from the most useful 20 per cent of your time. Similarly, 80 per cent of the profits of a firm are likely to come from 20 per cent of its products. Eighty per cent of the value in a book is likely to come from 20 per cent of its pages (this does not stop publishers churning out long books, because we consumers just won't believe that a short book is worth as much as a longer one!). And so on. Most people could add much more value to the world, and be happier, if they worked out what their most productive 20 per cent of activities were, doubled the amount of time spent on these, and cut out most of the rest.

The 80/20 Rule applies to business, but before you can use it, you need to know (a) what Business Segments you are in (the subject of this section) and (b) what the true profitability of each is (covered by the following section).

What do I mean by a Business Segment? Intuitively, this is anything that comprises a separate product, service or activity; or anything going to one group of customers as opposed to another group; or anything where the main competitor you face is different; or anything that may have different profitability.

Let me illustrate this with some extreme examples. For a publisher, each book published is a separate segment, since its profitability depends on how many copies it sells, and that is largely independent of how many copies of other books are sold (this would not be true, for example, if a well-known writer like Dick Francis or Jeffrey Archer *always* sold a given, large and predictable number of books, or if a publisher's cookery books *always* had the same sales, no matter who the author: in this case the segment would be all Dick Francis or Jeffrey Archer books, or all cookery books).

Another example is provided by a country's postal service. Since Rowland Hill's penny post, most postal authorities charge the same for delivering a letter, whether it goes to the next street or hundreds of miles away. But for the French post office, the letters delivered in Paris comprise a much more profitable segment than the letters going to a remote Pyrenean village near the Spanish border.

Similarly, different customers for the same product are very often different segments. A manufacturer of baked beans will get much less for them from the largest supermarket chains than from smaller chains or independent grocers. A branded tea supplier like Typhoo makes far more profit from Typhoo brand tea than from tea going to a retailer to be sold under his own brand.

Any supplier of services to different customers knows that some of them are no trouble, taking the standard product or service with no arguments about price or what is provided, while others haggle, quibble and are difficult to extract payment from. These customers (the easy ones and the difficult ones) constitute different segments.

Different segments can also arise if some customers require a basic product (or COMMODITY) to be adapted to their own requirements (a 'Special' product). This could simply be the requirement to deliver a product to the customer (rather than him or her collecting it themselves), or further stages of working on a product to adapt it to the customer's needs, or just an up-market version of the standard product. A higher price will usually be paid for a special product, but the extra price can be significantly more or significantly less than the extra cost (it is usually more), so the special product can be a different segment, with higher (or, usually, lower) profitability.

Different segments may be defined by any of the following:

1 different products or services

2 different customers receiving the same product or service

3 different regions receiving the same product, where the cost to serve the different geographical areas is different

4 different versions or variants of the same product, distinguished by the degree of value added, quality or personal service involved.

Although it is important to identify your separate segments, you should not go overboard on this and come up with a list that is so long as to be unmanageable. Also, potential separate segments may not be actually separate, if it turns out that their characteristics (especially profitability) are so similar to those of other activities that there is no point in singling them out.

Now is the time for you to think about your business and its segments. *Exercise 1* is for you to take a new page, type (or write!) *Potential Business Segments* at the top, and make a list of possible segments defined by the differences in (1) to (4) above. Depending on how big and complex your business is, you should have a list of between approximately five and 50 potential segments.

Exercise 2 involves turning this guesswork into a more objective *Definition of Business Segments.* I have compiled two tests that can be used for any of your Potential Business Segments, to see whether they are really separate or not. You need to set up the test by taking two possible segments, that could be separate segments, or that could alternatively just be one bigger segment. For example, let us assume that you are a butcher who has two shops, one in Madrid and the other in Barcelona. You want to know whether you should think of them as separate Business Segments.

The two tests are alternatives: *Test A* is a short, quick-and-dirty test, that will probably give you the right answer. *Test B* is longer and more certain to be correct.

Test A asks two simple questions:

1 Are your competitors in the two Potential Business Segments different or the same? *If the answer to this question is 'different', then they are probably separate segments, and you do not need to answer Question 2 below.*

2 If the answer to Question 1 is 'the same', do the competitors (including yourself) have roughly similar market share positions in the two Potential

Business Segments? In other words, if Competitor A is the leader in one potential segment, followed by B, followed by C, is this the same ranking in the other potential segment? *If so, the two areas are probably one single segment; if not, they are probably separate segments.*

To go back to our Spanish butcher, let us assume that the butchers in Madrid are different competitors from those in Barcelona; in that case he should think of the two shops as different segments (but if both shops were next door to the same hypermarket chain, they would probably be the same segment).

Or to take another example, a furniture manufacturer in Transylvania has two main product lines: sofas and sofa-beds. His main competitor is Dracula Sofas, which also makes sofa-beds. Question 1 produces the answer 'the same', since both firms make sofas and sofa-beds. But in the answer to Question 2, we discover the market shares shown in Illustration 1.1.

ILLUSTRATION 1.1 ◆ Transylvanian sofa and sofa-bed market shares

	Sofas	Sofa-beds
Our firm's market share	30%	50%
Dracula Sofas' market share	60%	10%
Our firm's relative market share	0.5×	5×

Our firm has only half the market share and sales in sofas that Dracula Sofas has, but has five times the market share of Dracula in sofa-beds, which is clearly our specialty and not theirs. We need to introduce our first piece of jargon here, which is the *Relative Market Share*, usually written as *RMS*. The Relative Market Share is simply your firm's market share divided by the market share of your largest competitor. If you are larger than anyone else in a product, your Relative Market Share will be more than 1.0 (written as 1.0×, or 1×); if you are smaller it will be less than 1, as in the example above in sofas where our firm is half the size of Dracula; this is written as 0.5×.

We conclude, therefore, that the relative market share positions in sofas are different from those in sofa-beds, and we should therefore treat them as separate segments. Our firm specialises in sofa-beds, and Dracula specialises in sofas. There must be good reasons for this difference, which are likely to result in different profitability. The chances are that our firm will be much more profitable in sofa-beds than in sofas, and more profitable than Dracula in sofa-beds. Conversely, Dracula is likely to make more money out of sofas than sofa-beds, and to have a higher return on sales in sofas than we do, but a lower return on sales in sofa-beds than us.

Why should it matter whether the competitive positions are the same? The reason is that if they are the same, it says that the way customers vote, and the ability of the two competitors to produce one product rather than another, is not much different in the two areas. The chances are, therefore, that Competitor A will have similar levels of profitability in each area, and that the same will be true for Competitor B (Competitor A is likely to be either more profitable, or less profitable, than Competitor B in both areas). But if one competitor is a specialist in one area, and has a higher market share in that area, there is likely to be something in consumers' preferences, or the firm's own ability to produce efficiently in one area, that means it is likely to be more profitable for him in one segment than in another.

Even if the profitability of two segments is not differential, the fact that a firm is relatively stronger in market share terms in one area than another indicates that this could be the basis of profitable specialisation.

Test B, to see whether segments are separate, takes longer than *Test A* but is even more reliable (though it usually comes up with the same result). We start with the same question – we have two product lines or potential segments, and we want to know whether they are part of the same segment, or comprise two different segments. Illustration 1.2 gives the tests for what some irreverent junior consultants of mine once called the Segmentation Mincer.

ILLUSTRATION 1.2 ◆ The Segmentation Mincer

		Column A Score	Column B Score
1 Are the competitors in the two products or areas the same?			
Yes: Column A	No: Column B	–30	+30
2 Are the Relative Market Shares (RMS) of our firm and the leading competitors roughly the same in the two products or areas?			
RMS similar: Column A	RMS different: Column B	–50	+50

3 Are the customers the same in the two products or areas? Yes: Column A	No: Column B	–20	+20
4 Are the customers' main purchase criteria and their order of importance roughly the same in the two products or areas? Yes: Column A	No: Column B	–30	+30
5 Are the two products substitutes for each other? Yes: Column A	No: Column B	–10	+10
6 Are the prices of the two products (for equivalent quality) or in the two areas roughly the same? Yes: Column A	No: Column B	–20	+20
7 Is our firm's profitability roughly the same in the two products or areas? Yes: Column A	No: Column B	–40	+40
8 Do the two products or areas have approximately the same need for capital per dollar of sales, i.e. similar capital intensity? Yes: Column A	No: Column B	–10	+10
9 Are the cost structures in the two products or areas similar (that is, roughly the same proportion of cost in raw materials, in manufacturing, in marketing and selling, and so on)? Yes: Column A	No: Column B	–10	+10
10 Do the products or areas share at least half of their costs, that is, the use of common labour, machines, premises and management resources for at least half of their total costs? Yes: Column A	No: Column B	–30	+30
11 Are there logistical, practical or technological barriers between the two products or areas that only some competitors can surmount? No: Column A	Yes: Column B	–20	+20
12 Is it possible to gain an economical advantage by specialising in one of the products/areas by gaining lower costs or higher prices in that product/area as a result of focusing on it? No: Column A	Yes: Column B	–30	+30

You now add the scores together to produce the result. If the result is a positive number, you should treat the two products or areas as separate business segments, and devise strategy for each of them separately. If the result is negative, they are currently the same business segment and should be lumped together, at least initially, in developing their strategy. The further away from zero the answer is, whether positive or negative, the more certain the result.

Let us take the Segmentation Mincer and apply it to our friend, the Spanish butcher. Remember that he has two butcher's shops, one in Madrid and one in Barcelona, and he is trying to find out whether he is in two businesses, two competitive systems if you like, or just one (see Illustration 1.3).

ILLUSTRATION 1.3 ◆ The Spanish butcher uses the Mincer

		Answer	Score
1	Are the competitors in Madrid and Barcelona the same?	No	+30
2	Are the Relative Market Shares of the competitors the same in Madrid and Barcelona?	No	+50
3	Are the customers the same?	No	+20
4	Are the customers' purchase criteria roughly the same?	Yes	–30
5	Are the two shops substitutes for each other (i.e. would a customer sometimes shop in Barcelona and sometimes in Madrid)?	No	+10
6	Are the prices for the same products roughly the same?	Yes	–20
7	Is the butcher's profitability in the two locations similar?	Yes	–40
8	Do the two shops have the same capital intensity (need for capital per peseta of sales)?	Yes	–10
9	Are the cost structures similar?	Yes	–10
10	Do the two locations share at least half their costs?	No	+30
11	Are there barriers between competitors participating in both areas?	Yes	+20
12	Can you gain an economic advantage by just competing in one area?	Yes	+30
Total score			**+80**

The result is +80, indicating that the two shops are different business segments and that the butcher should therefore develop a strategy for each shop, as well as a strategy for the business overall.

Now it's time to return to Pasadena, California, and see how Randy Mayhew and I are dealing with our first strategy question: defining United Tea Corporation's business segments.

Randy defines UTC's business segments

As you've probably gathered, Randy is a no-nonsense guy. When I told him we were going to define his business segments, he sighed. 'That's typical consultantese. Let me tell you a few simple facts about my business.'

'We have three businesses, or maybe four. Our biggest business by far, with over $700m of sales, is the Mainstream Tea business under the "5 Unicorns" brand. You know, we buy tea from plantations around the world, we put it into tea-bags, we put tags on the ends of the bags, we box them up with pretty packaging and we sell them to the grocery trade, especially to the big supermarkets.

'You can split this business into two if you want. The US business stinks. We have nearly $600m of sales revenue, but we make almost nothing out of it. We used to make a fair return, nothing great, but now the supermarket chains have tightened up on us and squeezed our nuts. Fortunately, the export business keeps us alive: we make $8.5m pre-tax out of revenues of between just $115m and $120m, something like that.

'Then we have two smaller businesses, but growing fast. One is Herb Tea. That's just $65m in revenues, but we make even more at the bottom line out of that than the Mainstream Tea exports. Finally there's the latest craze, Fruit Tea, and we make $3m profit out of just under $30m revenue. We bought these two businesses a couple of years ago and they're still separate. If I hadn't a done those two deals, I'd have been on welfare by now.'

Knowing that businessmen often misquote numbers, I asked to see last year's management accounts. But in this case, they proved that Randy was right (see Illustration 1.4).

ILLUSTRATION 1.4 ◆ UTC's previous profit report

Organisational unit	Sales $m	Profit ($000)	ROS% (Return on Sales)
Mainstream Tea US	589.6	233	0.0
Mainstream Tea Exports	117.2	8,510	7.3
Herb Tea Corporation	66.5	8,870	13.3
Fruit Tea Corporation	27.9	3,249	11.6
Total	**801.2**	**20,862**	**2.6**

'It's difficult to make money out of tea in America. We've put all our development effort into growing our export sales and profits. The exports deliver, but our advances here are overturned by the slide in domestic margins. Herb and fruit teas are very profitable and growing, and we have been successful in growing exports, which must also be the most profitable bit of the business.'

Randy was convinced that he had just four business segments, as shown in the accounts above. But I was not sure.

'Let's start with the Mainstream domestic [US] business,' I probed. 'Are there any chunks of the business where you face different competition, or have higher or lower margins, than the rest?'

'Nah, not really. Not unless you count the private label stuff we do for two of the supermarkets. It's true we're up against specialist players there, you know, commodity firms with no brands and no marketing overheads. Our biggest headache there is a guy we call Cheapco, 'cos he always undercuts us for the Big Boy Supermarket contract, or so Big Boy tells us.'

'Doesn't that make the private label business less profitable than the branded business?' Randy had to pause before answering. 'Well, maybe. But the branded business is no great shakes anyway. We're dealing with the supermarkets in both cases, and they're real SOBs.'

Despite Randy's reservations, I was convinced that Private Label business was a separate segment, because the main competitor was different. To cut a long story short, I then pressed my advantage, and discovered that there was another Private Label contract, for Small Fry Retailers, a contract that Cheapco did not try to win, because it was too small. The main competitor here was another commodity player, and I marked the Small Fry business down as another potential segment.

I was also unhappy at the way Randy lumped all the exports for the Mainstream Tea business together. Didn't he face different competitors in Canada, in Europe and in the Rest of the World [ROW]? 'Half right,' he conceded. 'In Europe and ROW the main competitor is the same as here, United Foods, but in Canada it's a local outfit, Canadian Tea.' I wrote down 'Canada' as a separate segment, but was not yet willing to give up on having Europe and the Rest of the World as separate too. 'How big are you relative to United,' I asked, 'here, in Europe, and in the Rest of the World?' 'Well, we're the biggest at home, but much smaller than they are in Europe. Hell, United Foods is based in Switzerland. In ROW, though, we're several times their size, which is stronger even than in America; they're probably about three quarters our size here in Branded Tea, though they don't do Private Label.'

I then asked similar questions about competitors in Herb Tea and Fruit Tea. I established that in both markets there were different foreign competitors, though one firm (Auntie Dot's) was the main competitor in the export markets for both Herb and Fruit teas.

While Randy visited the men's room, I wrote down my idea of UTC's segments on a paper napkin. Instead of his three or four segments, I thought there were at least ten:

1. Branded (5 Unicorns) Tea: US
2. Branded (5 Unicorns) Tea: Canada
3. Branded (5 Unicorns) Tea: Europe
4. Branded (5 Unicorns) Tea: ROW
5. Big Boy Supermarkets Private Label
6. Small Fry Retailers Private Label
7. Herb Tea: US
8. Herb Tea: Exports
9. Fruit Tea: US
10. Fruit Tea: Exports

When he came back, Randy rapidly agreed that we could take these ten segments, and got down to the serious business of ordering lunch.

You probably already have the idea, but in case you are in any doubt let's give one more example (skip this if you are confident you know how to 'mince'). Two firms, whom we shall call Heinz and Imperial Foods, are manufacturers of sauces. They both make tomato ketchup (catsup) and thick brown sauce. One of the firms wishes to know whether they are separate business segments for strategy purposes. At first sight it appears obvious that they are the same segment, because the main competitors are the same and because there is very high cost sharing between the two types of sauce: they are made in the same factories, using the same machines, by the same workforce; they are marketed to the same consumers and sold to the same customers (the supermarkets and other grocers) by the same salesforce. Nevertheless, it is useful to put these two potential segments through the mincer (Illustration 1.5).

ILLUSTRATION 1.5 ◆ Heinz versus Imperial Foods

Is tomato ketchup the same segment as thick brown sauce?

Test		Answer	Score
1	Are the competitors the same in the two sauces?	Yes	–30
2	Are the Relative Market Shares of the competitors roughly the same in the two sauces?	No	+50
3	Are the customers the same?	Yes	–20
4	Are the customers' purchase criteria roughly the same?	Yes	–30
5	Are the two sauces substitutes for each other?	No	+10
6	Are the prices for the two products roughly the same between the two competitors, with no brand premium?	No	+20
7	Is Imperial Foods' (or Heinz's) profitability in the two sauces similar?	No	+40
8	Do the two products have similar capital intensity?	Yes	–10
9	Are the cost structures similar?	Yes	–10
10	Do the two sauces share at least half their costs?	Yes	–30
11	Are there barriers stopping one firm or the other from competing as effectively in one sauce as in the other?	Yes	+20
12	Can you gain an economic advantage by competing in just one sauce?	Yes	+30
Total score			**+40**

The result is +40, indicating that, contrary to first impressions, the two sauces are separate business segments.

We need to explain why the questions were answered as they were. Heinz is the market leader in tomato ketchup, several times larger than the nearest competitor. But in thick brown sauces (under several brands, including Daddies), Imperial Foods is the market leader, where it is several times larger than anyone else. There is no particularly good reason for this difference, except (and it is a big 'except') that consumers are attached to the brands, Heinz in tomato ketchup and Daddies in brown sauce. The consumers obstinately and persistently vote massive majorities for the two brands in each of their areas. This has the result that Heinz commands a high brand price premium in tomato ketchup, and Daddies enjoys the same higher price in brown sauce because of the strength of the brand. Consequently, Heinz is very profitable in tomato ketchup (but not in brown sauce), whereas Imperial Foods is very profitable in brown sauce and not in tomato ketchup. Each area therefore deserves a separate strategy, with separate pricing and differential degrees of brand support. It would be wrong for either firm to treat both products as part of one sauce business and have the same strategy in each area.

The Segmentation Mincer does not always say businesses are separate segments! If red sauce is a separate segment, what about red cars? Clearly no-one can command a price premium or have lower costs by specialising in producing red cars today (though Henry Ford did once have lower costs by painting all Model T automobiles black), so the mincer would produce a high negative score (actually the maximum possible negative score, –290).

To come back to your business, apply the Segmentation Mincer to your list of *Potential Business Segments* to arrive at your list of 'real' business segments. You may now want to rank these in order of sales revenues, or, if you know it, absolute amount of profit produced by each segment. Now you should attempt to answer each of the questions below for each segment, either doing it one segment at a time (starting with the most important segment at the top of your list) or doing all segments at once.

CHAPTER 3

Where do you make the money?

Now that you have defined your business in a new way, by its real business segments, the most important thing to know is which of these segments generate most of your profits, both in terms of absolute amounts of money and in terms of profitability (measured by return on sales, or, preferably, return on capital employed).

It is possible that your accounting systems already provide this information, or that they can be easily tweaked to do so. If so, great. It is much more likely, however, that profit by segment, the way we have just defined them, is not readily available.

What usually happens at this stage is that your accountant, or your systems analyst, tells you that to restate the accounts in the way you want is a major job that will take several months. Should you give up, or wait?

Neither! You must find out your segment profitability – I can tell you in advance that it will be full of valuable surprises. And you are just getting into the game of developing your strategy, and to stop now would be defeatist. The answer is to estimate your segment profitability as best you can.

First, start with what accounting information you do have. You will certainly be able to discover your sales per segment, and probably also the gross margin (sales less cost of goods). You will also know the total costs for all the segments. It is quite likely that you will also know the profitability of certain segments on an aggregated basis: all sauces, for example, even if you can't yet split tomato ketchup from brown sauce. Now all you need to do, to arrive at the return on sales for each segment, is to allocate the costs to each segment on some reasonable basis.

The crudest way of allocating costs is on a percentage of turnover basis, and it might be a good idea to start just by doing this. A moment's reflection, however, will convince you that this is not terribly accurate, since some products take a lot more of some costs than other products: more advertising, for example, or more time selling, or more time in the factory because the production runs are shorter.

What you therefore need to do is to take each major category of cost, however arranged in your accounting system, and make a rough allocation of costs to each segment. You might want to start with the simplest, easiest-to-make-and-sell product, and say that it should have a cost of y per product in the particular department you are looking at. Then ask how much more difficult it is to make the next product, and allocate an appropriate cost: 1.5y for example, or 2y, or 10y. Do the same for each other product, then multiply by the factor (1.5y or whatever) by the volume of that product. Go through the same procedure for all other products, add up the total number of ys, and then allocate the departmental cost on the basis of each product's ys divided into the total number of ys.

Before long you will have arrived at a rough-and-ready estimate of the product's return on sales. If you want to take this to the stage of return on capital, you clearly have to follow a similar procedure to allocate the capital used by each product or segment. If this is going to be time-consuming, or if it seems unlikely it will yield any extra insight, stop for the moment at the return on sales.

Meanwhile, back in Pasadena, Randy's accountant and I spent Saturday afternoon beavering away to turn his previous profit numbers for four businesses (see page 29) into profits split by the new ten segments. Shortly after ten at night, we were satisfied that we had it about right (see Illustration 1.6).

ILLUSTRATION 1.6 ◆ Randy's profit numbers after proper segmentation

UTC segment profitability

Segment	Sales ($m)	Profit ($000)	ROS%
5 Unicorns Brand: US	200.1	17,800	8.9
5 Unicorns Brand: Canada	23.7	1,232	5.2

▶

5 Unicorns Brand: Europe	45.0	1,215	2.7
5 Unicorns Brand: ROW	48.5	6,063	12.5
Private label for Big Boy Supermarkets	353.6	(18,034)	(5.1)
Private label for Small Fry Retailers	35.9	467	1.3
Herb Tea US	55.5	7,715	13.9
Herb Tea Exports	11.0	1,155	10.5
Fruit Tea US	23.2	2,784	12.0
Fruit Tea Exports	4.7	465	9.9
Total	**801.2**	**20,862**	**2.6**

The following morning, I went through the numbers with Randy. He was stunned. 'You mean to say that we really do make good money out of the domestic branded business, but lose it all on the Private Label contracts? And that the US brand is more profitable than Canada or Europe? Perhaps we can do things to get even more Branded sales here. But I don't know what to do about the Private Label contracts. You may tell me to cut them out, but they're too big a part of our business and they still make a contribution to my overheads.' We agreed not to jump to conclusions until we had gone through my other questions.

This is, of course, only one example. But let me assure you that compiling segment profit data nearly always stands some perceived wisdom on its head, and provokes thought about the direction of your strategy. You generally discover that some business is *much* more profitable than you thought before, and that some business you thought worth having is in fact very unprofitable. It is wrong to jump to conclusions, however, before you have completed the strategic diagnosis. Our next port of call for more strategic insight is to look at our competitive position by segment.

CHAPTER 4

How good are your competitive positions?

For each of your business segments, we now want to find out how strong they are in competitive terms, because our strategy will be different depending on this. Assessing competitive strength is not as difficult as it sounds. Most of the insight available here can be gathered just by knowing four facts for each segment:

1 the business's *Relative Market Share* (RMS) in the segment

2 the *trend* in RMS

3 the expected annual future growth rate of the segment's market

4 the ROCE (Return on Capital Employed) of each segment business.

Remember that the *Relative Market Share* is the market share or sales that your firm has in the segment divided by the market share or sales of your largest competitor in the segment. Work this out now. If you are not exactly sure of your largest competitor's sales in the segment, make a note to find out later, but for the time being put down your best estimate. Now calculate the RMS. As an example, let's revisit Pasadena.

Randy defines his Relative Market Shares

After Randy's astonishment about his segment profitability (see Illustration 1.6), we spent the rest of Sunday morning with his marketing director, establishing how large UTC was to its major competitors in our newly-defined segments. By noon we had the answers (Illustration 1.7).

How good are these Relative Market Share (RMS) positions? First I explained to Randy and his marketing director some rules of thumb about these (see Illustration 1.8).

I then went on to tentatively classify UTC's segment position portfolio (Illustration 1.9).

This looked, on the face of it, pretty good. But before coming to any judgments, I wanted to look at the *trend* in RMS.

ILLUSTRATION 1.7 ◆ Randy defines his segment Relative Market Shares (RMS)

Segment	UTC Sales	Largest competitor	His sales	UTC RMS
Branded Tea: US	$200m	United Foods	$150m	1.33×
Branded Tea: Canada	$23.7m	Canadian Tea	$25m	0.95×
Branded Tea: Europe	$45m	United Foods	$200m	0.22×
Branded Tea: ROW	$48.5m	United Foods	$15m	3.2×
Big Boy PL	$354m	Cheapco	$490m	0.72×
Small Fry PL	$36m	George's Contracts	$45m	0.8×
Herb Tea: US	$55.5m	Herbal Health	$20m	2.8×
Herb Tea: Exports	$11.0m	Auntie Dot's	$20m	0.55×
Fruit Tea: US	$23.2m	Fruit-Tea Fun	$8.5m	2.7×
Fruit Tea: Exports	$4.7m	Auntie Dot's	$10m	0.47×

ILLUSTRATION 1.8 ◆ Rules of thumb concerning Relative Market Share (RMS) positions

RMS position	Name	Rule of thumb
4.0× or greater	Dominance	Extremely strong position
1.5× to 3.9×	Clear leadership	Very strong position
1.0× to 1.49×	Narrow leadership	Strong position
0.7× to 0.99×	Strong follower	Fairly strong position
0.3× to 0.69×	Follower	Moderate position
Less than 0.3×	Marginal player	Weak position

This requires going through the estimates of RMS again (as in Illustration 1.7), but this time for the position in RMS as it was three years ago. Since then, have you gained or lost in terms of Relative Market Share? The results for UTC's segments are shown in Illustration 1.10.

This looked like a deteriorating picture, although Randy's first reaction is that this is OK, since in the attractive export markets, the ones with the highest profitability, UTC was gaining share. I was not so optimistic, but before I could make any comments, Randy had stood up to march us off to lunch.

ILLUSTRATION 1.9 ◆ Strength of UTC segment positions

Segment category	Segments	Total % of UTC sales
Dominance	None	0
Clear Leadership	Branded Tea: US	
	Branded Tea: ROW	
	Herb Tea: US	
	Fruit Tea: US	40
Narrow Leadership	None	0
Strong Follower	Branded Tea: Canada	
	US Private Label	51
Follower	Herb Tea: Exports	
	Fruit Tea: Exports	3
Marginal Player	Branded Tea: Europe	6

ILLUSTRATION 1.10 ◆ Trend in RMS of UTC

Gaining share	Holding share	Losing share
Branded Tea: Canada	US Private Label	US Branded Tea
Branded Tea: Europe		US Herb Tea
Branded Tea: ROW		US Fruit Tea
Herb Tea: Exports		
Fruit Tea: Exports		
17% of sales	**48% of sales**	**35% of sales**

How does this picture compare to the trend in your segment positions?

It's time to introduce you to a new display, the growth/growth matrix (Illustration 1.11), which compares the growth in the market to the growth in your own business.

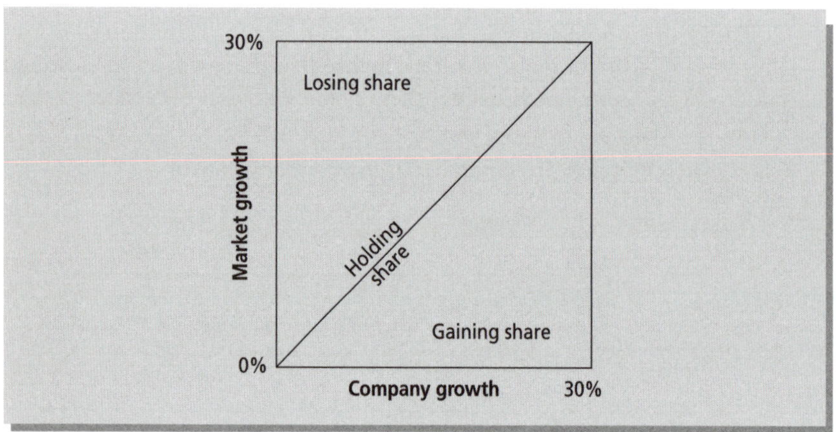

ILLUSTRATION 1.11 ◆ Growth/growth matrix

We can now superimpose bubbles on this representing your own segment businesses. By definition, where your businesses have grown faster than the market over the past few years, they will be bubbles (circles) below and to the right of the diagonal line (shown in Illustration 1.12 in grey); where you have grown at exactly the market rate the bubbles will be centred on the diagonal line (shown as clear circles), and where your business has grown slower than the market, the circles (shown in black) will be above and to the left of the diagonal.

Note that the size (area) of the circles is proportional to revenues (they can also be drawn with the area proportional to profits or to capital employed in the segments).

Before leaving this section on competitive positioning, I want to introduce you to three other charts on which to display your segment data. The first of these is perhaps the most famous strategic tool of all, the celebrated (and derided) GROWTH/SHARE MATRIX. We do not need to be detained by a lengthy explanation of the theory behind it (those who are interested should consult Part Four, pages 250–7); all we need to know is how to use it and how it helped Randy.

Randy looks at growth/growth bubbles

I thought that after lunch Randy, the marketing director and I should mock up some rough charts showing the growth in the market and in their sales for the ten segments. After asking them a few questions, the chart we generated looked like this (see Illustration 1.13).

Partly this was just a graphic way of showing the information from Illustration 1.10, but it also made us realise that there was an interesting pattern here. As we noted before, there is more area in the circles to the left of the diagonal (where Randy was losing market share) than to the right (where he was gaining share). But we could also note two other interesting facts:

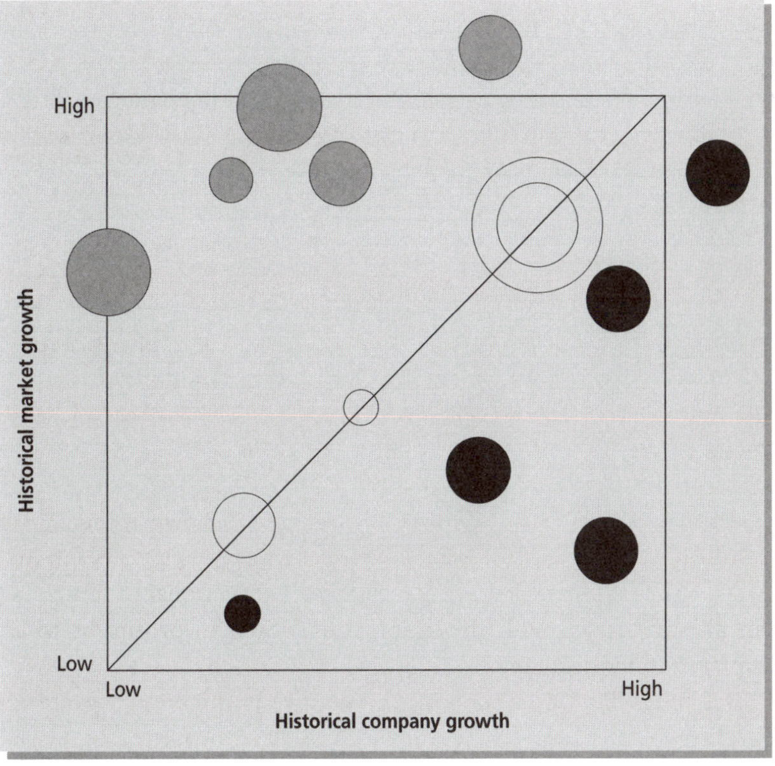

ILLUSTRATION 1.12 ◆ Growth/growth matrix with illustrative segment positions

1 The markets for Herb Tea and Fruit Tea were both growing very fast everywhere, at roughly the same rates (between 15 per cent and 20 per cent each year). Yet our growth rate was very different, averaging 5 per cent in the US and more than 20 per cent in the export markets. This was because more marketing effort was going into the smaller export markets, in the mistaken belief that these were more profitable. In fact we were losing market share in the profitable and high growth US markets. UTC was cutting itself off from most of the growth in the largest and most profitable segments: US Herb and Fruit Teas. Surely Randy could do something about this!

2 The branded Mainstream markets were low growth everywhere, while the Private Label market in the US was growing fast. This was bad news for UTC, because we made lower returns (in fact lost money overall) in the Private Label market. This trend explained why UTC's margins were sliding overall. But it also raised the intriguing question of whether private label was growing in some of the export markets, and whether we could profitably enter any of these.

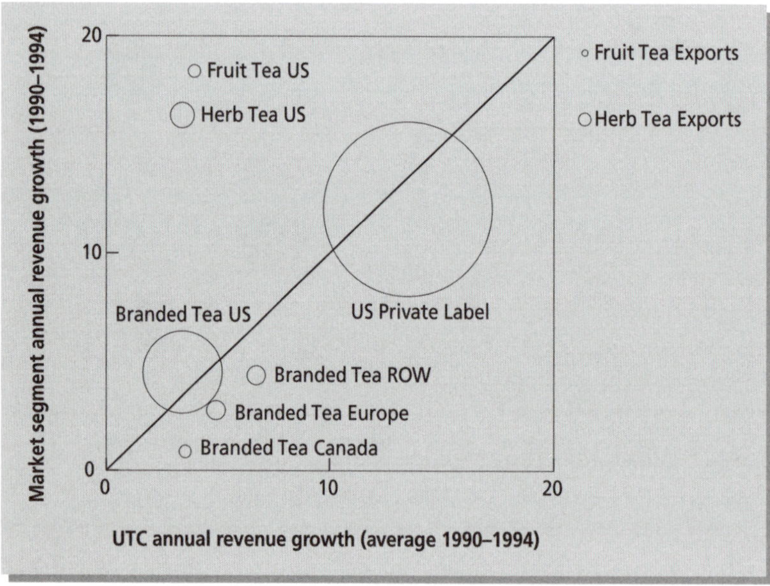

ILLUSTRATION 1.13 ◆ Randy's growth/growth bubbles

The Growth/share matrix uses the dimension of market growth that we've just looked at, except that you should plot your best estimate of the expected *future* annual market growth (this should also be in terms of units of volume of the product or service; if you find this more difficult to estimate than the value of the market in money terms, it is OK to use this although you should take real value growth and not include inflation). The other dimension is Relative Market Share (RMS) that we referred to earlier, though we did not then put it on a chart. Now just go ahead and plot your segment positions on the matrix (see Illustration 1.14), again making the area of the circles correspond to your sales in each segment.

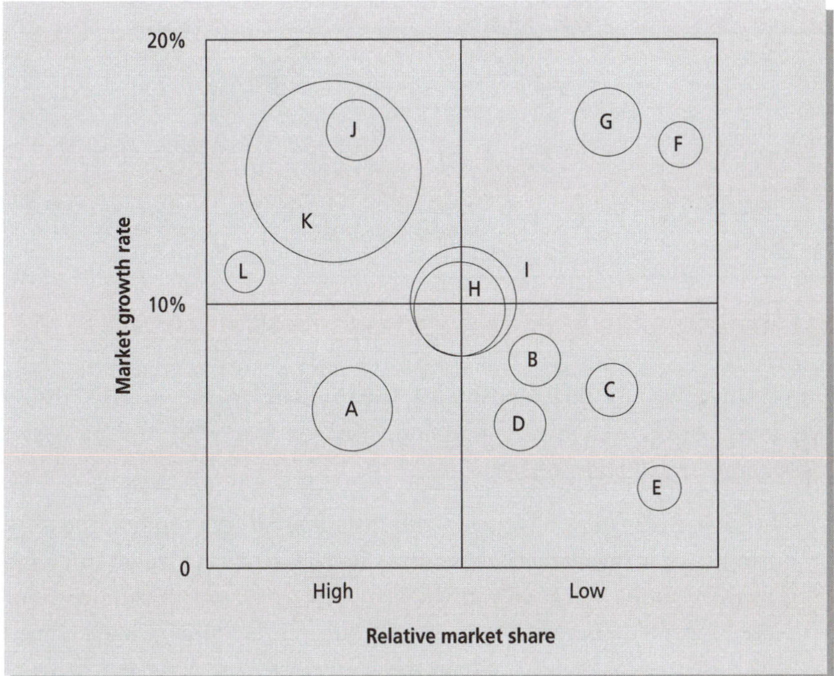

ILLUSTRATION 1.14 ◆ Growth/share matrix

Although many writers are sceptical about the Growth/share matrix or regard it as old hat and discredited, my experience is that sensibly used, based on the real business segments we have already discovered, the matrix is still a powerful diagnostic tool. The significance arises from the prescriptions accorded to each of the four quadrants of the matrix. First we need to give names to each of these (see Illustration 1.15).

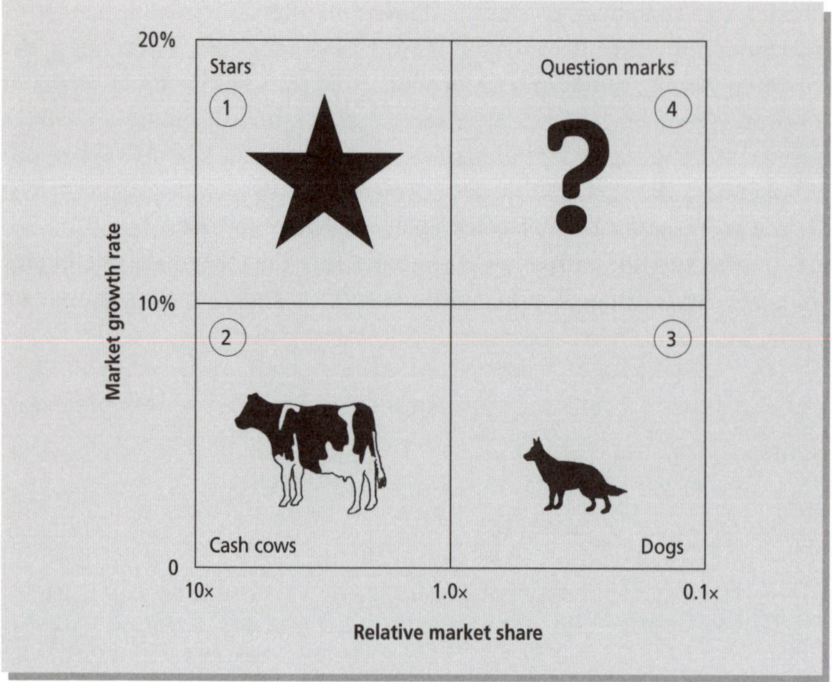

ILLUSTRATION 1.15 ◆ The Growth/share matrix quadrants named

I will now give my own comments (adapted from the original BCG prescriptions) on each of the quadrants. Your job is to see if this gives you insight into any of your businesses.

1 The most interesting businesses and insight are in the top left, the STAR quadrant. Star businesses are where you are the market leader in a high growth business. Most of you will have few or no star businesses. For those of you who have them, realise first of all how valuable such a business is. If you manage to remain the segment leader, your profits from the segment should be very high and growing all the time. When the market growth cools off, you will have a large, valuable business which should still be very profitable and will now begin to throw off very large amounts of cash (it will be in box two and will be a cash cow).

The rule for star businesses is to invest, invest and invest. *Do whatever is necessary to hold, or if possible, gain market share.* You will never regret doing so.

2 Box two contains the cash cows, business segments where you are the leader but where the growth is not particularly high. These businesses will generally comprise a minority of your sales, but a majority of your profits and cash generation. They are a classic illustration of the EIGHTY/TWENTY RULE: 20 per cent of the sales generating 80 per cent of the profits and cash (in fact, sometimes more than 100 per cent of the profits and cash). They are great businesses to have.

The rule for cash cows is to make sure that they have the highest grade grass, that they are well protected, and that they grow even bigger and stronger. Cash cows are generally quite easy to keep happy, since their appetites are nowhere near as voracious as those of stars, but remember: contented cows make bigger and better dollops of cash.

3 The bottom right box, labelled three, is the DOG kennel. Forget all you have been told about dogs. They are a motley crew, but some of these businesses are quite valuable.

If they are towards the centre of the chart, that is, if they are towards the left of the box (although still on the right of the middle of the page), they are MARKET CHALLENGERS or strong followers, and likely to generate nice profits and cash. Try to gain segment leadership if this can be done without too high a cost. Otherwise look after these businesses well.

For businesses towards the right edge of the box, the really doggy dogs, not too much should be expected. Find out if any of them are losing money and are a cash drain. Sell these, and if they can't be sold, close them.

4 Box four is in many ways the most intriguing, containing the QUESTION MARK businesses. They pose the greatest strategy dilemmas. On the one hand, it is nice to be in a high growth business, but on the other hand, it's bad news to be in a weak market share position. If you could be confident about becoming the market leader (driving the business to the star position) this would be a great move. But this will cost you. And if you don't make it, you will never get your money back.

The answer with question marks is to be very selective. Only back those you know can become number one in the segment. Otherwise, think about selling the business if it is not too closely connected with your other businesses. You could get a very nice price (people always pay a lot for growth businesses, even those in weak competitive positions) and you won't risk pumping cash into a black hole.

Randy draws a Growth/share matrix

Randy had liked his Growth/growth bubble-chart, which was just as well, because he couldn't believe I was suggesting making a Growth/share matrix. 'Jeez, Richard,' he protested, 'that stuff went out with the Ark.' I told him to trust me and drew a blank Growth/share matrix on the flip chart.

With only nine businesses to plot (we agreed to combine the two private label contracts) we did it fast. This is what we came up with (Illustration 1.16).

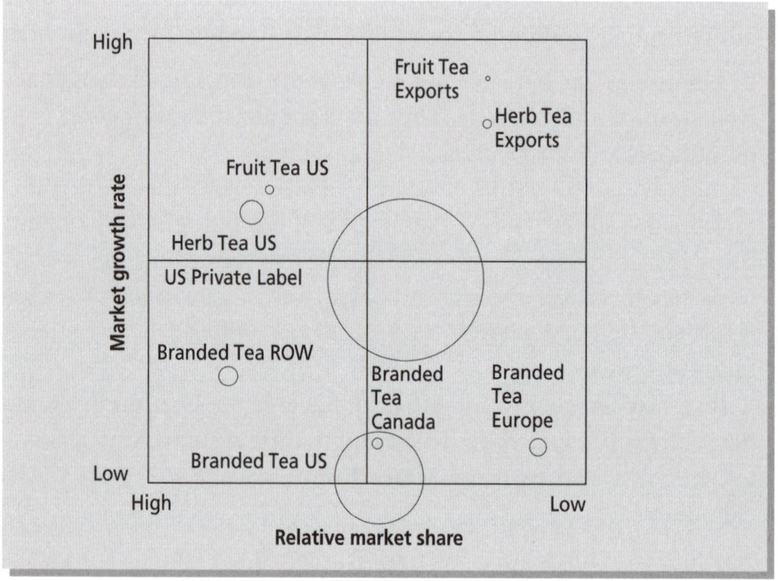

ILLUSTRATION 1.16 ◆ Randy's Growth/share bubbles

'So what do you make of that?' Randy asked me, not bothering to hide his scepticism. Brushing that aside, I made five comments.

'First, that's a portfolio many managers would kill for. You have leadership in four segments and a lot of growth. Most portfolios are much weaker than this. So we ought to be able to find a way round the present difficulties.

'Second, look at the US Herb Tea and US Fruit Tea businesses. The matrix says they are enormously valuable, but you haven't been treating them that way. If you carried on losing share they would drift over to the question mark box and end up as dogs. But it's probably not too late.

You should be investing whatever it takes to hold share and even regain share in these two businesses.

'Third, US Branded Tea is interesting. You're a leader, but not by a wide margin. And you're losing share, so this too could end up as a dog. You should probably aim to regain market share. But there's a question the Growth/share matrix can't answer about whether this is a good business to be in. It's under attack and losing to private label. You think it's a bad business. I don't know. A final view on this will have to wait.

'Fourth, Herb Tea exports and Fruit Tea exports are question marks. We're gaining share but we're still in very weak positions. We have to reach a view on whether we can gain leadership. That will have to wait until after we've studied competitors and talked to customers.

'Fifth, we have very different positions in Branded Tea in Europe, Canada and the Rest of the World. Europe is very weak and not very profitable. Canada is fairly strong and has OK profits. Rest of the World is very strong and profitable. I'd try to consolidate even further here. I'd want to know how much it would take to become clear leader in Canada. On the face of it, Europe looks a lower priority unless we can think of something dramatic to do there.'

By the end of my monologue Randy was looking more thoughtful.

You may want to draw two other charts for your business before leaving this section on competitive advantage. The first, called an RMS/ROS Chart, simply displays the data we already have on your segments' Relative Market Shares and Return on Sales. As before, I'll provide you with a blank chart on which to draw in bubbles showing your segments' positions (see Illustration 1.17).

The reason this is interesting is that there is often, but not always, a positive relationship between high Relative Market Share and high Return on Sales. If this does apply, it shows you the value of Relative Market Share, and should reinforce your desire to increase RMS wherever possible.

But if there is no pattern like this, this is also interesting. It may indicate opportunities or vulnerabilities for your business. I think you'll see why if we return to Pasadena.

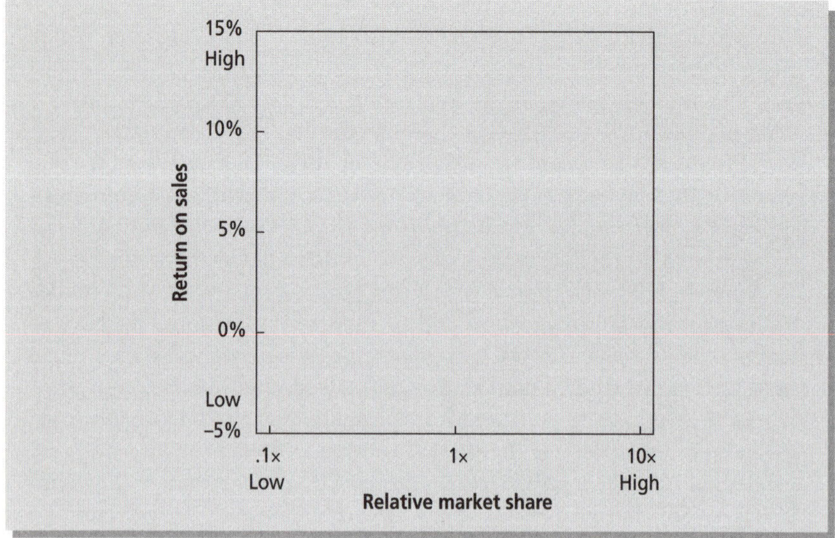

ILLUSTRATION 1.17 ◆ Your segments' RMS/ROS chart

Randy gets the message from his RMS/ROS chart

After the insight from the Growth/share matrix, Randy was subdued and patient as I sketched out UTC's RMS/ROS chart (Illustration 1.18). He even asked me politely what I made of it.

'Well,' I began, 'there is clearly a relationship: you tend to make the most money where you have the leading competitive positions. This should lead you to want to gain market share wherever possible, which we've just talked about. But the most fascinating thing is this big US Private Label blob, where the Relative Market Share is not bad at all, but you're losing money.'

'Can't do anything about it,' Randy interjected. 'Cheapco can always undercut us. We've got higher overheads, what with marketing and all.' He shot a glance at the marketing director, who started looking uncomfortable.

'We'll come to that later,' I retaliated. 'First I want us to draw up the final chart, which will end this afternoon's session. It's very similar to this one, except it looks at ROI or Return on Capital Employed, instead of Return on Sales. The bottom axis of the chart remains Relative Market Share, though I'm going to switch around the axes to keep you on your toes. In this chart (like the Growth/share matrix) the best, highest, RMS positions are on the left. We call this chart the Opportunity/Vulnerability matrix, or Bananagram. You'll soon see why.' Then I sketched it out (Illustration 1.19).

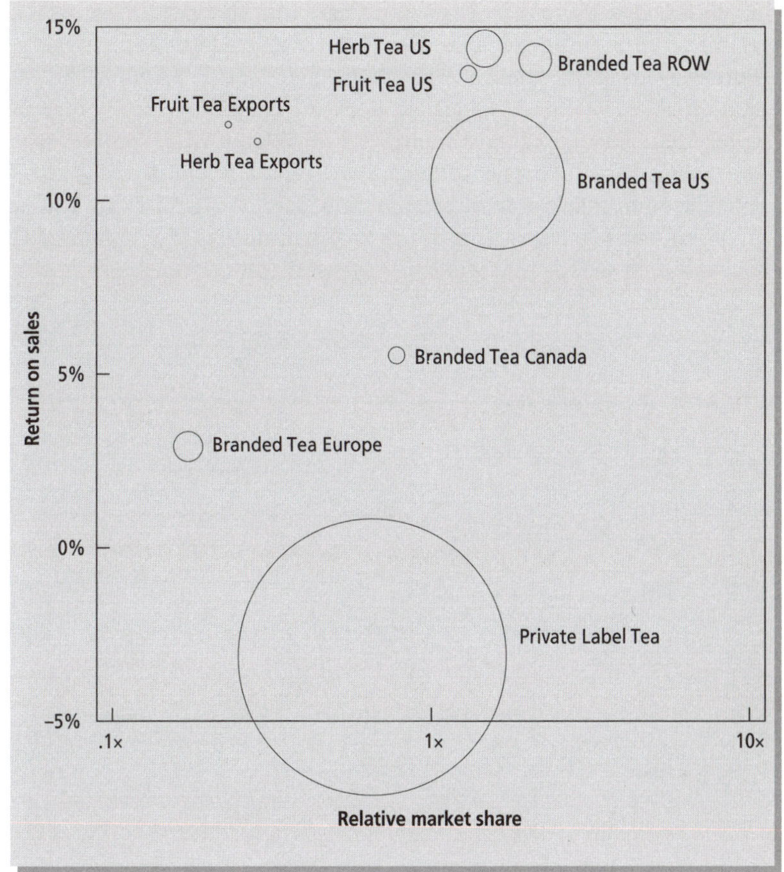

ILLUSTRATION 1.18 ◆ Randy gets the message from his RMS/ROS chart

Once I had drawn it, I took a yellow marker pen and coloured in the band in the middle (marked Normal Zone). 'This,' I asserted, 'is the Banana, more formally known as the Normal Zone or the Normative Curve. Experience and the collection of lots of boring data has shown that most business positions fall inside this band, because Relative Market Share does correlate with profitability (in this case with Return on Capital). Roughly three quarters of all businesses I have looked at fall within this band, after proper segmentation and product line profitability. In a way this just shows the RMS/ROS relationship in another way. You got that Randy?'

He grunted, which I took as agreement. 'But of your nine positions, only five of them fall in the banana. The exceptions are worth looking at carefully. This chart says, first of all, that you may need to be worried about anything above and to the right of the band. We call this the Vulnerability Zone, because you have high profits without the high market share we would expect to back them up. The theory says that either these businesses must improve their Relative Market Shares a lot, or you'd expect the profits to fall a lot.' I took a red marker and drew a circle around the two dots for exports of Herb Tea and Fruit Tea, and drew an arrow taking them down to the middle of the banana. 'The chart doesn't say that this will happen, just that it may.'

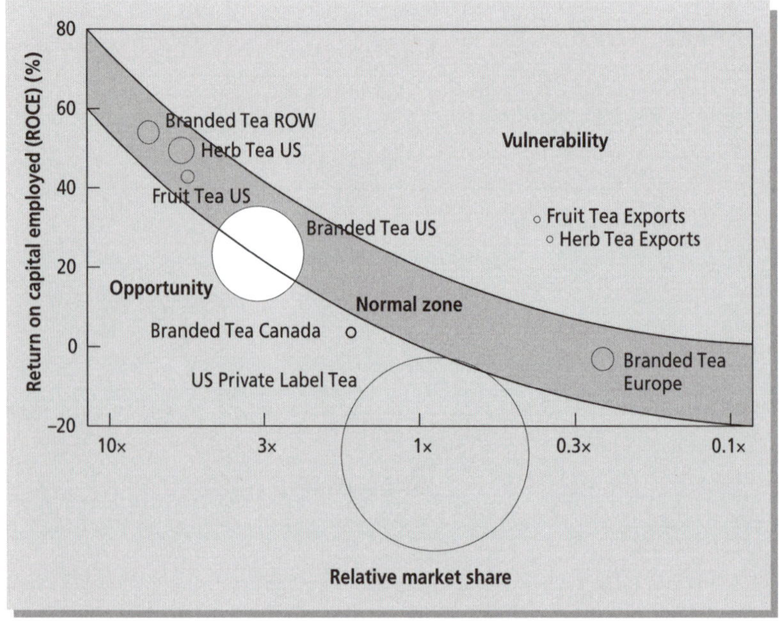

ILLUSTRATION 1.19 ◆ Opportunity/Vulnerability matrix

'But there's potential good news as well. Any business that is to the left and the bottom of the banana may be an Opportunity. That business has high market share but low profits. And if you could take this Private Label business...,' I circled it in green, 'and take it up to the line,' I drew an arrow up, 'you'd make several million dollars more profit.'

'Can't be done,' Randy returned to his refrain. 'Maybe not, but maybe yes,' I replied, 'I haven't given up hope yet. The same applies in a much smaller way to the Canadian Branded Tea business: you may be able to improve its profitability a bit.'

'To see if we can do anything about these businesses, we need to look at them in much more detail, understand their economics, whether they are bad businesses, and know what the customers think about you and their other suppliers, your competitors. We need a bit more investigation for that, which I'll do next week, and we'll fix a time to meet again next weekend.'

'Good. Time for cocktails, guys,' Randy concluded. He looked much more cheerful now, though whether that was due to the news about his business or the thought of a drink, I couldn't tell.

We've taken a long time exploring your competitive positions, but I hope you've found it rewarding. Segmentation, Profitability, and Relative Market Share are all related and looking at these three together is the fastest way to generate insight about a business. But we also need to understand what lies behind the strength in competitive positions.

CHAPTER 5

What skills and capabilities underpin your success?

Competitive positions should not be thought of independently of the skills and capabilities that make them possible. Where you are in leading positions, or gaining share, there must be a reason. Customers like what you have to offer, certainly, but *why*? Or, if you know that you are more profitable than other competitors, *why* is this? How can you make good money, and yet also have delighted customers?

When I asked Randy this question, he was pretty dismissive. 'It's because we've got good products, dummy,' he told me right off. 'Or,' he added after a brief pause, 'it's because we can make them cheaper and price them cheaper than anyone else.'

'Sure,' I replied, 'but why is that? How come? Why can you make something better and cheaper than any of your competitors? What's so special about you, smart guy?'

I wasn't about to mention the jargon phrase, 'core competencies', to Randy. That would just earn me more abuse. I had no intention of saying that, way back in 1955, Philip Selznick coined the phrase 'distinctive competence' to mean what a firm was peculiarly good at. Nor was I going to refer to the hugely popular article in the *Harvard Business Review* of May-June 1990 by C.K. Prahalad and Gary Hamel called *The Core Competence of the Corporation*: the *HBR* was not top of Randy's reading material. But I had the idea firmly in mind.

Randy was taken aback. I had to amplify, but tried to keep it snappy. 'Look: it's great to have good competitive positions, but you've got to ask what skills UTC has that have led to those good positions. What skills and resources, abilities and assets, what know-how, technology or other capabilities does UTC have, that give it leadership in Branded Tea and in Herb and Fruit Teas in North America? What is it about UTC that customers like? How rare are these skills? Can competitors imitate them? How does the organisation nurture these skills? And are the skills different across the different business areas? If you can't answer these questions, you don't know how secure your competitive positions are, how long they're going to last, or which new business areas to consider entering.'

'Whoa,' complained Randy, 'one question at a time please.'

'You're basically asking what we're good at,' he started again. I nodded. 'Well, the first thing, I guess, is the brand. It's not really the supermarkets that love the brand, they'd rather flog their own house brands where they make more money, no, it's the end consumers. They just love our brands. Some consumers just won't buy anything else. And why's that? Beats me. It's part of American history the marketing boys tell me, deep in the consumer's sub-conscious. Whatever. But it does mean very high quality too. We've always been hot on quality. Everything – the leaf tea we buy in, the way we process it, the packaging itself, to the product that stands on the shelves – it all has to be 100 per cent. We find a damaged carton, a damaged box, we don't let it stay in the warehouse or on the shelves. Everyone is committed to quality, and what they call the integrity of the brand. Don't laugh. (I wasn't about to.) It's very serious. Quality and the brand come first. We won't even change the advertising.'

'Is that true equally for all branded products?'

'Yep,' Randy replied confidently. 'The brands, the quality, they're equally critical for all the branded products.'

'But not the Private Label teas?'

'Not really. Well, obviously not, the brand isn't ours. Yes, we do still make a high quality product. Perhaps too much so. But the truth is, we don't really care as much.'

'And what about Fruit Teas and Herb Teas?'

'Same thing. The brand. It's just as important as in our regular Branded Tea. And, I guess, new flavours and new ideas. That's important too. We're good at that. Our R&D is the envy of the trade. Those guys are fantastic.'

'And what about my second question?' I asked. 'How rare are your skills in branding and quality, and product innovation?'

'Fairly. No, very. No-one in our market is as good. Objective outsiders say so, even the competitors themselves admit it.'

'Why can't your competitors imitate you? What's stopping them filching your best market and R&D people? Why can't they develop skills as good as yours, not overnight, but after a while?'

'Hmmm. Dunno. Part of it's attitude. They haven't really tried. But you make a good point. I should make sure that we keep our best people, and that the attitudes are reinforced throughout the firm. That we learn and deepen our unique skills. So that it's not just down to a few people, but really part and parcel of how we do business. I've always thought that was important. But we need to do more to protect our key skills. Now, did you have any more questions on this tack?'

'No, you've pretty much answered the questions. When we come on to consider new products, presumably we'll look for areas that can build on and reinforce these resources we've got: the brand, high quality, creative new product development?'

'Yep,' Randy concluded. I decided to quit while I was ahead.

Ask yourself the same questions I asked Randy:

- What are your business units particularly good at doing? What is it that the customers really value? What skills and other assets underpin this success?
- How rare are these 'core competencies'?
- How safe are you from competitors imitating them? How can you make this more difficult?
- How can you deepen and reinforce the core competencies throughout the business unit(s)?
- Are the core competencies different across the different business segments? Where are they most valuable?
- If you wanted to expand into adjacent segments, where would the core competencies be most valuable to customers and least subject to imitation by competitors?

CHAPTER 6

Is this a good industry to be in?

Competitive position and the competencies that underpin it are one thing – the attractiveness of an industry is something different again. One determines whether you win the race, the other how much the race is worth. There have been long and boring disputes about the relative importance of the two factors, but we need not bother with these. At the extreme, a business where no-one makes money and never will is of no interest, and a leadership position here is worthless; and there are some businesses (but very few) where almost everyone makes very high returns, regardless of competitive position. My own experience, for what it is worth, is that industry attractiveness on average explains about 30 per cent of the difference in firms' profitability, and competitive position within the industry (including the skill of the individual firm's management and the firm's culture) about 70 per cent. That is why I started with competitive position of the segments. But industry attractiveness is unquestionably important.

A good industry will have the following characteristics:

- high returns on capital for players accounting for most of the market
- a stable or rising average industry return on capital
- clear barriers to entry, keeping out many new entrants
- capacity at or below the level of demand, and low exit barriers
- reasonable or high market growth
- little or no threat from substitutes (competing industries)

- low bargaining power of suppliers relative to the industry
- low bargaining power of customers relative to the industry.

It is worth commenting briefly on each of these.

The best empirical measure of industry attractiveness is the *return on capital* for the industry, weighted by sales. Not everyone has to earn a high return, but the players supplying the bulk of the market should have a high average, well above the cost of capital. Many cute theories about particular industries' attractiveness or lack thereof can be quickly disproved by looking at the weighted average returns on capital in them. Many professional service businesses, for example, are alleged to be fiercely competitive and unattractive, but you wouldn't know this if you looked at the returns. Similarly, people often disparage 'commodity' businesses, without realising that many of these can be highly profitable.

The *trend in ROCE* is also important. If it is falling, from whatever level, this is often a warning signal. On the other hand, some industries invest very heavily at the outset but show steadily increasing returns on capital as volume builds.

Barriers to entry include investment scale, branding, service, cost to switch, a lock on distribution channels or sources of raw material, property/location, corporate expertise or access to highly skilled people, patents, ability to produce at low cost, corporate aggression vis-à-vis newcomers, and secrecy. Part Four, page 195–7, discusses each of these.

The industry *demand/supply balance* and *barriers to exit* are also clearly important. Barriers to exit include costs of firing employees, investment write-offs, disengagement costs, costs shared with other parts of a business, customer requirements for a 'package' of goods and services, and non-economic reasons like pride or desire to keep a large empire (these are elaborated in Part Four, page 195–9).

Market growth, especially the recent trend, shows how healthy demand currently is, and how well the industry is coping against competing products.

The *threat from substitutes* can arise from competing technologies (gas, electricity and nuclear power versus coal, or airlines versus railways), or simply from products that consumers tend over time to prefer (wine versus spirits, healthier versus less healthy foods, convenience versus labour intensive products, green versus non-green products, etc.). A threat from substitutes may exist and be very serious, but not yet show up in the statistics, as was the case with the threat to cross-channel ferries from Eurotunnel, the company that built a rail link under the sea between France and England.

The *relative bargaining power of the industry vis-à-vis its suppliers and its customers* is pivotal. Broadly speaking, if an industry has a more concentrated structure (fewer suppliers accounting for, say, 75 per cent of total output) than its suppliers or customers, it will tend to have greater bargaining power.

In the 1950s and 1960s, most grocery and fast moving consumer goods manufacturers had more concentrated industries than either their suppliers or their customers (the retailers). Since then, they have generally maintained the advantage vis-à-vis suppliers, but in most countries the emergence of a few large supermarket chains has wiped out the manufacturers' advantage over the retailers. Both groups are now highly concentrated. Both still have high returns on capital, but that of retailers has gone up while that of most grocery manufacturers has stabilised, indicating that the advantages from greater industry efficiency have tended to go to the retailers rather than the manufacturers.

The relative power of suppliers includes that of individual employees. In some industries (notably entertainment and investment banking) the power of the individual star can redirect profits from corporations to individuals. The singer George Michael can take on Sony. Bond or foreign exchange traders can try to double their pay, or threaten to go down the road for a multi-million dollar golden hello. Over the next decades, we will see a serious redistribution of corporate super-profits in 'knowledge industries' from shareholders to the most highly valued employees.

So you can see that industry attractiveness is a many-headed monster. One of the problems of such a long list of attributes is that it is difficult to provide an objective quantification, so that industry attractiveness is very much in the eye of the beholder. Talk to ten people in the same industry but in different firms, and you often get ten different opinions. In an effort to reduce the subjective element, I have distilled my *Industry Attractiveness Checklist* below, which you can now apply to your own business or businesses. If you find that you want to give different answers for different groups of your segments, you should go through the checklist separately for these. If you have ten segments, it is likely that you will have between one and three groups for assessing industry attractiveness purposes.

CHECKLIST

Industry attractiveness

1 **What is the weighted average ROCE (Return on Capital Employed) in your industry over the past five years?**

Score: whatever the average ROCE is, with a minimum of 0 and up to a maximum of 40.

2 **What is the trend in ROCE over the past five years?**

Score: (a) falling – no points; (b) erratic and no trend – 3 points; (c) stable – 7 points; (d) rising – 10 points.

3 **How substantial are the barriers stopping new entrants to the industry?**

Score: (a) few barriers – no points; (b) low barriers – 3 points; (c) fairly high barriers – 7 points; (d) very high barriers – 10 points.

4 **What is your best estimate of the next five years' average annual market growth?**

Score: (a) negative – no points; (b) 0–5 per cent p.a. – 3 points; (c) 5–10 per cent – 7 points; (d) over 10 per cent – 10 points.

5 **What is the current balance in the industry between customer demand and the total industry capacity?**

Score: (a) there is serious industry overcapacity, and no plans to remove it – minus 20 points; (b) there is serious overcapacity, but plans are in place to remove the excess – minus 10 points; (c) there is minor excess capacity – minus 5 points; (d) supply is in line with demand, or lower than demand – no points.

6 **What is the threat from substituting products, services or technologies?**

Score: (a) serious threat – minus 20 points; (b) may be a serious threat, but uncertain – minus 10 points; (c) only minor threats expected – minus 3 points; (d) threats do not appear to exist and are unlikely – no points.

7 **What relative bargaining power do the industry's suppliers have?**

Score: (a) the suppliers are more concentrated and can dictate terms to the industry – no points; (b) the suppliers are slightly more powerful and concentrated than the industry – 3 points; (b) the suppliers are slightly less powerful than the industry – 7 points; (d) the industry is more concentrated and more powerful than suppliers and can dictate terms to them – 10 points.

8 **What relative bargaining power do the industry's customers have?**

Score: (a) the customers are more concentrated and powerful – no points; (b) the customers are slightly more powerful than the industry – 7 points; (c) there is a rough balance between the power and concentration of customers and the industry – 12 points; (d) the industry is more concentrated than the customers and has more collective bargaining power because there are few suppliers and little choice – 20 points.

Interpreting the scores

The scores will range between minus 40 and plus 100. Industry attractiveness can be interpreted as follows:

Negative score [minus 1 to minus 40]: try to get out of the industry. If you are still reporting profits or anyone is foolish enough to buy the business, sell.

Score of 0 to 25: this is an unattractive industry. If you are not the market leader, sell the business.

Score of 26 to 50: the industry is not very attractive, but it is possible for segment leaders and very well run firms to make a living.

Score of 51 to 60: the industry is neither attractive nor unattractive. Competitive position is all.

Score of 61 to 75: the industry is attractive. If you are in it, consolidate your position and gain or maintain leadership. If not, consider entry if it is adjacent to your business and you have the expertise or can share costs with your existing business.

Score of over 75: the industry is unusually attractive. If you are in it, invest heavily for leadership. If you are not in it, you may find it difficult to enter without acquisition, but if there is a suitable way in, take it with both hands.

Randy tests industry attractiveness

The week after I saw Randy, I was busy on other assignments. But I did ask an assistant to check the ROCE for firms in the tea business, both branded suppliers and firms such as Cheapco that manufacture just for retailers' own labels. The following weekend, armed with my Industry Attractiveness Checklist and these data, I returned to Pasadena.

Randy rapidly agreed that we should do the Checklist separately for his Branded and Unbranded Tea businesses. 'That's what you persuaded me last time: unbranded stinks!' he said emphatically. He was therefore surprised to find that Cheapco and the other unbranded specialists had an average ROCE of 20 per cent, exactly the same as the average for the branded suppliers. He found that difficult to reconcile with his heavy losses in the unbranded segment. Still, he knew that barriers to entry were lower without a brand, and so was confident that unbranded would turn out to be a bad business. He wasn't sure that Branded Tea manufacture would score very well either.

When we went through the test, there were a number of surprises for Randy. Not only was the Unbranded Tea ROCE as high as Branded Tea, but it was also rising over time, whereas the Branded Tea average was stable. Branded scored higher on barriers to entry, but worse on market growth. And when we came to the last question, we realised that whereas the degree of concentration and power was roughly the same for Branded Tea manufacturers and the retailers, the latter actually had less choice when it came to unbranded suppliers. There were very few of these, since the manufacturing scale required acted as a barrier to most firms and none of the branded manufacturers apart from UTC would supply Private Label as a matter of policy.

The scores were as shown in Illustration 1.20.

As you can imagine, Randy and I had to battle to keep his prejudices in check. At the end, when he had finally accepted the scores, he restated his puzzlement: 'If Unbranded Tea supply is very attractive, how come I lose money in it?'

'I don't know for sure,' I replied. 'But Cheapco must be doing things differently. Perhaps they get a higher price than you do. Almost certainly they have lower costs. But if you did what they do, you could get costs as low. What we have realised is that the retailers are not as much in the driving seat as we thought. It's time to talk to them, the customers, and to look more closely at the competitors, especially Cheapco.'

'And another thing,' I added, 'cheer up, Randy. Your branded business is attractive too. And your segment competitive positions are not at all bad on average. So we should be able to find a way to make more money for you, so you can keep your job and keep buying me lunch.'

He was slow to take the hint. Randy was still scratching his head, and I surprised us both by being the first to suggest that it was time to eat.

ILLUSTRATION 1.20 ◆ Randy's industry attractiveness scores

Test		Branded Tea		Unbranded Tea	
		Result	Score	Result	Score
1	Industry ROCE average	20%	20	20%	20
2	Trend in ROCE	(c)	7	(d)	10
3	Barriers to entry	(d)	10	(c)	7
4	Future market growth	(b)	3	(d)	10
5	Capacity/demand balance	(d)	0	(d)	0
6	Threat from substitutes	(c)	–3	(c)	–3
7	Suppliers' power	(d)	10	(d)	10
8	Customers' power	(c)	12	(d)	20
Total score			**59**		**74**
Verdict		Attractive		Unusually attractive	

CHAPTER 7

What do the customers think?

I told Randy that I would show him the result of my customer interviews. Characteristically, he volunteered to guess what the results would be.

'They'll all say that we are lousy on price and pretty good on everything else. So the only way we could improve our market share is to buy it, to cut into our profits. As you know, lower prices would mean lower profits, a lower share price, and an enforced vacation for Randy Mayhew. But I suppose we might as well see the interview results,' he said.

If I had chosen to show Randy the average results of all the interviews, he would not have been too wrong. But I knew better than that. I showed him the results by segment, using a simple but very effective technique called Comb Analysis.

First I showed him the results from the US Branded Mainstream Tea business. You will recall that this was a large, important and profitable segment for UTC, but one in which it had been losing market share. Would the customer interviews explain this?

Comb Analysis asks the customers first of all to score what is important to them in deciding which supplier to use – their purchase criteria – on a scale of one (unimportant) to five (essential). We can then display the results on a chart like that in Illustration 1.21, which shows what was important to the supermarket buyers of Branded Tea.

It can be seen that Price is the most important criterion, scoring a very high 4.9, followed by Brand, also very important (4.7), Service (responsiveness to the customer and things like delivery efficiency), which was also important (4.0), with Packaging (3.8) also quite important, and Product Innovation (3.5) moderately important. Not surprisingly, the ability to supply proprietary product was almost completely unimportant (1.1) in the branded segment.

'Nothing new there,' commented Randy. I told him that the next stage in Comb Analysis was to ask the customers to score the client, in this case Universal Tea, on each of the purchase criteria, again on a one (terrible) to five (excellent) scale, and to overlay these scores on the previous chart, as in Illustration 1.22.

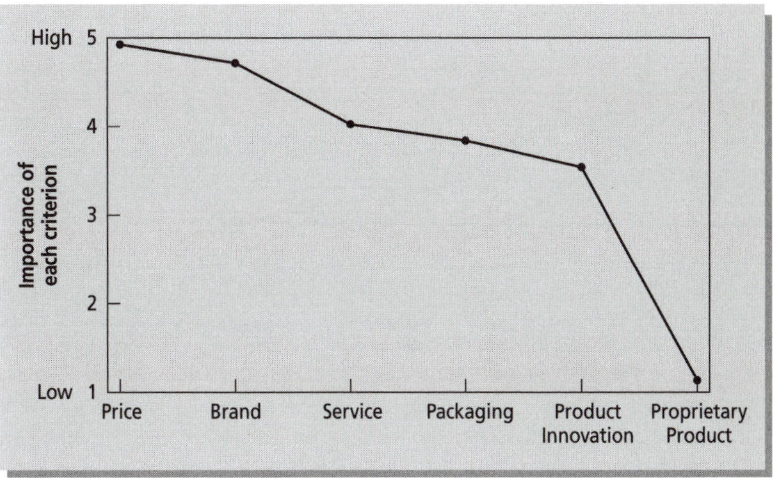

ILLUSTRATION 1.21 ◆ Segment purchase criteria for US Branded Mainstream Tea

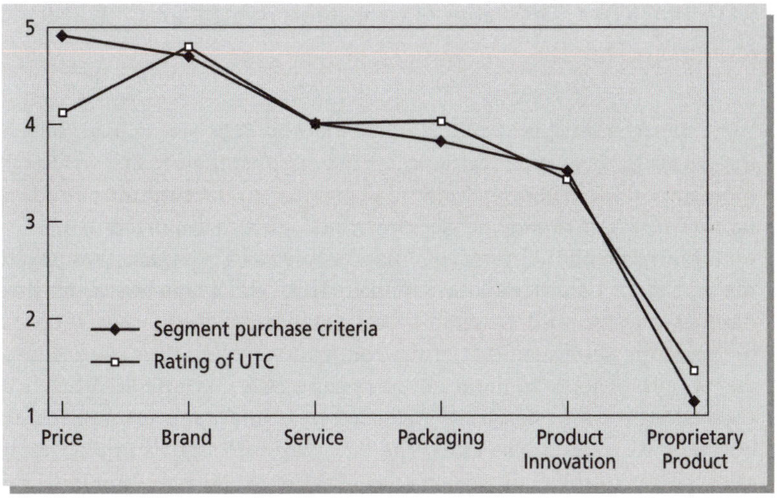

ILLUSTRATION 1.22 ◆ Rating of UTC's performance relative to purchase criteria for US Branded Mainstream Tea

'Still no surprises,' Randy said. I had to agree: UTC was very close to meeting all the performance criteria of the segment, with the single exception of price.

The third and final stage of Comb Analysis is to ask the customers to score the client's competitors on a similar one to five scale on each of the criteria, and to further overlay these results, as in Illustration 1.23.

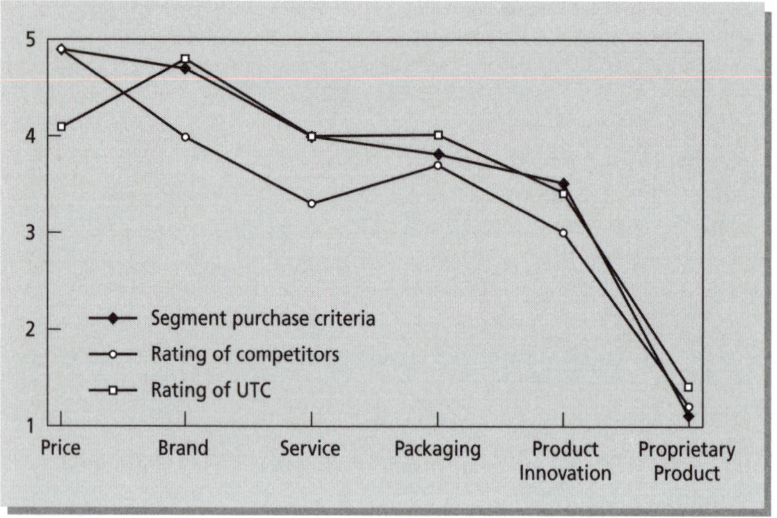

ILLUSTRATION 1.23 ◆ Rating of competitors overlaid for US Branded Mainstream Tea

'We can see from this,' I told Randy, 'that the only real selling point for the competition in this segment is Price. Unfortunately that is also the most important criterion. We at UTC appear to have significant advantages in terms of Brand and Service, which are also important.'

'Now remember,' I went on, 'that this segment is large and important for us, but we have been losing market share. But I conclude from these data that we should be able to do something about that. The gap between our rating and that of the competitor on price is not enormous, and we are at least as good on everything else. My guess is that if we showed a bit more flexibility on price we could get a lot more of the business. We should also stress the fact that our brand and our service are superior to the competition's, so perhaps we do not absolutely have to match their price to win more business.'

'But that would mean lower profits,' objected Randy, 'and what if they cut price still further? Only the customer would win.'

'Profits would not necessarily be lower,' I retorted. 'I think that if we did the sums, given the costs in the business that would not increase with more volume, costs like advertising and all the corporate overheads, not to mention the factory fixed costs, so that we could afford to cut price if we could be fairly sure it would give us more market share. Even if our return on sales dipped a bit, we'd make a much higher return on capital, and a lot more absolute profit, which is what concerns the shareholders.

'But as you say,' I went on, 'the key thing is the reaction of the competition. We shouldn't make any final decision until after looking at their position and likely behaviour. But bear in mind that our leading competitor, United Foods, has only $150m of sales here compared to our $200m. There is no reason, therefore, why they should have lower costs than us, if we were equally efficient.

'So, Randy, there are really only two alternatives. Either they are more efficient than us, or they are not. If they are, we can compensate for lower prices by becoming as efficient as them at lowering costs. If they are not more efficient, they must be accepting considerably lower profit margins than we are, and a further reduction in price to stop us getting more business could cut their profit margins to an unacceptable level, or even push them into making losses. We need to understand what United Foods characteristically does when faced with these sorts of decisions, so we can predict what they might do. But either way, we can probably get more volume and also increase our profits simultaneously.'

Without stopping to debate this further, I moved on to report on the second important segment, US Private Label. Here I saved time by displaying straight away all three sets of results: the segment purchase criteria, the rating of Randy's UTC, and the rating of his key competitor, Cheapco. In this case, the results had Randy jumping out of his chair, demanding to know if I had drawn the lines wrong on Illustration 1.24!

'That can't be right,' exclaimed Randy. 'The chart says that the buyers of Private Label for the supermarkets value product innovation and proprietary products most of all, even more than price. Our people tell me that the only thing these buyers, especially Big Boy Supermarkets, want is a cheap price. And you've seen for yourself how much money we lose in supplying them, because of the ridiculously low price they demand.'

'I agree that the data are surprising,' I countered, 'but I've double-checked the results of the interviews, and I think there are a number of things here that are interesting and potentially helpful for us.'

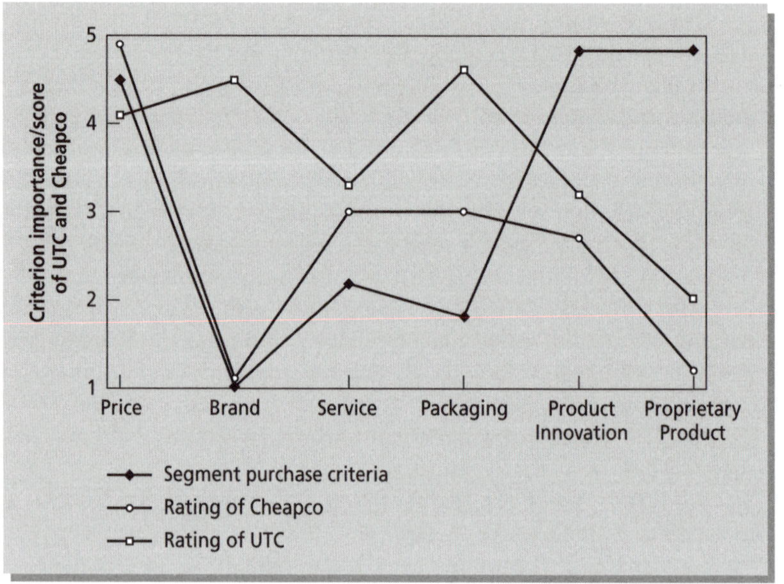

ILLUSTRATION 1.24 ◆ Comb Analysis of US Private Label Tea

'First, just concentrate on the segment purchase criteria compared to their rating of us. It's interesting that they give us a fairly high rating on price, not far below their purchase criteria, suggesting that they are surprised at how flexible we are on price. Look particularly, though, at the rating for our packaging, which at 4.6 is far higher than their purchase criteria at 1.8. This suggests that we might potentially give them cheaper packaging and save ourselves money, without in any way causing them concern. Now look at the surprising importance that they attach to product innovation and proprietary products. What the Big Boy buyer was saying was that they wanted to be able to offer a distinctive product under their own Private Label, where they would be selling a high quality product at a reasonably high price. This is a change in strategy for them, and they admitted that it is a recent development, but they're very keen on it.

'Now the interesting thing is, if we look at the rating of Cheapco, the Big Boy buyer is really saying that he couldn't see Cheapco coming up with a proprietary product for them, and although we haven't been at all responsive so far, he sees us as the logical supplier of this.'

By now I had Randy's interest, though not his agreement. 'So,' he queried sarcastically, 'you want me to do more unprofitable business with Big Boy, do you?'

'No, but I think it is possible that if you did supply Big Boy with a proprietary product, perhaps a different shape of bag, or product for different regions depending on the water quality, that you could negotiate a profitable contract with much higher prices than on the commodity business. It's also just possible that you could do this in exchange for negotiating slightly higher prices, maybe 5 per cent higher, on the commodity business. They want this proprietary product and you are virtually the only possible supplier. Also, given that Big Boy are very happy with the prices they are getting from you and Cheapco, it's likely that their margins on tea are above average and that prices could be edged up a bit. That depends upon the line that Cheapco take, so we can't be confident yet, but it's possible.'

Randy grunted. I decided to move on to the results for the US Herb and Fruit Tea segments, which were so similar that I put them together (Illustration 1.25).

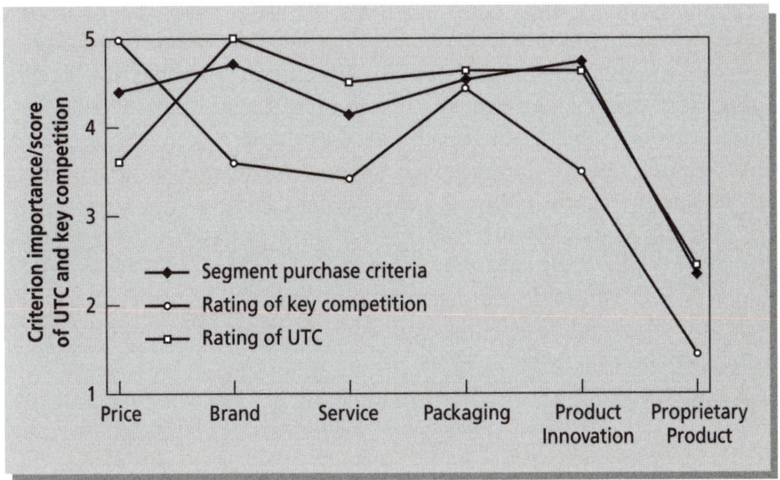

ILLUSTRATION 1.25 ◆ Comb Analysis of US Herb and Fruit Tea segments

'Now, this is a different picture, but also a very interesting one,' I lectured. 'We see that with the notable exception of Price, UTC is meeting the segment's purchase criteria very well. In contrast, our main competitor is rated a five on price, but under-performs the segment's purchase criteria on almost all other dimensions, especially brand strength and product innovation, both of which are very important to the buyers.

Note that this segment values product innovation just the same as the Private Label segment did, but in contrast to the latter, the buyers of Fruit and Herb Teas don't really want proprietary product – they want to sell it under the name of the known brand, which is us.

'Remember,' I went on, 'the data we showed earlier about these segments. They are extremely profitable for us, fast growing, and we are clear leaders, nearly three times bigger than Herbal Health in herb tea and Fruit-Tea Fun in fruit teas. Out of our $21m profits, we make half in these two segments. But we are losing market share in them. And why do you think that is, Randy?'

'Well,' he replied, 'it must be down to price, since we're far better than the competitors on everything else.'

'Right', I said, 'if we matched the competitors on price, there would be no reason for anyone to buy from them. Of course, they might undercut us again, and we could get dragged into a price war, so we'd need to understand their likely reactions. But the fact is that we could afford to cut price a bit. Another consideration is that we probably have some bargaining power with our buyers, since they need us for our brand strength and product innovation in particular. It's entirely plausible that we could negotiate higher quantities, and regain market share, if we were to shave our price just a bit. The other thing we could do is to speed up the pace of product innovation, and make more of the market in new products, where our competitors would find it harder to respond.'

I decided to draw the session to a close and stared hard at him. 'I think you'll agree, Randy, that we've learnt a lot from talking to the customers. But before drawing any definite conclusions, we need to take a closer look at the competitors and their freedom of manoeuvre. I'll see you back here in a week.'

CHAPTER 8

What about the competitors?

Modern management thought presents two opposite views on how important it is to analyse competitors. One view is that understanding competitors and how to beat them is at the heart of competitive advantage and strategy. The other is that the key thing is to get on with your own life, learn how to serve customers best and reduce costs, and not worry too much about what anyone else is doing.

My view is poised nicely between the two extremes. I would never start doing Business Unit Strategy by looking at the competitors, except to help define the segments. The key things to understand, to start with, are what your own firm is good at, where it makes the most money, and what your customers think of you. I also agree that it is more important to serve customers and make high returns than it is to 'beat' competitors, and that co-existence and implicit co-operation between competitors (especially if this involves tacit admission of each other's turf and avoidance of head-to-head competition by focusing on separate segments) is often a better route to sustainably high returns than a determination to do down the opposition.

My final concession to the 'worry about customers, not competitors' school of thought is to agree that strategy consultants often want to study competitors because they think this is a good thing to do rather than because they have very sharp and particular questions to answer. Such 'fishing expeditions' are usually a huge waste of time and money.

But in my experience, there is scarcely a business around that could not benefit greatly from asking a few very specific questions about its competitors.

Randy's business was no exception. For each of the three major business segments we were looking at, there were one or two questions about competitors that needed answering before we could work out a strategy to boost profits. The questions I wanted to answer are shown below.

Note that the questions I wanted to answer for Randy were very focused. Most of the answers, as it happened, came from a relatively straightforward look at relevant data on the Internet, at the financial documents filed by the competitors, combined with a press search and a few phone interviews with industry observers, brokers and some people within the competitor companies. My report back to Randy a week later is summarised below.

A few things that Randy really needed to know about his competitors

A US Branded Tea Segment

A1 *Is United Foods much more efficient and lower cost in Branded Tea than Randy's UTC? If so, why and how?*

A2 *How would United Foods react if UTC lowered its prices and started to regain market share in Branded Tea?*

B US Private Label Tea Segment

B1 *Is Cheapco much more efficient and lower cost in Private Label Tea than UTC? If so, why and how?*

B2 *What would be Cheapco's reaction if UTC raised its prices and attempted to move the general level of prices up?*

C US Herbal and Fruit Tea Segments

C1 *What is the profitability and relative cost position of Herbal Health and Fruit-Tea Fun, each compared to UTC?*

C2 *What would be the reaction of each of Herbal Health and Fruit-Tea Fun if UTC moved closer to them on price by cutting its currently high prices?*

What I told Randy about his competitors

A US Branded Tea Segment

A1 United Foods is making a return on sales of just over 7 per cent in the US Branded Tea business. Its prices in the supermarkets are on average some 5 per cent below those of UTC. The supermarkets are thought to be earning about 2 per cent higher margin on United Foods tea than on UTC tea. Therefore it seems reasonable to conclude that if United Foods had the same prices as UTC in tea, United Foods' return on sales would be 14 per cent (7 per cent + 5 per cent + 2 per cent). We know that UTC makes roughly 9 per cent return on sales in Branded Tea. We can therefore conclude, roughly, that United Foods has costs about 5 per cent below those of UTC.

Note, however, that United Foods has Branded Tea sales of only $150m in the US, compared to $200m for UTC. Normally, you would expect this to give UTC a cost advantage because of economies of scale, especially in marketing, that would be worth about 2 per cent return on sales.

It follows that the potential for UTC to reduce costs is in excess of 5 per cent of sales, with a rough target of 7 per cent.

UTC is losing market share to United Foods. We can conclude from the customer analysis that this is solely due to price – the lower prices being offered by United Foods to both consumers and to the supermarkets. Because UTC's brand, 5 Unicorns, is superior to that of United Foods, and because UTC's service to the supermarkets is better, it follows that market share loss could be arrested without completely matching United Foods' price.

If United Foods did not react to UTC lowering prices, it seems reasonable to conclude that a 4 per cent price cut (split between the consumer and the supermarkets) would stabilise market shares, that is, stop the loss of market share from UTC to United Foods. A 7 per cent price cut should lead to UTC regaining market share from United Foods, again in the absence of the latter also cutting price.

A2 United Foods is a well-run company, but it has publicly declared that it will seek to increase its earnings per share and stockholder dividends by a minimum of 10 per cent per annum. Analysts expect that to be difficult for United Foods to achieve this year, because of problems in the banana market. Tea is expected to comprise 25 per cent of United Foods' profits this year. It appears vital for United Foods to maintain its tea profits this year, and price-cutting would make a severe dent in these.

It seems reasonable to think, therefore, that unless UTC began to take large amounts of volume away from United Foods, the latter would be unlikely to cut prices.

B US Private Label Tea Segment

B1 By the same process of analysis as in A1, we conclude that Cheapco is a staggering 10 per cent lower cost than UTC in

Private Label Tea. A lot of this difference, perhaps up to 3 per cent, is due to the cheaper packaging used by Cheapco. As we have seen from the Comb Analysis, the buyers place zero value on UTC's more expensive packaging. UTC could therefore raise its margins, or cut its prices, by about 3 per cent almost overnight by a change in its packaging purchasing policy.

There is no discernible difference in prices between Cheapco and UTC in this segment.

There is the opportunity for UTC to lower its costs by up to 10 per cent. This could turn a business losing 5 per cent on sales into one making 5 per cent on sales, within say two years.

Cheapco currently makes 6 per cent return on sales on Private Label Tea.

B2 From sources I cannot reveal, I am fairly confident that a 2 per cent price rise by UTC would be followed by Cheapco.

C US Herbal and Fruit Tea Segments

C1 Herbal Health has a return on sales of 9 per cent (UTC: 14 per cent in herb tea), and Fruit-Tea Fun a return on sales of 8 per cent (UTC: 12 per cent in fruit tea). Both companies price about 5 per cent below UTC.

It is likely, therefore, that each competitor's costs are roughly the same as those of UTC.

UTC has a scale advantage, being nearly three times larger than either Herbal Health or Fruit-Tea Fun. This advantage should be worth about 4 per cent return on sales. There may well, therefore, be the opportunity to reduce UTC costs by up to 4 per cent.

C2 Moving closer to the competitors in price would probably reverse the loss of market share, unless they followed us down in price. Neither company can afford to do that. Herbal Health has just floated on the stock market by means of an IPO (Initial Public Offering), and Fruit-Tea Fun plans to do the same. For the next two years, both companies need to show steadily increasing profits, and they have no other businesses.

CHAPTER 9

How do you raise profits quickly?

This section should interest all readers. The way I will deal with it is to continue with the Randy/UTC example, before providing a more general checklist relevant to all businesses.

I had now reached the point where I felt sure of Randy's full attention. 'I'm going to summarise what we have learnt so far, and then outline how I feel you can increase profits,' I told him. I used an overhead projector and put up a slide, reproduced below.

Summary of findings for UTC

1 UTC is in ten different segments, each of which requires a different strategy.

2 UTC currently makes 85 per cent of its profits in the US Branded Tea business. UTC is the market leader, a third larger than United Foods. The segment is low growth, and UTC is losing share to United Foods. It is an attractive business to be in.

3 The supermarkets' most important purchase criteria are price and brand strength, with service and packaging also important. UTC scores better than United Foods on all criteria, with the important exception of price. United Foods prices its tea to consumers 5 per cent below UTC's prices, and also gives the supermarkets 2 per cent more margin than UTC. Price is the only reason why United Foods is gaining market share from UTC.

4 United Foods has 5 per cent lower costs in producing and selling its tea than UTC. Given UTC's greater scale, equal efficiency would lead to UTC having costs 7 per cent lower than today.

5 US Herb Tea comprises less than 7 per cent of UTC's sales but is responsible for 37 per cent of its profits (the reason that US Branded Tea and US Herb Tea provide over 100 per cent of current UTC profits is because of losses in Private Label). This is a highly attractive market, with 15 per cent market growth annually. UTC is a clear market leader, and enjoys a return on sales in this business of a staggering 14 per cent, but is losing market share quite fast to Herbal Health.

6 The most important purchase criteria in Herb Tea are brand and product innovation, closely followed by packaging, price and service. UTC performs better than Herbal Health on all criteria except price, where it is significantly less competitive, since Herbal Health prices 5 per cent lower.

7 Herbal Health has roughly equal costs to UTC, which, taking into account UTC's advantage of being nearly three times larger, suggests there is an opportunity to lower UTC costs by 4 per cent.

8 Herb Tea is a 'star' business, where market share must be defended for the sake of long term profits and cashflow. If UTC priced 4–5 per cent lower than today, to roughly match Herbal Health prices, it is unlikely that Herbal Health would reduce its prices. If this is correct, UTC could reverse the loss of market share and consolidate its leadership position.

9 The US Fruit Tea business constitutes under 3 per cent of UTC revenues but provides over 13 per cent of profits. Its characteristics are almost identical to those of Herb Tea, though the leading competitor (Fruit-Tea Fun) is different. This is another star business where UTC is losing valuable market share through pricing too high.

10 The export markets for Branded Tea together comprise 15 per cent of revenues but 40 per cent of profits. UTC is gaining market share in all major export markets, but is only the leader in Rest of the World (that is, markets other than Canada and Europe), which mainly means positions of strength in Asia. The Rest of the World Branded Tea business is highly profitable and well run.

11 The Herb and Fruit Tea export markets are very small, but profitable and fast growing. UTC is in weak but improving market share positions. Profits may be vulnerable if market prices fall, but it is worth while trying to attain leadership positions, particularly if this can be done by acquisition.

12 By far the biggest UTC problem, and by far the biggest opportunity, lies in the US Private Label tea business. The losses on the contract

with Big Boy Supermarkets come to $18m, or 86 per cent of the net level of profits. Yet this is an attractive business to be in, with few suppliers and a high average level of profitability (UTC is the only player losing money in it). UTC has a reasonable market share position.

13 The unbranded market has surprising purchase criteria, with the most important being product innovation and willingness to provide new and unique products under the supermarkets' brands. Price is also important. Packaging is not. UTC is rated well on price (as is Cheapco, the largest competitor), but performs poorly on product innovation and offering proprietary products to the supermarkets. It is important to note, however, that Cheapco performs even worse, and significantly worse, than UTC on these two most important criteria.

14 Cheapco has costs 10 per cent lower than UTC in Unbranded Tea, of which 3 per cent relates to cheaper packaging. There appears to be an opportunity to move the general level of prices up.

15 The most important opportunity for UTC in Unbranded Tea, besides lowering costs, lies in providing proprietary product to the chains. This could lead to large and profitable new business, since price sensitivity on unique product is lower and the volumes could be very large, without any need for expensive advertising.

As I went through the slide, Randy was uncharacteristically silent and attentive. At the end, he asked simply, 'But what do I do?' This was the perfect lead into my next slide, shown below.

Five key recommendations to Randy

1 In US Branded Tea, cut list prices by 2 per cent and offer another 2 per cent additional margin to the supermarkets, in order to stop market share loss.

2 Cut costs in US Branded Tea by 7 per cent within two years.

3 In US Herb and Fruit Teas, cut prices by 4–5 per cent to reverse the market share loss. Reduce costs by 4 per cent within 18 months.

4 In the US Unbranded Tea market, raise prices by 2 per cent immediately, and cut costs by a total of 10 per cent over two years, 3 per cent of which (relating to packaging) can be done immediately.

5 Mount a campaign to provide leading retailers (especially Big Boy) with unique new products to be sold under their own house brands. Target revenues of $100m by the end of year one and $250m by the end of year two.

I then moved on to a final slide, shown as Illustration 1.26, summarising the potential profit impact if the recommendations could be successfully implemented.

Note that the implied Return on Sales is calculated as a reality check. In this type of business, the successful competitors make 10 per cent Return on Sales, but anything above that across a business as a whole is not generally sustainable. It can be seen that although I estimated that Randy had the potential to increase his operating profits to more than 450 per cent of today's level, the third year Return on Sales, at just over 7 per cent, still looks reasonable.

ILLUSTRATION 1.26 ◆ Potential profit impact of recommendations to UTC: Effect on operating profit ($m)

		Year 1	Year 2	Year 3
1	US Branded Tea 4% price cut	(8.0)	(8.0)	(8.0)
2	US Branded Tea new volume	0.8	2.0	4.4
3	US Branded Tea cost cutting	3.7	7.3	12.8
4	US Fruit and Herb Tea 4–5% price cut	(3.5)	(4.1)	(4.7)
5	US Fruit and Herb Tea new volume	0.9	2.1	3.5
6	US Fruit and Herb Tea cost cutting	1.1	2.4	2.7
7	US Private Label Tea 2% price rise	7.8	7.8	7.8
8	US Private Label Tea cost cutting	12.0	24.1	40.2
9	US Private Label Tea unique new products	1.5	8.8	12.5
	Net change	16.3	42.4	71.2
	Previous budget	22.0	24.2	26.6
	Total profit	**38.3**	**66.6**	**97.8**
	Total revenues after new initiatives	950	1265	1370
	Implied return on sales	4.0%	5.3%	7.1%

So much for Randy's business, which is a disguised example of a real-life business that did make similar (actually slightly larger) profit increases with these sorts of actions. Illustration 1.27 provides a diagnosis of profit improvement opportunities that can be used for any business.

Some of these themes will be expanded in the next chapter, which covers the development of secure, high-quality, long term profits, and expansion into related and new businesses.

CHAPTER 10

How do you build long term value?

Short term profit improvement is almost always possible as a result of cost reduction and a refocus of the business on fewer segments, where your firm has a clear competitive advantage. It may also be possible to push through some tactical price increases, particularly if the product or service can be improved. But the sources of long term profit improvement are generally different. Paradoxically, because they are long term, they need to be worked on now, immediately after you have worked out how to raise short term profits.

ILLUSTRATION 1.27 ◆ General diagnosis of profit improvement opportunities

Profit improvement type		Diagnosis
A Cost reduction	1	The business is unprofitable
	2	Competitors have higher return on sales
	3	Customers do not value some part of your product offering
	4	Unit costs have been rising historically
	5	Some competitors outsource large parts of the process that you produce yourself
B Price increases	6	Competitors would probably follow a rise
	7	Segment profitability is low
	8	You are gaining market share
	9	Customers rate you highly
	10	You have lower prices than competitors

C Price decreases	11	Competitors are lower price
	12	You are losing market share due to price
	13	Competitors are unlikely to match your cut
	14	Profits are above the 'normal zone' on the bananagram
	15	Customers say price is the most important criterion
D Changes in business mix	16	You have wide differences in your segment profitability
	17	... and in your relative market share positions
	18	... and in customers' rating of you in different segments
	19	You have the opportunity to seize leadership in a segment, provided you focus on it
E Changes in activity focus	20	You are clearly best at just one part of the 'value added chain' (such as R&D, manufacturing, marketing, etc.) and should concentrate only on that and outsource everything else
	21	You can 'lock up' a channel or business by integrating forward or backward
F Expansion in existing market	22	You have the knack of growing faster than the segments
	23	You can mop up competitors by acquisition without paying a fancy price
	24	You can attain higher prices and/or lower costs than any competitor in your chosen segment
G Expansion into adjacent segments	25	There are business segments which can use your skills segments or cost base well that you are not currently doing
	26	No competitor in those adjacent segments is bigger or better financed than you
	27	The adjacent segments are at least as profitable as existing segments
H Invention and innovation	28	You are good at it
	29	The industry has not historically been very innovative
	30	Suppliers have been innovating
	31	New customers can be created by innovation
	32	You can copy new trends from other industries, that have not yet been applied in your industry
	33	You spot innovation in your industry currently only applied in other countries

Long term profit improvement almost always rests on one or more of the following five sets of actions:

1 actions to increase market share in existing segments
2 actions to 'recompete', that is, to change the basis of competition in your key segments, nearly always involving a transformation of the cost base
3 actions to enter new segments that your firm is not currently serving
4 actions to transform the firm's total cost base
5 actions to increase the firm's competencies and ability to learn.

Now let's discuss each of these, with a checklist for you to review what may be relevant to your firm.

CHECKLIST

How to raise long term profits

A Actions to increase market share in existing segments

Note: you should aim to increase market share only if the segment is a core segment for you and the market is attractive. In certain segments you should actively aim to 'sell' market share, to pay for market share expansion in your key segments. Be selective.

1 **Cut prices.** Price should be cut if (i) the market or an important and profitable part of it is price sensitive, and (ii) you can be fairly confident that competitors will not match your price cuts for long, or, in any case, if you are lower cost than your competitors in serving the segment. In the latter case it will not matter much if the competitors cut price, because sooner or later they will be forced to raise prices again or exit the segment (unless the segment is so important to them that they will lose money in order to hold market share).

Price sensitivity varies enormously between markets, but few segments can resist the allure of higher value for money over the long term.

Cutting price is not a very popular tactic, but is nearly always effective in increasing market share. The payback may not be quick: cutting price usually leads to substantially lower profits for the first three to five years. But there are very few examples of price cutting, which, consistently followed, have not worked and led to a much more valuable business long term.

Price cutting should lead to a virtuous circle: increases in market share, immediate pressure on internal costs because of lower profits, higher volume leading before long to lower unit costs, still greater market share gains, pressure on competitors to leave the business or retreat to higher price segments, further increases in market share, further reductions in unit costs, and so on.

The only cases where price cutting has hurt the initiator and everyone else is when there is serious excess capacity in the business and there are also non-economic barriers to exit. Otherwise, it is a very good bet.

2 **Build in extra features, value, service and quality.** This tactic should accompany cost reduction, and not be seen as an alternative. Having said that, it is a much more popular tactic than price cutting, and one that succeeds much less often. This is not because it is inferior, but simply because it is much more difficult to do. Firms that are successful in the long run, however, almost constantly strive to deliver more to their customers – more than they did the year before, and more than the competitors.

3 **Remove a competitor**, either by buying it or forcing it to exit from the segment. In one sense, all profitable business activity involves establishing a very high relative market share of a segment, or, to use emotive words, setting up a monopoly or at least an oligopoly. In general, the best way to achieve this aim is to provide a better and cheaper service to your customers.

But there is also no doubt that 'taking out' competitors helps enormously. Fortunately, anti-trust/anti-monopoly constraints do not operate with sufficient precision or pervasiveness to stop this happening in most cases.

Almost the only case where removing an important competitor does not help is when the barriers to entry are low and removing one firm may simply lead to another one entering the market, so you will need to assess the chances of this happening. If the chances are low, buying a competitor or pricing so that he or she has to leave the market will nearly always pay off handsomely in the long run, whatever your cost/benefit analysis shows today.

4 **Invest more, and more intelligently, than competitors.** Market share goes in the end to the competitors who are most committed, who invest the most. Traditionally, investment meant laying down physical capacity, in terms of plants, distribution networks, service centres, retail outlets and/or computer systems. These are still important in some industries, but increasingly the most effective investments are

in software, research and development, training, brand-building, getting close to customers, design and innovation.

But investments are not investments unless they are costly. By definition, investments do not have an instant payback, and usually not a short one. Make a checklist of all possible investments you could make. Then assess the potential benefit in terms of market share in ten years' time. Force yourself to guess these on a consistent basis for each possible investment. The numbers will be wrong, but still helpful. Then guestimate the cost of each investment, and rank them according to cost-effectiveness. Then make all the investments you can possibly afford.

The second way to raise the quality and quantity of long term profits is to change the rules of the game in a key segment. In stratspeak, this is often called '*recompeting*'. Examples include Kwik-fit in the UK, which set up specialised exhaust and tyre fitting services with a very quick and low cost formula, completely outwitting the traditional suppliers, the broad-line garage repairers/service stations. Another example is IKEA, the Swedish furniture retailer, which engaged the customer in providing much of the labour (such as selection and assembly of the product) traditionally taken on by the retailer, making it possible to provide high design at a low price, combined with instant availability.

Or take the example of First Direct in banking or Direct Line in insurance. Customers can obtain superior and faster service by using the phone, without needing to visit a bank branch or insurance agency, rendering existing competitors' cost bases (expensive retail networks) unnecessary. Home delivery of pizza and other fast food provides another example of successful recompeting.

Some hints about possible ways to recompete are provided below.

CHECKLIST

How to raise long term profits

B Actions to recompete

Note: Recompeting is a terrifically powerful weapon, but may not be possible, or may not be appropriate, for a particular firm. But it is always worth engaging in the most creative thinking you can regarding recompeting, if only to be aware of potential dangers to your traditional business. And you may just hit the jackpot ...

1 **Think of radical ways to cut costs in any activity,** to below half of their current level. This will not be possible without doing something radically different. Brainstorm possible ways, however bizarre.

2 **Think specifically of where less might be better,** for example, self-service in supermarkets and petrol retailing, where, simultaneously, cost can be removed and the customer might prefer to be more actively involved.

3 **Think of the most expensive part of the existing industry's operations,** and brainstorm how it might be removed.

4 **Imagine what information technology and the Internet,** creatively applied, could do to the industry. What might it look like in a generation's time?

5 **Put yourself in the position of the customer.** What irks him or her today about the way they are served. How could it be done better? Could the customer be engaged in providing some of the service?

6 **Roll back history and pretend the product/service does not exist today.** How would you set up the industry from scratch, if you could not simply replicate how it developed historically? You are not allowed to use the existing systems in answering this question.

7 **What would a 'greener' industry look like? A more socially responsible one? One that is more in tune with social changes? One that is more fun, for both operator and customer?**

8 **Steal ideas from other industries where recompeting has taken place.**

9 **Steal ideas from other countries, where they do it differently or more cheaply.**

The third way to raise long term profits is to enter new segments, particularly those which are 'adjacent' to your existing profitable segments. Some ideas are given below.

More detail is provided in the entries in Part Four on the ANSOFF MATRIX and ADJACENT SEGMENTS.

The fourth route to long term profit improvement is to transform the firm's total cost base, via a customer-focused '*re-engineering*' exercise.

CHECKLIST

How to raise long term profits

C Entering new segments

1 **Think of ways in which you could use your existing cost base in a** new segment...

2 **...or use your existing skills,** where you believe these are better than competitors'.

3 **Imagine products/services that your existing good customers might want to buy from you.**

4 **Dream up other uses for technologies you have.**

5 **Make a list of all the segments your competitors are in. Why aren't you?** (But beware: there may be good reasons.)

6 **Look at the range of services provided by your counterparts in other countries and/or similar industries.**

7 **Are there any competitors who are leaders in a segment adjacent to your own? Could it make sense to acquire them or form a joint venture?**

This is much more than finding short term cost reduction opportunities. It is concerned with the whole way that a firm should operate.

Peter DRUCKER is right again: 'So much of what we call management consists of making it difficult for people to work.' Re-engineering, often called BUSINESS PROCESS RE-ENGINEERING or BPR, attempts to remove the obstacles placed in the way of satisfying customer needs by traditional, hierarchical management.

BPR is a huge subject well beyond the scope of this book, but let me do two things here: first, to explain the basic principles and why BPR is important; and second, to explain the linkage between strategy and BPR, and why strategy for any business should be arrived at before undertaking BPR. If you wish to, you can then look up the entry on BPR in Part Four.

Most people, when asked to describe a business, fall back on a *structural* view: so many employees, this and that factory, here's the organisation chart, the places where different functions are located, the sales offices are there, and so on. This is the old-fashioned mentality from which BPR seeks to liberate us.

In contrast, BPR takes a *process* view and a *skills* view.

The *process* view is how the firm's people interact in order to produce something that customers want: for example, how marketing and R&D jointly develop new products, or how customers' orders are fulfilled, or how a product is made in the factory by a sequence of process steps.

The *skills* view looks at how effective the firm's people are at doing what customers want, or finding new customers: how pleased customers are with how they are treated and what they receive, how quickly and efficiently goods are made and delivered, how good the firm is at developing new products or finding distributors, and so on.

This leads to the second point. Conducting BPR using a process and skills view can lead to dramatic cuts in cost, and even more importantly, increases in sales through greater customer satisfaction and loyalty. But BPR is an expensive and time-consuming one-off exercise. It should be undertaken after, rather than before, a strategic review. If a business is competitively weak or worth more to another firm, a decision may be made to sell it, so that time spent on a BPR exercise might be wasted if BPR were to be undertaken before looking at strategy.

In thinking about both processes and skills, time is a critical dimension. Here the old adage that 'time is money' really comes alive. If something can be done more quickly, it can kill two birds with one stone – both please customers, and also do things at lower cost.

The process view therefore aims to streamline operations to reduce throughput time: how long it takes to manufacture a product, how long it takes to deliver it to customers (from the time the order is taken to the time the customer has it in his hands), how long it takes to bring a new product to market (from having the original idea to having it in the shops), and so on.

The process view looks at flows: of money (cash flows), of physical product, and of information. Compression of cycle times in delivering product to customers is the key to reducing the costs and increasing customer satisfaction, and therefore the firm's market share.

Through looking at processes, it is possible to work out better and cheaper ways of doing what the firm already does. Through looking at skills, it is possible to work out which skills customers value the highest, which skills are areas where the firm can be better than its competitors, and how these core skills can be enhanced and made 'world class'. Since this is easier if fewer things are attempted, the skill-based view usually ends in the firm deciding to use outside contractors for some of its activities (those where it does not currently have, and would find it difficult to build, skills superior to those of its competitors).

The relationship between BPR and strategy is summarised in Illustration 1.28. BPR should be conducted only after a strategic review, for core businesses that are to be retained. It should not be conducted for weak businesses with poor competitive positions, except as a last resort.

The fifth way to raise sustainable profits is to *deepen and enrich the company's distinctive culture, its competencies and its ability to learn*. This is true at the operating company or divisional level as well as at the overall corporate level.

Very often a company's success derives not so much from its products, technology, strategic positions or other 'hard', structural reasons, but from 'softer' influences – operational excellence; good service to customers; employees' ability and energy levels and the way that they co-operate with each other; and the company's whole personality, culture and way of doing business.

Different firms in the same industry (and sometimes different divisions or operating companies within the same corporation) frequently have different average levels of employee ability and commitment. Some companies attract the best people; others repel them. Some companies get the most out of all their people; others systematically get the worst out of their people. Some companies exhibit teamwork; most do not. It is not surprising that these differences lead to greater or lesser efficiency and customer satisfaction.

Ultimately, a company will only be successful if it has people who are above average in their skills and in their commitment to the company. Such commitment will only be forthcoming if they believe in what the company does and feel that they are a key part of it.

Recently, theories such as those of Peter SENGE have focused on the LEARNING ORGANISATION, claiming that the real source of competitive advantage is in how well firms are able to learn. Even more interesting is the idea, associated with Senge but particularly also with Arie DE GEUS, a manager-turned-business philosopher, that companies are 'alive'. The scientific concepts of chaos and complexity do in fact indicate that organisations are not machines but rather 'complex Self-Organising Systems' with a life and will of their own. This exciting idea is explored in

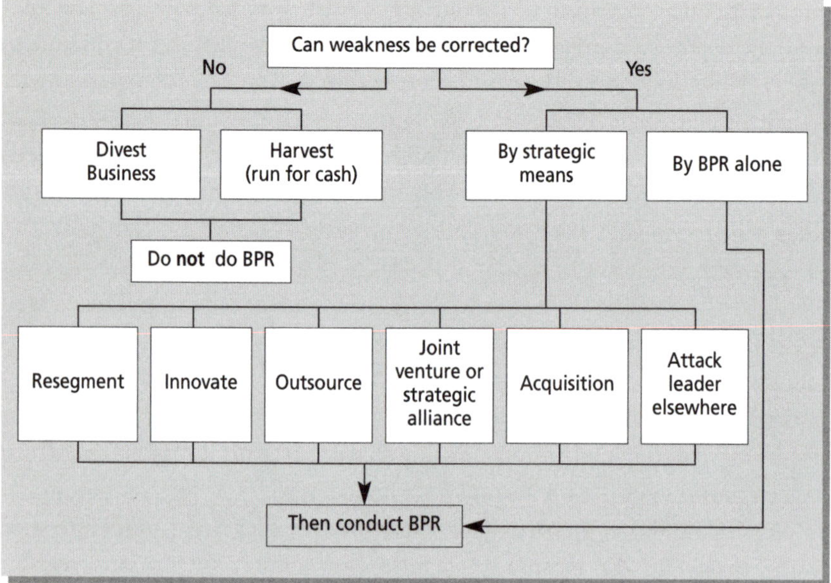

ILLUSTRATION 1.28 ◆ When is BPR appropriate?

my book, *The Power Laws*, and the scope of the idea lies well beyond this text. Some hints are contained in the entries on Senge and De Geus in Part Three and, in Part Four, on Chaos Theory, Complexity, Core Competencies, Culture, Knowledge Management Structure, Learning Organisation, and Self-Organising Systems.

You can make a start on thinking about these issues, however, by asking yourself the following three questions:

1 Is our company above-average in terms of the way that we execute what we do, in terms of operational excellence and service to customers?

2 Do we find it easy to attract and keep above-average staff? Do they enjoy their work and feel personally committed to the company?

3 What, specifically and in very concrete terms, are we particularly good at doing, in the eyes of our customers and in terms of making the highest profits?

Unless you can honestly answer yes to questions (1) and (2), you should think seriously about the company's culture and how to change it.

Question (3) is not easy to answer, but if you persevere you may gain a very useful insight into how to develop the firm. To illustrate this, answers that certain firms have arrived at include the following:

> *'We are good at supplying high margin, branded stationery items in Europe, delivering high quality product quickly. We cannot be efficient or low enough in cost for lower margin or unbranded product, and we are not operationally effective in America or the Far East.'*
>
> *'We are excellent at product invention and innovation. We are poor marketeers and inefficient at manufacturing.'*
>
> *'We are good at churning out high volume, standard products at low cost. When we go up-market or try to meet special requirements we fall flat on our face.'*
>
> *'We are good at pleasing customers who have rigorous engineering requirements. We are bored and slow when it comes to satisfying standard needs.'*
>
> *'We are good at project management on complex, high value projects.'*
>
> *'We have no advantage in terms of product, brand or geography. But our people love meeting customers and delivering exactly what they want, fast. We prosper because our customers, in turn, love us.'*

Once you have discovered the specific source of your company's success, or where it is most successful, there are three things that you could, in theory, do, only two of which are generally sensible:

1 Most people's first instinct is to *correct* their *weaknesses*. For instance, we are good in Europe but not in America, *ergo*, let's sort out America.

   This usually ends in tears. There are generally good, deep-rooted reasons for failure in America (or wherever). It normally requires a lot of time, energy, skill, money and luck to turn bad into good. Most of the time it is not worth the effort and the risk.

   Far more productive, in most circumstances, are the following two approaches:

2 *Further enhance your areas of strength.* Take what is very good and make it excellent. Take what is better than competitors can do, and make it

so much better that they give up entirely. Take something that is excellent by local standards, and make it world-beating. Take something that is excellent but brittle, and dependent on a few people, and make it broader-based and so deeply rooted in the company's mentality and way of doing business that it could survive the departure of the current experts and leaders.

3 *Focus on the functions, parts of the* VALUE CHAIN, *products and/or markets that really play to your strengths*, gain market share and sales in these areas, and migrate out of other areas. It may be that only 20 per cent of your sales are in the areas of real strength, though these generate 60 per cent of your contribution and 90 per cent of your fully costed profits. In that case, aim to migrate, over time, out of the 80 per cent of sales that do not play to your strengths. Plan so that in 5–10 years, your 20 per cent of profitable sales have been tripled, the 80 per cent of unprofitable sales eliminated, and the surplus cost associated with the latter also eliminated. You will have a smaller, simpler, more focused business, and profits nearly three times as great as today's.

Some of you may feel that I have strayed well beyond the province of strategy, to talk about operational excellence, culture and competencies. This accusation may even be correct, if 'strategy' is thought to be confined to hard, analytical issues. Yet 'strategy' should mean thinking about how to improve a company's worth and competitive positioning, and such thinking should not ignore non-analytical issues.

A firm's competitive strategy cannot be confined to purely structural issues. Operational issues and strategic position are all of a piece. Awareness of structural strengths and weaknesses, and operational strengths and weaknesses, are simultaneously necessary. Only then can the company focus on what it does best, and make excellence permanent and deeply engrained. Only then can customers be delighted, won and retained. Only then can competitors be outpaced. And only then can short term profits and long term shareholder value be raised.

CHAPTER 11

Conclusion

We have now reached the end of the section on Business Unit Strategy, for those running real businesses with customers and competitors. This is where the greatest value of strategy lies: in detail, at the sharp end, with those who are in the thick of the battle. I hope that, if you have read this far, you are now convinced of the value of strategy to operating line managers.

But for 30 years the conventional wisdom has been different. The accepted view or assumption of strategists throughout this period has been that the main value of strategy is at the overall corporate level, at the Head Office. In the process, more value has been subtracted than added.

To understand why this is the case, and what are possible antidotes to value destruction at the central level, we shall shortly turn to Part Two: Corporate Strategy.

CHAPTER 12

Additional note on the theory of Business Unit Strategy

The view I have presented above is a practical distillation of what I consider useful for practising executives trying to develop a strategy for their own business. MBA students and others who are interested in the theory of strategy should be aware of the following controversies that I have ignored or side-stepped in the text above:

- the resource-based view of strategy versus the positioning view
- the boundaries between Business Unit Strategy and Corporate Strategy
- planned strategy versus emergent, crafted and evolutionary strategy
- strategy as art versus science.

In this note I outline the main issues and protagonists, before giving my verdict on the controversy.

The resource-based view of strategy versus the positioning view

I have presented what is basically a 'positioning' view of Business Unit Strategy, which says: identify and worry about the competitive positions that you have in each business segment. This is the view most commonly associated with BCG and with Michael PORTER, the Harvard Business School professor.

There is another view, the resource-based view of strategy, that says that it is wrong to start with the individual segments. Rather, it says, we should start with the total corporation and think about its core COMPETENCIES, and then decide which BUSINESS SEGMENTS to enter.

The issue is: where does competition really occur? Is it at the level of whole corporations, or between business units within different corporations? Michael Porter states bluntly: 'Corporations don't compete, business units do.'

But Michel Robert of the resource-based view disagrees: 'It is companies that compete and not business units. In fact, what will determine a business unit's ability to compete is determined even before that business unit is formed.'

Robert goes on to assert: 'Successful companies are those that can leverage their unique set of capabilities (driving forces and areas of excellence) across the largest number of products and markets.' He quotes a number of examples, mainly of Japanese companies, where the key expertise is technological and extends across different product applications. For instance, Honda's real skill is in motors – specifically in multilevel cylinder heads with self-adjusting valves – and these skills are deployed across quite different markets – motorcycles, cars, lawnmowers and power generation equipment. In the US, Hewlett-Packard's key competency is in instrumentation technology, used in a large range of markets from oscilloscopes to cardiac analysers; Northern Telecom Switches has a key skill in digital switch technology, which is used in PBXs, in hybrid analogue-digital switches, and also in fully configured offices.

Although in my account I have folded in the idea of core competencies (in section 5) to take account of what underpins competitive position, the resource-based school would say that I have put the cart before the horse. If we can define the core competency or competencies, they say, we will know where we should focus, and we can then hive off or sell businesses that do not fit the core competencies.

My verdict is that the resource-based view is perfectly legitimate and it makes some good points. The companies cited by Michel Robert have generally been successful, quite possibly as a result of a top-down resource approach. I do not, however, find this a very satisfactory approach for most practical business people, for three reasons:

1 It is more difficult to define a corporation's core competencies objectively than it is to observe where the corporation is strong in its individual competitive segments, measured in terms of its relative market share, trend in market share, and return on capital. Competitive strength is the verdict of the market and has a great deal of objective reality. To say, for example, that Hewlett-Packard has a core competency in instrumentation technology does not take us very far in deciding where to focus.

2 As a matter of fact, Michael Porter is more often right than Michel Robert: competition occurs more frequently at the level of business units than whole corporations. Honda competes against Yamaha in motorcycles, and against Toyota, General Motors and Ford in cars; Yamaha doesn't make cars and the car-makers don't make motorcycles. Honda's approach based on its core competency may be valid, but it still has to take account of different competitors in individual segments, and only a segment-based positioning approach can do this. To focus exclusively on the core competency runs the risk of ignoring competition where this does not coincide with the company's own approach (which is nearly all of the time) – a very dangerous policy.

3 The resource-based approach blurs the distinction between Business Unit Strategy and Corporate Strategy. I will comment more on this in a moment, but the practical disadvantage for business unit managers with the resource-based approach is that they either have to wait for the corporation to sort out its view on its core competencies (which may take forever), or they have to treat their own business unit as a separate mini-corporation, and work out their own core competencies, regardless of those of the whole corporation. This is not necessarily a bad thing, but unless the corporation is willing to split itself up according to differences in core competencies, it is likely to lead to conflict between the Centre and the business units. A bottom-up resource-based view is likely, in my view, to present a more honest and valid picture of a corporation's real core competencies that the top-down approach favoured by most resource-based theorists. Yet the bottom-up view is likely to be too polyglot and variegated to ever lead to an integrated, holistic view of corporate competencies, which is what the resource approach is gunning for.

My overall view is that the resource-based view has a valid point, especially for small and simple corporations. There is not necessarily an inconsistency between the resource-based and the positioning schools: it is just a pragmatic decision on whether to start at the top or the bottom. If you start at the top, you either have to de-emphasise, demerge or sell the activities that don't fit the overall core competencies. If you start at the bottom, with a positioning approach, you should be extremely mindful of the core competencies that underpin your strong positions; you should nurture and deepen those core competencies and make them more difficult for competitors to imitate; and you should think carefully about new business segments where you can deploy those competencies, preferably where you can avoid competition altogether, or, as a second prize, where you can establish leadership in the new segment.

In Part Two I go beyond both schools of thought, developing an 'ecological' theory of strategy. See pages 103–110.

The boundaries between Business Unit Strategy and Corporate Strategy

This is really an extension of the resource-based versus positioning debate. Do you treat the division or SBU (Strategic Business Unit) as an autonomous corporation or sub-corporation, or do you start with the whole corporation, or at least the whole SBU? To the extent that you start with the whole corporation or a bigger part of it, you will need to work out the overall Corporate Strategy first. To the extent that you start at the bottom with a positioning approach, you are in effect ignoring the overall Corporate Strategy or putting it on hold for the moment. The boundary between Business Unit Strategy and Corporate Strategy is not as clear-cut as I have presented it in Part One; it is often blurred and messy.

For example, unless we have each SBU as a self-sufficient mini-corporation, with its own balance sheet and control of its own cash flow and financing, there must be a central process of resource allocation, either at the divisional or corporate level. Therefore, the division may have to exercise some of the functions of 'the Centre', and, in effect, have a Corporate Strategy. In a way, Randy Mayhew of UTC is in fact a Centre manager: he has to allocate resources across his segments, he has to nurture his core competencies, he has to lead and motivate, he has to be a catalyst for corporate learning, and he has to control budgets and cash flows at a 'mini-central' level before reporting to his head office. I discuss these points further in Part Two. For the moment, just remember that the boundaries between the role of the Centre and the roles of the business units are permeable and to some extent subjective, and certainly not as clear cut as Part One implies.

Planned strategy versus emergent, crafted and evolutionary strategy

'Strategic planning' has an old-fashioned, Stalinist ring to it. In the 1970s multi-national corporations built up huge planning departments at head office: General Electric had 200 such planners, and also bought in large amounts of strategic consulting to bolster these meagre resources. It was widely recognised, in time, that such efforts did more harm than good. They took power and initiative away from the operating managers, and increased the power of the Centre. In 1983 the new chief executive of General Electric, Jack Welch, wisely dismantled the whole department.

More recently, the whole idea of 'strategic planning' has come under attack, regardless of who does the planning. Partly this is because it is recognised that it is difficult to predict the future, and to plan for it implies lack of respect for the chance occurrences of life. It is better to 'go with the flow' and respect market feedback than to stick to a plan that won't work. Partly, it is the related idea that strategy should be 'crafted' rather than 'planned': it should be a creative and intuitive interaction between the firm's aspirations and results in the marketplace. This view, eloquently espoused by Henry MINTZBERG, the Canadian academic, claims that planning necessarily involves over-definition and categorisation of business reality, which is fluid and constantly evolving. Data-gathering and analysis are the key to planning, Mintzberg says, whereas the true key to good strategy is sensitivity to market opportunities, the creation of superior products and service, and the crafting of strategy by those at all levels in the organisation.

Mintzberg really does have a point. I am all in favour of strategy that emerges from the lower reaches of the organisation, as a result of trial and error and continual experimentation. I do not believe that strategy has to be written down or incorporated into fancy charts with masses of numbers as back-up. The best strategy is one that is simple and that everyone can remember. But my experience as a consultant has convinced me that one effective way of getting the debate on strategy going – and casting a great deal of light on a firm's real strengths, very quickly – is to go through the sort of exercise described in Part One. The value of the exercise is not so much in the data and analyses generated – though these do have some value – as in the concepts that lie behind the framework. It's all very well for a professor of strategy to dream about crafting strategy as he goes along. He'd probably make a good job of it, because he knows the basic concepts. For the rest of us, structure helps. But the structure is only a guide and a beginning; and we can layer on top of it all the good things that Mintzberg extols.

Strategy as art rather than science

Another related debate – Is there really such a thing as 'management science'? Are there general rules, or is business just 'one damn thing after another'? If business is really a science, then strategy textbooks, professors of management, business schools, rational analysis, and billions of dollars spent on young and inexperienced, but formidable intelligent, consultants – all these things make sense. If business is really just an art, with no general rules, then experience, judgment and luck are all that matter.

I steer a middle course on this. I'm very influenced by the idea from chaos theory that business is 'fractal', which basically means 'the same pattern but with infinite variety'. Coastlines, clouds, trees and leaves are all fractal. Each one is different, but recognisably similar. If you've observed vast stretches of coastline, you stand a better chance of knowing which way it will go beyond the horizon; but you may still be wrong. Rules of thumb about business are useful, but they are more useful when they are specific to particular types of business. Each business is different, but some are more similar than others. Market share is nearly always of some value, but more valuable in particular types of business than in others.

PART 2

Corporate Strategy*

* This part is totally new and replaces the part on Corporate Strategy in earlier editions. My new views have been greatly enriched by the work of Andrew Campbell and of Peter Johnson and my many discussions with them (see the Preface). I must stress that my views are not, however, identical with those of either Andrew or Peter and they are not be held in any way responsible for my idiosyncrasies.

CHAPTER 1

The joy of Corporate Strategy

Economists, who are meant to provide an accurate and insightful account of how the economy works, can do no such thing, because they lack a coherent 'theory of the firm', of how corporations work, of Corporate Strategy. Most economists would prefer to ignore firms altogether, and show no curiosity about how they work. Economists are happiest describing markets, without the need to describe how those supplying markets are organised. If they do deign to describe firms, economists mainly assume that all firms are similar and that it is impossible for a firm, except when the market is not working properly (under monopoly or oligopoly), to earn a profit over and above the normal cost of capital.

Yet the joy of Corporate Strategy is that the economists are hopelessly wrong. Firms *are* important to the economy. Firms *are* the main vehicles for the creation of new products and services, and for delivering better and better goods at lower and lower costs. Firms *are* the main way that economic resources are exchanged and increased.

Firms are gloriously different from one another. By being different, in creative and new ways, they can be highly profitable, miles above the cost of capital, and make their owners and executives rich. And it is mainly when firms are doing things right, for customers and the economy, that this happy state of affairs prevails.

Most marvellously of all, firms are at root driven and made successful not by money or luck or machines – though both money and luck and machines are essential – but by collaborative human effort and, above all, by an internal compound of co-operation and raw brainpower. Firms are not just economics entities, but *social* entities, in which conscious deliberation by individuals and teams can achieve extraordinary and mind-boggling results. It is corporations and human beings creating and directing them that have made the modern world, that have made human beings an astonishing biological success, able to conquer hunger, disease and untimely death and shape the whole world for human purposes. None of this was possible before the eighteenth century. It only became possible because of the widespread development of corporations, of business firms, of 'organisations'.

All this makes Corporate Strategy rather interesting. It is the difference between what firms do and are that can allow them to defy the economists' drab, homogeneous world, and create extra wealth. It is the *choice of Corporate Strategy* – in practice, what firms do that is different, not a set of fine words written down in the annual report – that drives progress and make the world rich in all senses.

But what *is* 'Corporate Strategy'? Nobody can agree on a definition but I look at it this way. In Part One, you and I explored *Business Unit Strategy*, in fact a simplified view of how a single-product[1] business could exploit its position to make more money. The focus was very much on the structural positioning of a business in terms of customers, costs and competitors. There was very little discussion of what happens when firms attempt to manage a whole variety of products or business units. There was also very little about how firms evolve over time; how they attract and keep talented people; how they collectively 'learn'; how they get much bigger and more valuable; or how they make and can perhaps avoid huge blunders that make the firm much less valuable or cause it to disappear. All of these matters have two things in common that define Corporate Strategy as opposed to Business Unit Strategy.

First, they are about how *firms grow and develop over time*, how they evolve and increase or decrease their value; how they contribute more or less to the economy and to their owners, employees and others who rub up against the firm.

Second, they are about *human beings* and *human creativity*, as well, of course, as human stupidity and miscalculation – the role of conscious thought and intent in shaping the world, and the ability or otherwise of people to work together to achieve something new and great. Corporate

Strategy is about how people – mainly intelligent and dedicated people – make decisions and defy the odds, either to build something fantastic, or to destroy value on a colossal scale.

Corporate Strategy is about guiding the evolution of a firm, determining its character and leadership, deciding where and how to compete, and, in all this, finding a way to make the firm different from any other firm in a way that appeals to certain customers, so that the firm can make super-normal profits and increase its value to both owners and customers.

Note that by this definition, every firm – even simple firms, even one-product firms – needs a Corporate Strategy. Indeed, every firm in fact *has* a Corporate Strategy, if only by default. The strategy is manifest in the actions of the firm and its direction. Even if those who run a firm have never thought explicitly about Corporate Strategy, they have one. It is what they do.

The essence of a firm lies not in its competitive position at a point in time in one business arena, or (if the firm operates in more than one arena) in all its arenas. The essence of the firm lies in what it is and what it can do for customers. '*What it is*' means what the firm knows and how it behaves, which comes down to the knowledge the firm has and how it uses it. What the firm is determines what it can do for customers. But firms can change, and do more or less in the future than they can now.

Not everyone agrees with my broad definition of Corporate Strategy. Some excellent strategists, such as Andrew CAMPBELL, confine Corporate Strategy to firms that operate in more than one 'strategic business unit', and in particular to the 'multibusiness corporation' that has more than one division. To make this distinction clear, Andrew talks of 'corporate level strategy', which means the strategy determined by the Centre of the corporation. Andrew does not neglect the importance of corporate development for single business corporations – he just puts that under the rubric of Business Unit Strategy. This is entirely a matter of taste. His view has great clarity, and is perfectly defensible. I prefer my approach on two grounds. First, the most natural understanding of Corporate Strategy is that it refers to the strategy of *corporations*, regardless of what type of firm they are. Second, it seems to me that the most exciting laws of strategy apply equally to corporations, whether they are mature and complex, with a large Centre directing them, or whether they are newly formed, single businesses run by an entrepreneur. It seems to me logical, therefore, to discuss these laws of strategy – what I call Corporate Strategy – at the same time.

Strategy, I claim, is about how firms are different, how the people in them collaborate to create and satisfy customers, and how they therefore advance the economy and make a killing for their owners. How could all this fail to be fascinating? And yet, how often does the heart sink and the mind wander when the phrase Corporate Strategy is heard? In my view, this is because the excitement, richness and diversity of Corporate Strategy has been, with a few honourable exceptions, very poorly explained or appreciated. Let us see if we can do better.

CHAPTER 2

An ecological view of Corporate Strategy

Writers on Corporate Strategy generally fall into one of two competing camps. In the red corner, there is the *positioning* or *portfolio-based* approach. This says that companies should seek to be in attractive markets where the firm can establish a competitive advantage. The high priest of this movement is Harvard Professor Michael PORTER,[2] who believes in micro-economic analysis of the segments where competition occurs and who states bluntly that 'Corporations don't compete, business units do.'

In the blue corner, however, sits the *resource-based* view of strategy, which stresses the uniqueness of each corporation (not business unit) and claims that the success of firms is determined by the strength of their 'core competencies' – above all the people and learning embedded in a corporation. The arch gurus of this school are C. K. PRALAHAD and Gary HAMEL, who invented the phrase 'CORE COMPETENCIES' in 1990.[3] Another resource-based thinker, Michel Robert, has put the rejoinder to Michael Porter:

> ***'It is companies that compete and not business units. In fact, what will determine a business unit's ability to compete is determined even before that business unit is formed ... Successful companies are those that can leverage their unique set of capabilities (driving forces and areas of excellence) across the largest number of products and markets.'***[4]

I have sympathy with both schools of thought. As will have been evident from Part One, I believe that different business segments can have hugely different attractiveness and that the front line of the competitive battle is fought in a great variety of particular, closely defined areas or segments. On the other hand, my experience tells me that the most important determinant of success or failure for any substantial, multibusiness firm, more important ultimately even than the aggregate strength or weakness of its segment competitive positions, lies in its people. I was a management consultant for 15 years, and it slowly dawned on me that it was not enough for a firm to have great strategic positions if the people in the firm couldn't capitalise on them; and that, conversely, some firms with little obvious competitive advantage could do very well based purely on the skill and creativity of their people. After giving up consulting, I became a professional investor, and it became evident to me, as to all venture capitalists and private equity specialists, that 'there are only three things that are important in making an investment decision – people, people, and people.' I never make a private equity investment without believing both in the people and in the structural opportunity to dominate an attractive market segment.

My view of Corporate Strategy, while acknowledging the truth held within both the resource-based view and the positioning view, goes beyond both of them. It is a biological or ecological view, originally triggered by Bruce HENDERSON's remark that 'no two businesses can survive that make their living in exactly the same way.' In ecology, a viable 'niche' – what Charles Darwin called 'a place in the economy of nature' – is defined partly by the place where a particular creature lives, but also – and critically – by the *way* it makes its living.

It is precisely the same with corporations. Each firm operates within a number of 'ECOSYSTEMS', which are the segments or niches where it conducts its business.[5] But each firm also has a genetic structure – a combination of skills, approaches, ways of doing business and interacting with customers, suppliers and other outside parties, knowledge, assets, and most important of all people, who are used to working together. The firm's genetic structure may be more or less suitable for the ecosystems in which it operates. The firm's genetic structure also *penetrates, influences and changes* the ecosystems where it operates. Indeed, the firm may have created one or more of the ecosystems where it lives, and will retain an obvious advantage there if the balance of the ecosystem remains undisturbed. In turn, the ecosystems and the firm's genetic structure can be influenced and changed by the action of competitors, or by events in adjacent ecosystems and technologies. From time to time, a competitor, usually a new rather than an existing competitor, dramatically changes an ecosystem and may make it much less hospitable to the original firm.

The key thing to grasp is the huge variety in ecosystems and in the genetic structure of firms, as well as their dynamic nature – they may change gradually over time or abruptly at a point in time. The variety in ecosystems and in the genetic structure of firms explains why many apparent competitors can sometimes all make returns well above the cost of capital.

What do I mean by the variety in ecosystems and their dynamic nature? Well, aside from pure agricultural markets, such as those for barley or rice, most markets exhibit a high degree of specificity and therefore heterogeneity – they are different from all other markets, heavily conditioned by the way that particular customers, particular firms and particular suppliers to those firms interact with one another.

Consider the market for cars. In the 1890s, although the automobile market in the United States was very small, there were over 500 firms making cars. Every vehicle was handcrafted and often tailored to the requirements of the buyers, who were almost without exception rich and usually eccentric enthusiasts for the new technology. The car market was quite unlike any other market, and nearly all the firms catering to the market were new and focused on that market. The car ecosystem was unique.

Yet, that ecosystem was not stable. Why? Because one man – Henry Ford – had a bee in his bonnet. He wanted to 'democratize the automobile'. Initially he had no idea at all how to do this. But he conceived the idea that if autos could be made much cheaper, they could be sold to different customers – to the middle classes and eventually to skilled workers. Ford believed that standardisation and scale could reduce the cost of making and selling cars to a fraction of their cost in 1900. Ford's lieutenants eventually discovered the assembly line with its many integrated feeders. This they improvised and improved until they achieved – and then greatly exceeded – Ford's targets for cost reduction. In the process, the car ecosystem was utterly transformed. By 1910, some 438,000 Americans owned cars, which was more than ten times as many as in 1900. By 1920, the number of car owners had multiplied another 18 times, to 8,225,000. The new ecosystem emerged in the shadow of Henry Ford – the Ford Motor Corporation was ideally matched to the new ecosystem.

The car ecosystem was transformed again in the 1920s and 1930s by Alfred P. Sloan Jr, President of General Motors from 1923. General Motors took a quite different tack from the Ford Motor Corporation. Instead of paring costs to the bone by standardisation, GM invented 'a car for every purse and purpose', using marketing to create separate identities and loyalties for five new car brands. In ascending order of aspiration and price, customers could choose from Chevrolet, Pontiac, Oldsmobile, Buick and Cadillac, and from a huge diversity of colours and features. Instead of centralising the corporation like Ford, Sloan decentralised GM into separate divisions, one for each brand. Instead of emasculating subordinates and employing spies to report on his staff, as Ford did, Sloan delegated to his managers and indeed did much to create the whole concept of management. Instead of making his corporation as much like a machine as possible and giving orders from the top, as Ford did, Sloan led by example, worked out of two small cubicles in Detroit and New York, and allowed himself to be overruled by his associates. Sloan spent most of his time making decisions on people – 'the most important decisions an executive could make,' he said.

In creating a new type of corporation and reaching out to new customers, the genetic code of GM was very different from that of the Ford Motor Corporation. And it worked. By 1937, GM had overtaken Ford, capturing 42 per cent of the market. Ford slumped into third place with only half that level.

Since then the auto ecosystem in the United States has been transformed by changes in technology and the action of competitors, first from Europe and then from Japan. New segments or ecosystems – the sports car market, the mini-van market, the sport-utility market, the small car market – were created and moulded by new competitors. Ford and GM didn't evolve the genetic code for these ecosystems in time – they were dominated by Porsche and later by Mazda (sports cars), by Chrysler (mini-vans), by Jeep (sport-utility) and by Volkswagen (small cars).

If you compare any two 'competitors' today, in any industry or any country, you will find that the more you know about the companies, the less similar they appear. They are likely to serve different types of customer, with subtly different products, different mixes of products, different component makers and other suppliers, different degrees of sub-contracting, different proportions of the value added provided by each firm, different channels of distribution, and different price realisations. At each stage of production the 'competing' firms will likely have different costs. Most of the differences may cancel out, but they reflect significant differences in the way the firms compete, and they are likely to influence customer preferences. The firms will probably have subtly or radically different cultures, degrees of decentralisation, and a different mix of employees defined by any criterion. Unless they have the same unions or draw on an identical geographical and demographic catchment group, the firms will pay their people differently. If you ask different groups of customers, they will have different opinions about each of the companies and their products on several dimensions. The genetic structure of all firms is unique, and all successful firms are quite distinctive from their competitors. This is almost the complete opposite of the picture held by most economists.

Head-to-head competition is rare. Where it does occur, as in commodity-like markets such as steel or semiconductors, profit margins are slim or non-existent. Firms can be profitable to the degree that they identify a group of customers that like their products *and* to the degree that the firm is quite unlike any other firm. Put another way, firms are successful if their way of business is highly adapted to and popular in viable ecosystems and if they are more adapted to those ecosystems than any other competitor. It is the fit between the genetic structure of the ecosystem and the genetic structure of the firms that determines success.

Let's go back to the debate between the *positioning* school and the *resources* school. The *ecological* view of strategy sides most obviously with the resource view. In the ecological perspective, the essence of any firm is not just a collection of transactions or market positions. The firm is a living and unique organism. It is more than the sum of its parts. It has a unique genetic structure which can be mapped on many different dimensions: the particular ecosystems in which it competes; the way it approaches them; the mix of value added it has; the suppliers with whom it collaborates and the way it does so; and above all, the people it employs and how they go about serving and creating ecosystems where the firm can flourish.

Behind all this, the firm has a *business model* that it has evolved in its most important and profitable markets, which – if the firm is very successful – is very well matched to the needs of those ecosystems. The business model encapsulates everything that the firm needs to do to satisfy its most important and profitable customers and to innovate in new ecosystems that are similar to the existing ones or where it can use its business model effectively.

The key to great Corporate Strategy, therefore, is to ensure that the firm operates *in as many profitable ecosystems as it can effectively service*, provided that those ecosystems are susceptible to the firm's business model and genetic code; to evolve the firm's genetic structure to dovetail more perfectly with those ecosystems; but also to ensure that the firm does not operate in any ecosystems that are not profitable or where other competitors have a better business model or genetic code. Since markets differ greatly and can be divided into a great variety of separate ecosystems, the art is to compete only where the firm is more suited to the ecosystem than any other competitor.

Certainly, if a market is large and highly profitable, a firm may want to adapt its genetic code to serve that market, even if the existing business model is not ideally suited to it. But this is often a trap. A firm's GENETIC CODE can be modified over long periods of time, by incorporating new learning or new people and by improving the way it serves its customers. Yet a firm's genetic code cannot be changed radically or quickly except at a time of crisis and through extreme measures, such as firing the entire senior management and importing a new top team used to a different business model.

Any attempt by a firm to change its business model to serve a new ecosystem is fraught with danger. If the change is successful, it will dilute the genetic code that the firm is employing successfully in other ecosystems, and open those up to challenge by new competitors. But most likely the change will not be successful, and it will squander resources in the vain pursuit of a new profitable ecosystem, while detracting from the successful maintenance of the existing business model in the other key ecosystems. This is another way of saying what all experienced managers know – that a new business initiative may distract attention away from the core business, and the pursuit of growth may weaken the firm.

Note that the ecological view places a great deal of emphasis on identifying the differences between ecosystems and the fit between the firm's resources and each ecosystem. While this has the clearest affinity with the resources school, it also encapsulates the best insights from the positioning school. The choice of ecosystems – the micro-characteristics of markets that define the boundaries of different ecosystems – matters a great deal. From the firm's viewpoint, ecosystems differ in only two crucial respects: the extent to which the firm's business model and genetic code fits the ecosystem better than any other firm; and the extent to which the ecosystem is profitable. Different ecosystems, even in the same industry, can have extremely variable profitability. For example, in the personal computer market, the software ecosystem dominated by Microsoft is extremely profitable, the market for direct ordering of computers dominated by Dell is rather profitable, and nearly all other ecosystems (other than routers and specialist software) are marginally profitable at best.

The resources school stresses one of these aspects (the fit between the firm and its markets) and the positioning school stresses the other aspect (the importance of differences in profitability in different segments of the market). Both are crucial. Corporate Strategy is about hard decisions and tradeoffs, because a firm often cannot be configured to serve different types of market effectively and profitably. Indeed, the best and fastest way of diagnosing a firm's genetic code – of defining its 'core competencies' – may well be through the *positioning* route, by seeing in detail where it is most profitable and then trying to work out why it is ideally suited to serve those ecosystems.

Some animals focus on just one ecosystem and one source of food. Ecologist Robert MacArthur points to different species of warblers and says that each one inhabits a different part of a spruce tree and eats different insects. Each warbler species has its own particular ecological niche and lives on one type of insect.[6] On the other hand, some species of animal – humankind for example – have genes that enable them to take advantage of many ecosystems and many different sources of food.

It is the same with corporations. Some are only adapted to one type of ecosystem, and lose money whenever they venture beyond it. Other firms – of which private equity houses are currently the most successful example – manage to operate in diverse ecosystems and apply a few limited but powerful insights across all of them. Trying to take a firm that is only adapted to one type of ecosystem and move it profitably to serve another type of ecosystem is a big gamble – sometimes you hit the jackpot, but usually you lose your shirt.

Let's try to summarise the ecological view of Corporate Strategy:

- Corporations are important to the economy because they comprise unique ways of serving customers. Each corporation evolves its own business model that is peculiarly suited to certain customers and leads to a good fit between the ecosystem (market niche) and the firm's genetic code (way of doing business and corporate character).
- The most successful firms are ones that serve large and profitable ecosystems and are more suited to do so than any competitor. The more different the firm from other firms, the more likely the firm is to be highly profitable on a sustained basis.
- Because competition is heterogeneous, successful firms can obtain a return on capital that greatly exceeds the required rate of return.
- Different types of ecosystem require different types of operations to serve them. These differences, though vitally important, are often subtle and easy to miss or misread from the outside. Indeed, the biggest blunders in Corporate Strategy happen when a firm enters a new ecosystem thinking that it is similar to others in which it operates successfully, but the new ecosystem turns out to be very different.
- It is unusual for a firm to serve different types of ecosystem successfully. But it is possible, in two circumstances. One is when there are different divisions operating largely or totally autonomously within the same corporation. The other case is when the Centre of a firm – either a head office or active owners of the firm such as a private equity house – has insights that can operate in the different ecosystems.
- The art of Corporate Strategy is to find and if possible create profitable ecosystems that are ideally suited to the firm; and, conversely, to make the firm the best possible firm to supply the profitable ecosystems where it operates. Everything about the firm should be geared to the needs and wishes of the ecosystems – even when customers in the ecosystem are unaware that it exists or unaware of what they will like.

CHAPTER 3

Five dimensions of Corporate Strategy

Five dimensions of Corporate Strategy are worth exploring, each with their own principles of good strategy:

1 Evolve the firm's genetic code

2 Back winners and cull losers

3 Become the best possible parent

4 Place astute bets on growth

5 Create a new ecosystem.

1 Evolve the firm's genetic code

For every firm, evolving its GENETIC CODE in a way that fits its most important and profitable markets is essential for success. Unless the firm is better adapted to its most profitable ecosystems than any other firm, it cannot go forward and will inevitably slip back.

The idea of a firm's genetic code incorporates (but goes beyond) the idea of a firm's 'distinctive competences' or 'CORE COMPETENCIES'. In remarkably modern language, Philip SELZNICK wrote in 1957 that the most important task of leaders was to identify and build on the organisation's distinctive competencies:

> ***'Leadership goes beyond efficiency (1) when it sets the basic mission of the organization and (2) when it creates a social organism capable of fulfilling that mission ... [this] is not so***

> ***much technical administrative management as the maintenance of institutional integrity ... It is a practical concern of the first importance because the defence of integrity is also a defence of the organization's distinctive competences.'*** [7]

It is interesting to compare Selznick's view to the definition that C. K. PRAHALAD and Gary HAMEL gave of 'core competencies' in their famous 1990 *Harvard Business Review* article:

> ***'... the collective learning in the organization, especially how to coordinate diverse production skills and integrate multiple streams of technology ... unlike physical assets, competencies do not deteriorate as they are applied and shared. They grow.'***

Although both definitions are useful and complementary, I think Selznick's offers the greater insight. In talking of 'a social organism' and the defence of the firm's integrity, he stresses the *choices* and *tradeoffs* that leaders must make. Firms have a collective character and must be true to themselves. This means that they can only be effective in certain distinctive ways and in distinctive ecosystems. As Selznick observes, a distinctive competence in one area necessarily implies a 'distinctive incompetence' in many other areas. Selznick told of a high-quality, bespoke master boatyard that decided to expand into mass production of inexpensive speed boats, a much higher growth market. The boatyard's culture did not fit the requirements of the market; the move failed because the yard's distinctive competence of care and quality carried with it distinctive incompetence in low-cost mass production.

Firms frequently fool themselves into believing that they can cover the waterfront, serving different types of market. I've done it myself! For several years I've been the lead investor in a hotel business called Zola, which, thanks to the skill of the two operating partners, has been consistently successful. Our distinctive competence is in buying badly run three-star hotels in small English towns where there is substantial business trade, improving the quality and increasing the number of rooms, and selling the hotels two or three years later at a substantial profit. A few years ago we ran out of suitable new investments and relaxed our criteria so as to allow us to buy badly run three-star hotels in small English towns where the main trade was for vacations rather than business. We bought two hotels in seaside towns catering mainly to holiday-makers. We sold the hotels a couple of years later, making almost no profit on our investment.

The needs of the business market we understood. Those of individual vacationers we didn't. The properties and business formula seemed very similar. Not similar enough. It is salutary that even a great firm like Coca-Cola can't make a go out of entering non-cola beverage markets. Heed the warning – avoid superficially similar ecosystems.

Define your firm's distinctive competences. Now define all the significant ecosystems where you operate. Which ecosystem is the one that most appreciates your distinctive competences? That is where you should focus.

Why talk about a firm's genetic code rather than its distinctive competences? Is it just a preference for new and proprietary jargon? I don't think so. A firm's genetic code is a deeper and more useful concept than its distinctive competences, although in talking about a firm's 'integrity' – necessarily implying its character – Philip Selznick was groping towards the genetic idea all those years ago. The firm's genetic code incorporates all the differences between one competitor and another, both objective differences and also 'softer' differences such as culture and ways of behaving.

To get some idea of the millions of permutations that could define genetic differences between firms, consider some of the dimensions of difference. First, some objective differences:

- the type of people it employs, and their variety or homogeneity
- the number of levels in the organisation
- the extent of delegated authority at each level
- the proportion of employees that deal face-to-face with customers
- the firm's revenues in each ecosystem
- the proportion of value-added in its revenues (what it 'makes' as opposed to buys in from the outside) in each ecosystem
- the customers and type of customers (for example individual consumers, other business firms, specialist organisations such as hospitals) in each ecosystem
- the firm's revenues in each ecosystem split by channel of distribution (for example, through agents, distributors, the Internet, call centres, retail)
- the applications that each customer uses in each ecosystem (for example, is computer software used professionally or personally?)

- the firms that are supply partners in each of the ecosystems
- the proportion of revenues the firm spends on various activities of importance to customers, for example, research and development, advertising and other marketing initiatives
- its market shares and relative market shares in each ecosystem
- the ratio of top-paid to bottom-paid employees
- customer retention levels (consistent repurchase over time)
- employee retention levels
- the firm's profitability in each ecosystem
- the firm's financial leverage.

Here are some of the 'softer' yet even more vital differences between firms:

- the dominant value systems in the firm – what qualities are most admired (for example, dedication to customers, product innovation, intellect, short term results)
- the personality and legacy of the founder or founders
- the personality of the CEO and senior executives
- the diversity or homogeneity of the firm's ecosystems
- the degree to which different business units are totally separate from each other (at one extreme) or collaborate very closely every day (at the other extreme)
- the degree of friction or warmth between the Centre and the operating units, and between one unit and another
- the degree to which financial targets and results are top of mind – is missing budget tolerated?
- the degree of formality or informality in the firm
- the degree to which the firm is hierarchical or meritocratic; and the extent to which the firm has 'single-status'[8]
- the degree to which information is shared freely within the firm
- how open or closed the firm is to outsiders
- whether friendliness or fear is the dominant motif
- how quickly decisions are taken

- whether the firm's environment is predictable or fast-shifting, or both (in different ecosystems)
- whether customers tend to love or hate the firm, or be indifferent, or all three (in different ecosystems)

Firms are all different. Yet my long lists can mislead. Typically, only a few of the dissimilarities will matter. It is the *pivotal differences* between apparently similar competitors and apparently similar ecosystems that matter – the variances that can explain why one competitor is growing faster or is much more profitable than other firms, or why two apparently head-to-head competitors can both experience high growth and profitability.

For instance, to the informed outsider, there might appear to be little difference between the two strategy consulting firms Bain & Company ('Bain') and the Boston Consulting Group (BCG). If you walked about their offices – which tend to be located in the same cities and districts of those cities – you'd see a bunch of high-energy young people frenetically staring at computer screens, on the phone, or meeting in glass-fronted goldfish bowls. BCG and Bain recruit from the same talent pools, work for similar firms, and tend nowadays to have similar levels of growth (good) and profitability (very good). Both firms use the same intellectual techniques and believe in the power of arcane data-gathering and analysis. They pay their people similar large amounts and require them to work the same ridiculously long hours. They charge similar (very high) fees.

Yet if you knew both firms intimately – if, for instance, you'd worked in both of them – you'd know there were some profound differences between the firms, reflecting the personalities of their different founders (Bill Bain contrasted with Bruce Henderson), even though the founders are long gone. BCG is decentralised, even anarchic; Bain & Company is centralised, even Stalinist. BCG admires intellect; Bain admires results. BCG is individualistic; Bain believes in teamwork. BCG loves innovation; Bain loves discipline. The business formula of each firm is different. BCG promises its clients a creative solution. Bain promises them increased market value. (Both generally deliver on their promise.) BCG will work for competitors, whereas Bain & Company will not. BCG will work on important projects for clients who are not the top dog in the whole organisation. Bain will not (or at least did not for the first 15 years of its existence). Bain has a private equity arm; BCG does not. The personality traits of the successful BCG person and the successful Bain person are completely different.

The point is not that Bain is better than BCG, or BCG better than Bain. Both are excellent firms. They have different genetic codes and therefore their work is substantially different. Even though they might compete for the same assignment, they would structure it very differently and deliver different things. They operate in different ecosystems, the one they created. Were it otherwise, they could not both be so profitable.

Another point. The crucial thing is not what a corporation *can* do, but what it *does* do, and how well this fits each customer ecosystem. A firm may operate in many ecosystems, some of which may be subtly or sharply different in character from one another. Yet the firm can only have one genetic code, one personality, one way of acting with integrity. It follows that a firm must make choices. It cannot operate effectively in ecosystems that have different requirements of the firm. The firm should only operate in ecosystems where its genetic code gives it an advantage over all other firms.

Whereas 'distinctive competences' or 'core competencies' are additive, the genetic code is not. This is a much more realistic map of what leads to success. A firm can have unparalleled knowledge and skills that are highly relevant to many ecosystems. But if the ecosystems are different in character, no firm will be able to marshal its different competencies to satisfy all the ecosystems.

Some 30 or 40 years ago, Xerox Corporation had skills and knowledge that, with hindsight and appropriate deployment, could have made the owners of Xerox as rich as the owners of Microsoft. In California's leafy Palo Alto, the Xerox boffins invented the personal computer, the mouse, software similar to Windows, the laser printer, the paperless office and Ethernet. But none of these innovations was commercially introduced by Xerox. They had no product champions within Xerox.

Xerox's genes were incompatible with the nurturing of ground-breaking technologies. The firm's genetic code was framed by its experience in the copier business, a business that it had dominated for a long time. Xerox's business formula was based on commercial exploitation of one huge success, and by financial rules to optimise that success (for example, leasing rather than selling copiers). Xerox was bureaucratic and controlled by financial types who valued constantly increasing short-term profits. The corporation believed in milking its existing products, not in creating dramatically different new ones.

The only way that Xerox could have used its technological competencies would have been by totally changing its character – absent a crisis or a visionary CEO from outside, impossible – or by spinning off Xerox Parc into a new corporation. If a SPINOFF had been made, Xerox Parc would almost certainly have become much more valuable than its original parent. Although Xerox remained a valuable corporation, the value not realised from Xerox Parc was stupendous.

A firm's genetic code partly relates to its structural position, which can be mechanically described: its products and technologies; its cost position relative to competition; the strength of its brand in various ecosystems; the ecosystem market shares and relative market shares; whether it developed those ecosystems itself or followed a firm that created them; its important customers and suppliers; any other competitive or regulatory advantages or disadvantages; and other external facts that are 'sticky', that is, relatively insensitive to actions by the company. *But a firm's genetic code relates mainly to its people.* What matters most is the quality, creativity, self-perception, patterns of thought and actions of the people, especially – since almost no firms are democracies – the people at the top, and the way that people throughout the firm relate to one another and to outsiders.

It follows that if there is a serious problem in a firm – if, for example, it is losing market share or producing disappointing numbers – there really is a problem with the people in the firm. Above all, probably, if they have been there some time, there is a problem with the people at the top – almost certainly with the CEO. This is, of course, the dilemma of consultants and why so much expensive consulting work, done by excellent consultants, has no useful outcome. If the CEO is the problem, and the CEO is paying the consultants, very few of them – in my experience, none – will tell the CEO that he or she is the problem and must go.

The main reason for poor Corporate Strategy is that firms don't replace under-performing CEOs quickly enough. Private equity firms replace failing CEOs much faster than the public markets – one reason why private equity is more profitable and growing faster than the public markets.

Sometimes, however, the problem is not so much inappropriate top management as a change in the firm's ecosystems which renders the old genetic code of the firm less relevant; or else because the firm is trying to serve different ecosystems which require different corporate genetic codes.

Take the case of Hewlett-Packard (H-P). This fine firm used to have a close fit between its genetic code and the needs of its ecosystems. Up to the 1970s, Hewlett-Packard operated in fast-growth, fast-moving, free-wheeling, high-margin ecosystems, where innovative products and creative engineers at all levels were the key to success. H-P's markets all shared these characteristics.

In the 1980s, however, three of H-P's most important ecosystems – calculators, minicomputers and instruments – started to mature and become more predictable. H-P's entrepreneurial enthusiasm became less useful in these markets. Margins shrank. Control by numbers and low-cost production became more important. H-P's growth and profitability came under pressure, and the firm found it difficult to change its genetic code, simply because it was rooted so strongly in the culture and had performed so well for so long.[9]

Hewlett-Packard also became a firm where different ecosystems came to require different genetic codes. Although H-P had three important mature businesses by the late 1980s, it also operated in a large number of smaller, fast-growth ecosystems where the original H-P genetic code was just as appropriate as ever. What H-P required was what is impossible in one corporation – two different genetic codes. The firm has never fully resolved this dilemma. With hindsight, H-P should have split into two firms, by spinning off the mature businesses into a new corporation with a new CEO used to such ecosystems and able to build a new genetic code.

There are seven action implications:

1 CEOs and corporate strategists should understand and describe the firm's genetic code, the extent to which it fits or does not the requirements of each of the firm's key ecosystems, and whether in each ecosystem a competitor has a genetic code more adapted to the ecosystem.

2 As no firm can successfully serve different types of ecosystem, business in ecosystems where the genetic code is less adapted should be sold or spun-off.

3 In cases where the firm has the best genetic code for the ecosystem, the firm should focus heavily on growing its sales and profits in the ecosystem, and seek to accentuate the differences between itself and competitors.

4 Where the firm does not have the best genetic code for an ecosystem, the firm has a choice. It can either sell or spin off the business, which is the easier and usually more profitable solution. Or it can attempt to change its genetic code to provide not merely a better fit with the ecosystem, but a better fit than any other competitor.[10] The chance of success here may be low.

5 If a profound change in a firm's genetic code is attempted, it should be led by someone with empathy for the key ecosystems, and a track record in a firm successfully serving them.

6 All firms, especially those where performance is deteriorating for unexplained reasons, should look carefully at the trend in the nature of its ecosystems and whether a new competitor with a different and more adapted genetic code has emerged in one or more important ecosystems. If the nature of the ecosystems is changing, the firm must change too, or else dispose of the relevant business.

7 If a firm is performing badly and the CEO has been in place a long time, the firm's owners should, as a general rule, remove the CEO.

2 Back winners and cull losers

The positioning school has part of the puzzle. In several hundred exercises I have performed or seen, analysis of a large corporation's portfolio always shows dramatic differences in the profitability of different segments or ecosystems.

Chris Zook and James Allen of Bain & Company analysed data from 185 companies in 33 industries and showed that profitability was clearly related to market leadership.[11]

Market position	**Return on capital**
Weak follower	4%
Strong follower	9%
Parity (1x RMS)	14%
Weak leaders	22%
Strong leaders	25%

These differences in profitability arise partly because of micro-economic influences such as Porter's Five Forces:

- The bargaining power of customers
- The bargaining power of suppliers
- The threat from substitute products
- The threat from potential new competitors
- The competition amongst existing competitors.[12]

But the differences in profitability in a company's portfolio also arise because of the fit between the firm's genetic code and its ecosystems, and in particular because of the specific relations between the firm and its important customers. Where for some specific reason a firm is blessed with large customers who like the firm's product a great deal or who are price insensitive, or where the firm for some specific reason can serve the customer at a cost lower than competitors can (for example, because it is next door, or uses a cheaper material acceptable only to that competitor), then the firm's business in a particular ecosystem can be unusually profitable. In my experience these specifics between important customers and a firm explain as much or more of the differences in segment profitability for the firm as do the general market forces stressed by Porter. The specific differences are often taken for granted by managers in the firm and little thought may be given to them, despite the difference they make to results.

Two rules of thumb follow from large differences in the profitability of different chunks of a firm's business (whether the chunks are defined by ecosystem, product, or customer):

1 Where there are exceptionally profitable chunks of business, the firm should do all possible to expand sales there and to find similar new business.

2 Where business is unprofitable, the price should either be increased, or the cost to serve the customer decreased, or both. If neither is possible, exit from the business.

But product, customer, and ecosystem positions are not the only 'winners' and 'losers'. There are also winning and losing executives, and winning and losing projects and investments. The prescriptions are similar, obvious, and usually ignored, except by private equity professionals.

3 Become the best possible parent

The idea of becoming the best possible parent applies only to 'multibusiness corporations', those with more than one major division.

In 1950, the large majority of firms in the United States and the UK operated largely or entirely in just one business. But by 1980, most large firms had become 'multibusiness', with a number of separate divisions controlled by a head office (also known as 'the Centre'). Surprisingly little research was conducted on the influence of the Centre on its separate businesses, until the publication in 1994 of *Corporate-Level Strategy*, authored by Michael Goold, Andrew Campbell and Marcus Alexander of the Ashridge Strategic Management Centre.[13] This landmark work, based on 11 years of painstaking research, spawned two essential concepts of Corporate Strategy: Value Destruction and Parenting theory.

One might have expected that multibusiness companies (MBCs) grew because their centres were making positive economic contributions. Not so.

As Goold, Campbell and Alexander explain:

> ***'The research on which this book is based suggests that while a few multibusiness companies have corporate strategies that create substantial value, the large majority do not; they are value destroyers. This disturbing conclusion, which applies to multibusiness companies in many different countries and cultures, and of varied size and complexity, casts serious doubt on whether multibusiness companies should continue to play a leading role in the world economy.'***

The book said that the head office (or 'parent') of MBCs is highly influential. Occasionally it has a really positive impact on the company's operating companies. Rarely, it was neutral. Usually, its net impact is negative – it destroyed value. How?

First, through *demotivating operating managers*. Those in charge of subsidiaries find their decisions second-guessed and challenged by the Centre, taking away the vital sense of being responsible for running their own show. Alienation aside, there is also the danger of cosseting and insulation from hard commercial reality – 'businesses that are part of a well-resourced parent organization may not feel the same urgency to perform as an independent entity.'

Second, through *wrong influence and decisions*. Goold, Campbell and Alexander quote an example of an oil company that acquired a minerals company and suggested new approaches to exploration that were appropriate to the oil industry but quite inappropriate for minerals. Managers in the acquired company felt compelled to follow the advice, until it had racked up large losses from doing so. They also highlight a frequent blunder, which is to intimate that all businesses in the portfolio should target the same annual percentage growth. In the case of one low-growth 'cash cow' business, the result was a fruitless search for growth that detracted from the health and profitability of the core business.

The authors explain why bad decisions are typical in an MBC. Information passed up from the divisions to the Centre is filtered and biased to fit the preconceptions of the Centre and display the divisions in the best possible light. Inappropriate goals and advice are given by the Centre, both because they don't know the businesses as well as the divisional managers, and because the experience of those at the Centre may be in subtly different kinds of business where key factors for success are different. The basic problem for corporate parents, the authors say, is 'the 10 per cent versus 100 per cent paradox'. Why, they ask, 'should the chief executive in 10 per cent of his time be able to perceive better strategies for a business than energetic managers devoting 100 per cent of their time to the business?'

Evidence of the value-destroying nature of MBCs comes from spectacular increases in profits that can follow management buyouts of divisions. Premier Brands was a buyout of Cadbury Schweppes' food division by Paul Judge and other ex-Cadbury managers in 1986. When owned by Cadbury in 1985 the firm made £6.6m profit before tax. After the buyout, just three years later, profits surged to £31m. Why? The debt taken on as part of the buyout made performance improvement essential. 'Opportunities were found to reduce indirect workers by 500 (25 per cent of the workforce) and to cut working capital in half ... Suddenly there was a new sense of urgency and an ability to grasp issues' previously swept under the carpet. New investments were made and new products introduced which had previously been rejected by the parent; they were highly successful.

The business, bought from Cadbury for £97m, was sold three years later to Hillsdown Holdings for £310m. Since there were no private equity investors, the great majority of the £213m profit went to the ex-Cadbury managers.

Aside from the impact on operating companies, there are the new initiatives taken by the Centre of companies, especially acquisitions and other growth strategies. These, too, destroy value more often than they create it, as we shall see shortly in section 4 below, 'Place astute bets on growth'. First, however, let's look at the positive side of Parenting theory.

The parent's role, according to Goold, Campbell and Alexander, is to create value over and above its cost and any negative influence it has on its operating companies. The parent should create PARENTING ADVANTAGE, which is like competitive advantage, but refers to the activity of the Centre. Not only that. Unless the parent is the *best possible parent* for any operating company, it should not own the company – economic value could be created by selling the company to its best possible parent.

The Ashridge writers identify three essential features of successful parents:

1 value creation insights

2 distinctive parenting characteristics

3 heartland businesses.

Value creation insights are ideas about specific businesses that point the way to superior performance. The Swedish-Swiss engineering company Asea Brown Boveri (ABB), for example, developed these value creation insights:

- It is most profitable for engineering companies to dominate tightly defined product niches, on a global basis.
- Many European engineering businesses have too many products, most of which are unprofitable.
- These European engineering businesses can be acquired and performance greatly improved by paring the product line back to the highly profitable products and selling them globally.

Canon has evolved these value creation insights:

- Diverse products such as cameras, business machines and specialist optical products can share the same technology base.
- Better products can be made by cross-fertilising technological ideas across the different product areas.
- Similar marketing approaches for these three product areas can be used throughout the world.

Emerson, an American manufacturer of mid-tech electrical, electromechanical and electronic products, has this value creation insight:

- It's possible to acquire steady businesses in these product areas making 5–10 per cent return on sales and take them to 15 per cent by tightening the product focus and reducing manufacturing costs the Emerson way.

Distinctive parenting characteristics comprise specific ways that the Centre adds value, helping the entire company to exploit the value creation insights.

ABB's distinctive parenting characteristics comprise:

- the ability to integrate autonomous business units into a global sales network
- a process to improve the performance of acquisitions – radical simplification, reducing overhead costs, identifying key customers and their needs, focusing on high profit segments, and raising margins in less profitable areas.

Canon's distinctive parenting characteristic is to make cross-fertilisation happen

- across technologies
- across markets
- between technical and marketing executives.

Emerson's distinctive parenting characteristics comprise:

- its ability to raise profits in its business units
- its Best Cost Producer (BCP) programme to reduce manufacturing costs
- skill in helping managers reach the 15 per cent return on sales target
- identification of acquisition candidates that have the potential for performance improvement.

The last key idea behind parenting theory is that of HEARTLAND BUSINESSES. These are ones where the value creation insights can be applied by the parent. According to Parenting theory, the company should *only* own heartland businesses; others should be sold to another parent whose heartland they fall into. Goold, Campbell and Alexander identify five levers the parent can use within heartland businesses to add value:

1 *Build*: Use the value creation insights to build the business, often into new markets by means of acquisitions and alliances.
2 *Develop*: The classic core competency strategy, *develop* often involves technology-based expansion, as in Canon's case.
3 *Leverage*: Exploit corporate assets, brands, know-how or relationships. Richard Branson's Virgin group cleverly leverages Virgin's brand and its lifestyle connotations.
4 *Link*: Encouraging synergies across business units. In financial services, a service network or distribution channel often sells several products. In some industries purchasing power can be pooled across business units. The marketing expertise of Unilever and Proctor & Gamble links many different product areas successfully. It is worth noting, however, that successful link strategies are heavily outnumbered by clumsy and value-destroying attempts by parents to get sister companies to collaborate, despite little or no real SYNERGY.
5 *Stretch*: The parent encourages all operating companies to reach higher levels of performance than they currently exhibit. Within heartland businesses, where the parent has a deep understanding of potential growth and profitability, stretch can be very valuable. Both ABB and Emerson employ stretch goals successfully. Outside of heartland businesses, stretch goals are dangerous. In particular, the pursuit of short-term profit growth, beyond what the market will accept, always destroys value and, sometimes, the entire business.

Parenting theory sets the bar for corporate Centres appropriately high. Centres that own only heartland businesses, where they deploy value creation insights and distinctive parenting characteristics – in the terms we have used, with a unique genetic code – add value to their shareholders and to the world. But what do you do if you are setting Corporate Strategy for a multibusiness corporation that doesn't have a clear parenting formula and can't think of a sensible one?

4 Place astute bets on growth

There are three quite different ways of answering the question just posed:

- Abandon the MBC format – slim down to the most attractive single business cluster and sell or spin-off all other divisions.
- Don't worry about growth.
- Use 'TRAFFIC LIGHTS' to assess the growth gamble.

Curiously, all three answers can be valid. Let's see why and when.[14]

Abandon the MBC format

There is nothing sacrosanct about the modern divisionalised multibusiness corporation. It is the product of fashion and a particular point in capitalism's history. The MBC's hegemony may already be passing. If so, we should not mourn its fall. Without divisionalised corporations, or with very few, it's probable that good Corporate Strategy would be much more prevalent and bad Corporate Strategy would lose its current popularity.

Divisionalised companies were invented in the 1920s, to solve a particular problem. General Motors and Du Pont were becoming too big and complex to manage. The top executives couldn't make all the decisions rising to the top. The solution was to decentralise, to break GM and Du Pont each into several business divisions – to invent the MBC. Industrial capitalism had been going for over a century and a half, with stunning success, without divisionalised companies.

The MBC took time to catch on. It only became dominant and unchallenged as the main model for organising big companies in the period between 1960 and 1990. In 1949, less than a quarter of all *Fortune 500* firms were divisionalised. By 1959, a bare majority were divisionalised. In the later 1960s, 1970s and 1980s, however, a large majority became MBCs.

It is not clear that this was a good thing. In the 1920s and 1930s, DIVISIONALISATION was a sensible tactic, but only to avoid disaster. The top level of corporations had become a bottleneck. CEOs were overloaded. As a result, they were starting to make bad decisions. Divisionalisation solved the problem, or at least reduced the VALUE DESTRUCTION at the top. Divisionalisation improved things, because it was a step toward decentralisation, so that more decisions could be taken by executives closer to customers and to the different operations of the company.

Probably, though, it would have been better to decentralise more completely. Instead of dividing GM into five divisions, it could have been divided into five companies, each fully competing with one another, each arranging its own funding from banks and the stock market. Almost certainly, this would have been a better solution for customers and the public generally. It would have increased competition and accentuated the differences between these car companies, increasing choice. Also, there might not have been the same collusive pricing as happened between the divisions within GM, where a cost-plus formula determined all pricing decisions.[15]

The breakup of GM would probably also have been better for its shareholders. Instead of holding one share in GM, they'd have held one share in Buick, one in Cadillac, one in Chevrolet, one in Oldsmobile and one in Pontiac. According to the ecological theory of Corporate Strategy, the companies would have diverged from one another, developing their own increasingly distinctive genetic codes. Paradoxically, therefore, although customer choice would have been increased by making each GM brand a separate company, the extent to which each division *truly* competed against one another would have been decreased; the different brands would have become less and less like substitutes for one another. By breaking GM up into five separate companies in the 1920s, or any time before 1970, the American car industry would have been better able to face the onslaught from German and Japanese rivals. After 1970, imported cars increasingly plugged the gaps left by the three look-alike US domestic producers.

Not only was divisionalization an inferior solution to the true 'division' or breakup of overloaded companies. Divisionalization also created or at least encouraged one of the most pernicious trends ever to emerge within capitalism – that of DIVERSIFICATION. By 1969, 44 per cent of all MBCs had diversified. By the 1980s it had become very hard to find any large American corporation that had not diversified way beyond its base business. The high tide of diversification came, perhaps, in 1982, when the Coca-Cola Corporation, up to then a model of sober single-business success, fell prey to diversification. Coca-Cola bought Columbia Pictures and then the Taylor Wine Company.

Plaudits for diversification were short-lived. Within five years it became clear that, in the main, it hadn't worked. Michael Porter reported in 1987:

> ***'I studied the diversification records of 33 large, prestigious US companies over the 1950–86 period and found that most of them had divested many more acquisitions than they had kept. The corporate strategies of most companies have dissipated instead of created shareholder value.'*** [16]

Coca-Cola sold Columbia Pictures in 1989 to Sony, a great move for the seller and a terrible one for the buyer. Coca-Cola also divested Taylor Wine Company. Since it reverted to being a one-business corporation, Coca-Cola has gone from strength to strength, whereas its main rival, PepsiCo, has struggled mightily. Pepsi is a highly diversified company, operating not only in cola, but also in other beverages, several fast-food restaurant chains, snack foods and many other products.

In the late 1980s, corporate raiders – including Michael Milken, Carl Icahn, T. Boone Pickens and leveraged buyout specialist KKR – began to pick over the bones of failed diversification strategies by launching bids for even the largest of America's corporate under-performers.

The big trend in the 1990s was the voluntary dismemberment of many of America's biggest MBCs. To defend themselves against external breakup, they broke themselves up, into two or more separate companies – just as General Motors could have done, so many years before, as an alternative to divisionalization. The US firms splitting themselves included Anheuser-Busch, Baxter International, Corning, Dun & Bradstreet, Dial, General Mills, General Motors, Grace, ITT, Lilly, Marriott, 3M, Pacific Telesis, Ralston Purina, Sears and Tenneco. In the late 1990s, breakups became the bigger than all other disposals on the stock market and also bigger than the 1980s leveraged buyout craze at its height.

British breakups have included BAT, British Gas, Courtaulds, ECC, Hanson, ICI, Lonrho, Racal and Thorn EMI. In Continental Europe Chargeurs, Hoechst, Lufthansa, Sandoz and Sonae have all split themselves.

Breakups release value. A study by investment bank JP Morgan showed that on average, during the first 18 months of its life, a spinoff performed 25 per cent better than its peers during the same time, and was clearly still on a rising trend. For smaller spinoffs, median out-performance was 45 per cent.[17]

The only way to explain this surge in value is the removal of value destruction by the firms and centres previously controlling the divisions spun off. Nothing else was altered. Coming on top of the indictment of

MBCs contained in Goold, Campbell and Alexander's 1994 book, the breakup movement and the performance of the firms spun off may mark the end of MBCs as the dominant form of industrial organisation.[18]

Don't worry about growth

Many large company executives feel a strong imperative, even a kind of moral obligation, to expand their company. Others simply respond to the demands of equity markets for growth. Such pressures are misguided. If one company does not grow, another will. There is no shortage of entrepreneurial initiatives. Since 1980, large American corporations have retreated,[19] yet the US economy has been very strong.

This is where markets really do work well – not in doing away with companies, but in allowing smaller and newer companies to break through when larger and older firms have shot their bolt. According to the ecological theory, the economy grows through divergence of ecosystems. New companies are more suited to create new ecosystems than old companies, tied by their genes to old markets and traditional ways of competing.

Deciding not to grow, or to accept a reduced level of growth, is not giving up. Such decisions can be excellent Corporate Strategy. Many, perhaps most, large and established companies would do better for their shareholders if they targeted low growth or no growth in revenues. Profits and market value can still increase, or, what is often just as important, decline more slowly than would likely happen with a dash for growth.

In their book *The Growth Gamble*, Andrew Campbell and Robert Park give two fascinating examples of successful low-growth strategies. In 1891, Crown Cork and Seal was founded in Baltimore to make better bottle tops. The firm eventually became world leader. By the mid 1950s, however, Crown Cork had diversified unsuccessfully into beer cans. At that stage a local entrepreneur, John Connelly, bought the firm and pursued a retrenchment strategy. He shut the beer plant, closed central research, removed layers of management, halved the number of staff jobs, and devolved control and profit responsibility to plant managers.

All went well until the late 1970s and 1980s, when large can buyers started to make their own cans. Crown's competitors responded by diversifying into fibre-foil, paper, plastic and other packaging solutions. But not Connelly. He remained entirely focused on crowns and cans, expanded internationally, and invested in plants near his customers' canning lines. This strategy proved highly profitable and cash positive.

Even so, margins came under pressure. Connelly's reaction was to focus even more on cash generation. From 1970 onwards he used excess cash to buy back shares – by 1987 he had bought in more than half the 1970 level. Despite low growth, Crown's earnings per share rose from $1.41 in 1970 to $9.29 in 1987. The shares surged tenfold.

By diversifying beyond cans, Crown's competitors doomed themselves. Since most can companies moved into other packaging products, the result was over-capacity and falling margins, even though the new markets grew impressively. Between 1985 and 1988 the three largest American can companies, apart from Crown, were acquired at modest prices.

Louis Gerstner's time as CEO of IBM provides another vignette of how attractive a low-growth strategy can be. Shortly after he took over in 1993, IBM's shares were on the floor at $41. Yet by March 2004, Gerstner's strategy had taken the shares to the equivalent of $367 – a compounded annual gain of 22 per cent, despite IBM's revenues growing less than 2 per cent a year, well behind average American growth. In addition, shareholders enjoyed nearly doubled dividends. Gerstner's simple strategy was to focus on cash generation, reinvest in the base business, offset the decline in hardware sales by developing a major service business, and – this is the most vital part – use the cash to buy back shares. Between 1993 and 2003, IBM invested $56 billion on R&D, earned $51 billion after tax, and spent $53 billion gross ($44 billion net) buying back its shares.

When is it right *not* to grow? When a low-growth strategy of cash generation is likely to be better than a high-growth strategy of using cash to expand. When is that? Whenever new business projects cannot be relied upon to earn more than the cost of capital. When is that? Usually. The onus shouldn't be on managers who eschew growth to prove that is the better strategy, but on managers who advocate growth to argue that they can defy the odds. Most companies have few new opportunities warranting investment. Most companies spend too much, not too little, on new ventures. The problem is that managers, with few exceptions, are too keen to grow and are not realistic about growth prospects. Most managers overestimate the likely payoff from growth initiatives, and underestimate the dangers. The methodology to be explored in the next section provides a more rigorous assessment of the chances of success or failure. It is a much-needed antidote to managerial over-optimism.

Use 'traffic lights' to assess the gamble on growth

It is possible for companies to transition successfully from one business to another. The Edison Light Company, which was founded in 1879 by Thomas Edison to make the electric lightbulb he had invented, turned into General Electric, which has diversified into a huge range of activities, including financial services and private equity. Hewlett-Packard moved from instruments into computers. Finland's Nokia evolved from making low-tech products such as rubber boots to become the world's biggest mobile phone company. England's WPP, now a huge international marketing services company, began life making wire trolleys for supermarkets.

Against these success stories, there are many more stories of failed diversifications. For the past ten years, Andrew Campbell has been researching why some companies are able to beat the odds and succeed by gambling on growth. In 2005, he and Robert Park came up with five major insights and a new tool, 'Traffic Lights'. The insights and the new tool are fully explained in Part Four, pages 300–4, under TRAFFIC LIGHTS.

5 Create a new ecosystem

All the greatest and most rewarding examples of Corporate Strategy, from Ford to Microsoft, result from creating a new ecosystem, a new market category. Creating a new ecosystem is typically easier for a young or small company, or for an entrepreneur, who has little or nothing to lose in the old category, and no identification with it in the eyes of the customer. As we have just seen, mature corporations can also create a new ecosystem – albeit with a high risk of failure, and often with serious consequences, even when successful, for the existing business. For the new entrepreneur there is no such dilemma.

The interesting point, for entrepreneurs or managers, is that there is a tried and tested method to create a new ecosystem. The method is to take an existing ecosystem and split it into two (or more) new ecosystems.

There was a car market before Henry Ford, but he created a new ecosystem, one based around the mass-produced Model-T for a new, middle-class clientele. He divided the auto market into the old, luxury ecosystem and the new standardised mass-market ecosystem. More than a decade later, General Motors divided Ford's ecosystem into five new ecosystems, adding variety and choice based around five new brands.

The mainframe computer ecosystem, dominated first by Remington Rand and then by IBM, diverged when Digital Equipment created a mini-computer ecosystem, again when IBM created the personal computer ecosystem, once more when Sun Microsystems created the workstation ecosystem, then split again with the 3-D workstation ecosystem pioneered by Silicon Graphics, the laptop ecosystem from Toshiba, and the direct-to-customer ecosystem from Dell.

The gaming market used to be controlled by bookmakers or by state monopolies. The market diverged to produce legal and illegal bookmakers, track betting and off-track betting, fixed-odds bookmakers and spread betting, lotteries, amusement machines, computer games, telephone betting, casinos, online betting and betting exchanges. Each new category enlarged the market and also challenged previous categories.

The process of creating new ecosystems is sometimes called *value innovation* or *blue ocean strategy*, expressions coined by INSEAD professors W. Chan Kim and Renée Mauborgne.[20] I believe that the risks inherent in creating new ecosystems can be considerably reduced, and the potential returns greatly increased, by following a three-step procedure:

1 Target a new core customer group

For the product category where you want to innovate, target a subgroup of customers who might have different characteristics and needs from other customers, and who might potentially be very profitable to serve. The target group may be younger than the average customer, or older; richer or poorer; fashionable or frumpy; a lover or hater of technology; male or female; from a particular type of background or affiliation; or any other distinction that conduces toward special needs or desires.

2 Vary the business model profitably

Think of a way of doing business that is different from the current way and that might appeal particularly to your target group. List the attributes of the products currently provided. Now make two changes:

1 *Subtract* something from the standard product offering that is either completely unimportant to your target group, or not particularly important to them. Preferably, subtract something that costs a great deal to deliver.
2 *Add* some attributes that are particularly important for your target group. Think of delivering the benefits in a new way, ideally one that is cheaper as well as different from any existing product offering.

Some pointers: Go back 50 years, and every airline ran pretty much the same way. National or regional airlines had their 'hub' or base of operations, the place from where they ran their planes to many destinations. If you used the airline you could connect to anywhere, through that airline or another, and when you checked in your bags would be sent – probably – to your final destination. The setup had just one disadvantage – it was expensive.

Then came America's Southwest Airlines. Southwest targeted customers who wanted to travel locally and cheaply, and whose main alternative was not another airline, but driving. Southwest *subtracted* some things every other airline offered. It doesn't use large airports and extended routes, travelling from one point to another, period. It doesn't offer more than one class. It doesn't ticket your bags to through destinations.

Southwest *added* some attributes too, that were ideal for its target customers. It runs a very frequent service between its selected cities. You can pay at the gate. You can check in and board quickly and without waiting a long time before the flight. And, above all, it's inexpensive, so that it can cost no more to fly than to drive.

Since then, a raft of imitators have taken the Southwest idea and tweaked it. Many airlines run shuttle services between two cities along similar lines. And in Europe, the low-cost airlines, led by Ryanair and Easyjet, have taken the idea further. They have subtracted something more. There's no onboard service. There are no assigned seats. There are no frills at all, and only rudimentary customer service of any kind. But there are rock-bottom fares, and that fills planes.

Amazon.com is another illustration. In its original books business, Amazon targeted technophiles who wanted to be able to buy books without walking or driving to a bookstore. Amazon *subtracted* the pleasure many people get from browsing in a real bookstore, being able to inspect and open a book, and sit down with it over a cup of coffee. Amazon *added* one thing you can't get in any bookstore – an enormous range of books, easily accessed and assessed in a few minutes. Amazon also added objective reviews of books and a rating system based on the opinion of previous buyers of the books. And lower prices than in most bookstores.

In the gaming market, Betfair, the original and largest betting exchange, in which I became the largest outside investor shortly after it was set up, is another great example. It targeted Internet-savvy gamblers who bet large amounts of money. It *subtracted* the real-world excitement of betting at a racetrack or in off-track betting shops. It *added* extraordinary value, the ability to place a bet against an outcome, the ability to trade in and out of positions, and the ability to bet when an event is taking place.

For a new ecosystem to be viable, the new business model has to work better in relation to the new target subset of customers than the current business model. The variation must be profitable. This can only be true if the volume of business is more intensive as a result of the new way of doing business, or if the price charged is higher, or if the costs of serving the new market are lower, all relative to the current way of doing business.

In airlines, the new business model worked because low fares could fill the planes. In some years, Southwest has been the only profitable US airline. In Europe, Ryanair's value on the stock market exceeded, for a time, that of British Airways, a hugely bigger, traditional operation that claims to be 'the world's favourite airline'. Maybe, but not the favourite of investors.

It's the same story in the wagering market. Betfair has much wider profit margins than its traditional competitors, despite charging its customers only a tenth or less of the 'take' scooped up by bookmakers. In the year to April 2004, Betfair made after tax profits around £20m ($36m) and analysts expect it to make over 50 per cent more in 2005. Not bad for a company that's only been around for five years and was started with almost no capital.

3 Create or re-create the corporate genetic code ideal for the new ecosystem

Imagine you've created a new ecosystem in the image of your product. What security do you have against competitors? Being first gives you a great advantage, especially if you establish your brand as synonymous with the new category. As Al and Laura Ries point out in their terrific book *The Origin of Brands*, Coca-Cola has been the number 1 cola brand since 1886, GE the number 1 lightbulb brand since 1902, and Kleenex the number 1 tissue brand since 1924 – all created these markets.[21]

It's difficult, even for a powerful and well-run company, to become number 1 in a new ecosystem it didn't pioneer. The fizzy, caffeinated citrus category was created by Mountain Dew. Coca-Cola tried to enter the new ecosystem with Mello Yellow and foundered. Then they tried Surge, which misfired too. Dr Pepper was first into the spicy cola ecosystem. Cola-Cola tried to displace Dr Pepper with Mr. Pibb. That failed too. Snapple created the natural beverage category. Cola-Cola responded with Fruitopia, another damp squib. Red Bull created the energy drink ecosystem. Coca-Cola eventually tried to challenge with KMX. No dice. Finally, the sports drink category was created by Gatorade. Coca-Cola imitated with Power-Ade, a distant second in the market.

But creating an ecosystem provides no guarantee that the pioneer will stay ahead. Duryea created the automobile ecosystem in America, but soon lost leadership. Du Mont created the US television ecosystem. Who has heard of them now? The same with Hurley, the pioneer of washing machines.

Remington Rand created the mainframe computer market, but lost leadership to IBM pretty quickly. Ford created the mass car market, but lost out to GM and Chrysler. In the 1960s and 1970s, Porsche was dominant in volume sports cars, a lead long ago lost to Mazda. British firms Norton and BSA created the motorcycle ecosystem, but by the 1970s the British motorcycle industry was almost dead, supplanted by Honda and Yamaha. In all these cases, the initial advance by the challenger was made by dividing the old ecosystem into two or more new ones, by dominating the new ecosystem, and then by forcing the original leader to retreat and lose overall leadership.[22]

Firms retain leadership in the ecosystems they create *if and only if their genetic code remains better adapted to the needs of the ecosystem than the code of any competitor*. This very often comes down to one person or very few people, who provide or fail to provide the leadership required. When Betfair is established, as it will almost certainly be, as a company valued at several billion dollars, its progress there from scratch and its leadership in the betting exchange ecosystem will appear to have been inevitable. I can tell you this was not the case.

The first betting exchange was not launched by Betfair, but by an American-originated firm called Flutter.com, the brainchild of Vince Monical and Josh Hannah, who had the idea when they were consultants at Bain & Company's San Francisco office. They moved to London, the betting capital of the world, and launched their site in May 2000. Betfair was started shortly afterwards by two Brits, Andrew ('Bert') Black and Ed Wray, who realised the strategic importance of the UK horseracing market and quickly became the leaders in that ecosystem.

But when I invested in Betfair early in 2001, it quickly became clear that Betfair's lead over Flutter was slipping. This was partly because Flutter had more money, but mainly because it had a better chief technology officer, a brilliant, charming and dedicated American called David Yu. Flutter's technology was more reliable and more user-friendly, and this was why it was gaining market share at an alarming rate, even in the UK racing ecosystem that Betfair had pioneered. Luckily for Andrew Black, Ed Wray, and myself, we merged the two businesses in December 2001 under the Betfair brand but with David Yu as CTO (he is now the CEO). I am sure that otherwise Betfair would have lost leadership in the ecosystem it created, and be worth only a small fraction of its current value.

The implication for ecosystem pioneers is to be paranoid about loss of relative market share. If a new competitor enters the ecosystem and starts to gobble up share, this is an indication that the competitor's genetic code is more adapted to the ecosystem than the genetic code of the pioneer. This is nearly always a question of people. If it possibly can, the pioneer should try to hire away the few people responsible for the advance of the challenger. The owners of the pioneer should consider replacing the CEO of their company with the CEO of the challenger. Very often such a move will require the two companies to merge. But this will only have permanent benefit if the people who are better at serving the ecosystem emerge in the right jobs after the merger.

For the economy to progress, there has to be profitable variation. Just as the ecosystem has to be different, so too the genetic code of firms has to be different. An unusual strategy, but one that has worked for me, is to deliberately change the genetic structure of the firm and then create an ecosystem suited to the new structure. This reverses the standard and common-sense order, but it makes sense if the new genetic structure gives the firm and therefore potentially the market 'better value'. This was the case shortly after I and two other partners of Bain & Company left to set up our own consulting firm, LEK.

Experienced MBAs refused to join our firm, rightly considering it high risk. But top-notch undergraduates signed up by the busload. In our second year we had three partners, two consultants and 30 fresh-faced 'research assistants'. The latter were high-energy, highly intelligent kids in their early twenties, whose only liability was a complete absence of knowledge about business or consulting. To earn money we had to find something for the kids to do, yet we couldn't risk setting them loose inside client organisations. Eventually we stumbled on the solution – get the kids to do computer analysis and investigation of clients' competitors.

LEK made a speciality of intensive analysis of competitors, very useful both for establishing competitors' costs relative to those of the client in every product line and stage of production, and also for analysis of acquisition targets. The kids were ideally suited to this work and it was commercially valuable. Our competitors, the more established firms like Bain & Company and the Boston Consulting Group, couldn't do this work as well or as cheaply as we could – we had the secret weapon of masses of kids. We established a new ecosystem – the market for analysis of competitors and acquisition targets – *after* having created, accidentally, a different genetic structure for our firm. The upshot was that we grew extremely fast, doubling our revenues, profits and employees each year for the first five years. And we had higher profit margins than any other consulting firm.

The consulting industry provides other excellent examples of how to establish new profitable ecosystems and new genetic structures for firms, and how related these two are to each other. In 1963 Bruce HENDERSON set up the Boston Consulting Group and broke new ground by basing the firm on intellect rather than experience.

Whereas previously the typical lead consultant had been a silver-haired distinguished gentleman with an impressive collection of hats, a gnarled veteran who had seen it all and done it all, Bruce hired newly minted MBAs from Harvard Business School who might never previously have held a proper job. 'The younger you are as a Vice-President,' one of BCG's officers – who was 25 years old, but looked 19 – once confided to me, 'the more it terrifies the clients.' Terrifying clients, in his book, was clearly a good thing. This was consulting, but not as clients had known it. The firm's new genetic code defined the new ecosystem it created – a new type of 'strategy consulting', which combined the previously separate arts of market research and financial analysis, and quadrupled the margins on them.

Ten years after BCG's startup, Bill Bain took a team from BCG to start up Bain & Company as a competing firm. Bill Bain had a very different background from most of the senior BCG folks. Bill had been a Bible salesman in the Deep South, selling Bibles from door to door, and then became employed by a Southern university to raise funds from its alumni. When he joined BCG, Bill knew nothing about business. Yet he proved even better at selling consulting than selling Bibles. Bill hit upon the absolutely brilliant idea of dividing BCG's strategy consulting ecosystem into two by creating a firm that would exclusively sell to the group CEOs of large companies, and only serve one firm in an industry. This means a *relationship of equals* between the consulting firm and the CEO – and it was very much the CEO whose interests were served. Bain earned fees in a single client that were quite unprecedented, and grew at the rate of 40 per cent a year for its first ten years, overtaking BCG for a while.

As a final example of creating a new ecosystem, consider Bain Capital, the private equity firm established by Mitt Romney, now Governor of Massachusetts and formerly one of the most senior associates of Bill Bain, as an autonomous new venture still linked in many ways to Bain & Company. Mitt reckoned that as Bain was adept at multiplying profits for its clients, it would be possible to set up a private equity firm that would do the same on its own account. Bain Capital became the dominant force in all its investments, working out strategies to add extraordinary value. During its first ten years, Bain Capital doubled the value of its investments every year, making its partners rich. Bain Capital was unique in the private equity industry in three ways – its genetic code, the new private equity ecosystem it created, and its results.

CHAPTER 4

Conclusion

Hatching wealth is a creative task, a human task, a task of individuals and teams. This was true at the dawn of industrial society and is even truer today. For part of the nineteenth and twentieth centuries it looked as if the power of capital might crush the entrepreneurial spirit, but today creative individuals have the upper hand and those who rely purely on capital are lucky merely to preserve it. Corporate Strategy is a game of imagination, a sport for human beings with nimble brains and the gift of inducing profitable collaboration.

Creativity does not imply randomness. It is probably true that we are only at the early stages of attaining a rigorous or scientific understanding of what drives business success. But, in devising business strategy, there are clearly certain principles or rules of thumb that work better than others, indeed that work rather well. The rules of thumb are often instinctive, prosaic and not yet grounded in reliable theory. They are no less useful for that. Part Two has tried to draw together the rules that work best.

In so far as we can glimpse a grand theory that links and explains the particular rules of thumb – that may in future be subject at each stage to rigorous proof or disproof, to detailed quantification – the best hope may lie in an ecological theory, the bare bones of which have been sketched here. Ecological theory combines three main motifs:

1 *The ecology of market niches*, each one subtly different, able to give one firm – and usually only one firm – returns far above the cost of capital

2 *The primacy of human innovation* and skill in creating and improving each of these ecosystems

3 *The ecology of firms as living entities*, systems that are usually much more, or much less, than the sum of the parts. These parts are the resources – cash, technology, market positions, ideas, ways of working, but above all people – that make firms what they are. Good Corporate Strategy makes the firm and its results more than the sum of the parts. Bad Corporate Strategy makes them less. This is just another way of saying that nearly all firms have returns above or below the cost of capital, and there are reasons why.

Good Corporate Strategy requires flights of fancy, the urge to build something permanent, and also depths of humility in the face of events beyond control. Though enterprises sometimes scale new heights, create awesome wealth, and dazzle us with their ingenuity and attainments, markets always have the last laugh. Civilisation rests on human striving, but the fruits of civilisation are always fragile. Nowhere is this more evident, more quickly, than in the achievements of firms. The consolation for the wise strategist, as decades of ingenuity and toil tumble down in a few months, is that destruction is always creative. It releases new opportunity. It frees up resources for better use elsewhere. There is no waste in nature, and there is no permanent waste in business. It just feels that way. New and better ecosystems can be, and endlessly are, about to be created.

PART 3

Strategic thinkers

ADAIR, JOHN (b. 1934)

British pioneer of 'action-centred leadership' who stresses the role of leadership and that leadership skills can be taught. Tall, courteous and softly spoken, yet not above banging his own drum. He defines leadership as three overlapping circles, compromising the Task, the Team and the Individual. Well worth reading.

Of his recent books, I'd single out *Effective Innovation* (1996, Pan Books, London) which is good primer on creativity.

One of his unverified but intriguing ideas is Adair's Fifty-Fifty rule, which says that half a person's motivation comes from inside, and the other half from external factors, including leadership. He also says that 50 per cent of success comes from the team and 50 per cent from the leader.

ALEXANDER, MARCUS (b. 1968)

One of the Directors of the Ashridge Strategic Management Centre who have undertaken pioneering work on Corporate Strategy (see CAMPBELL and GOOLD for a description of their main work). Marcus Alexander's own focus has moved from traditional Western corporate structures to more exotic variants. This partly reflects the growing importance of different regions (such as the Middle East, China and India), but also the growth of different ownership structures in the West, such as private equity and regional clusters.

'Ownership,' says Alexander, 'is too often confused with control, for which it is neither a necessary nor sufficient requirement.' His previous work on outsourcing and strategic sourcing emphasised the costs and risks of ownership, and the importance of non-ownership control mechanisms. 'First, you need to decide what it is that you really *want* to have control over; then you have to think through how you can achieve this most cost effectively.'

He points out that the starting assumption of many resource-rich corporations is that more ownership is better, whereas organisations and individuals that are resource-poor have learnt to be more nuanced and selective. This does not mean that ownership has no valuable role, but that its relative merits are seldom explored objectively. 'I have been struck,' he commented in a recent *Financial Times* article, 'by the almost equal balance of passionate advocates and bitter opponents to the notion of outsourcing.' His argument is that the interplay between value creation (or destruction) and value capture (or loss) is often misunderstood due to basic, but faulty, assumptions.

More provocatively, he believes that the economic inefficiency of current 'sourcing' decisions will continue until there is as strong a professional and strategic focus on this area as has been developed with others.

> ***'People "did" finance and marketing before there was an explicit finance or marketing function, but they did it in a more piecemeal, rudimentary and intuitive way. To unlock the real economics of "sourcing", we need a similar focus on something that is no more just about "purchasing" than finance is just about accounting or marketing is just about sales.'***

ANDREWS, KENNETH (b. 1945)

Probably responsible, more than any other single person, for the most influential, if not the best, model of strategy.

The classic model is what Henry MINTZBERG calls the 'Design School' or 'Strategy formation as a process of conception': the outcome of thinking, using a very simple model. At the heart of it is the SWOT (Strengths, Weaknesses, Opportunities and Threats) diagnostic, taught to generations of business school students and well known throughout industry everywhere in the world.

In 1965, Ken Andrews edited and wrote the renowned Harvard Business School textbook *Business Policy – Text and Cases*. This has been the standard text for many 'business policy' courses up to today. In 1971, Andrews wrote *The Concept of Corporate Strategy* for practising managers, which was most recently reprinted in 1987.

Its model requires executives, and particularly the chief executive, to think initially about two streams: an *external appraisal*, compromising threats and opportunities in the environment; and an *internal appraisal* of the strengths and weaknesses of the organisation, and therefore its distinctive competencies.

Strategic options are then constructed and evaluated according to four components of strategy:

- what a company MIGHT DO – the market opportunities
- what it CAN DO – its corporate competencies and resources

- what it WANTS TO DO – the aspirations of the key executives
- what it SHOULD DO – its social responsibilities.

One strategy is then chosen, with particular emphasis on the fit between external opportunities and the firm's own competencies, and then promulgated by the chief executive and implemented. The organisation's structure should be modified, if necessary, to facilitate the implementation of the strategy.

The model has many virtues, including simplicity; the idea of fit between what the organisation can do and what the outside world wants; the way in which it forces strategy to be explicitly considered; and the primacy to which the model elevates strategy. It strikes a nice balance between analysis and intuition, allows full rein to creativity, and yet takes account of external and internal realities. The model also *works*, in the sense that it is easy to understand and use; if this were not true, the model would not have become so influential.

Sadly, the model also has some grave flaws, and looks increasingly dated. It is a top-down, which is not wholly bad, but certainly unfashionable, and in many circumstances inappropriate. It assumes that the chief executive (or other strategists) can know the organisation's strengths and weaknesses, largely as a result of a cerebral process. Where is the scope here for external perspectives, for data collection, for economic analysis, or for experimentation to see if the market agrees with the hypothesis? Moreover, the assumption that structure should follow strategy is too clear-cut, and often wrong: strategy is often determined by structure, and the best solution is to allow strategy and structure to shape each other.

The promulgation of one strategy is also questionable: this can lead to inflexibility. It is usually best to let strategy emerge from a process – sometimes quite a long one – of experimentation, thinking and action, where the market is actively involved in determining the outcome.The Andrews model runs the serious risk of detaching thinking from acting: there are those who think, and those who do. The best strategies usually come from mixing the two processes, so that the operating managers in the thick of business do the thinking as well as the acting.

Perhaps the most serious objection to the model, however, is that it is too vacuous. The procedure is there, but the model gives little helpful guidance on how to evaluate the strengths, weaknesses, opportunities and threats. Having sat through hundreds of sessions where managers, with no further help, try to divine the SWOT elements, I can only say that they usually come up with the wrong answers. Thinking and self-diagnosis are not enough. A much better framework is available – in Part One of this book, to mention just one place!

ANSOFF, H. IGOR (1918–2002)

Russian-American engineer, mathematician, military strategist and operations researcher who wrote the highly acclaimed *Corporate Strategy* in 1965. The book is quite readable and provides a model for deriving a Corporate Strategy. The model assumes that the purpose of a firm is to maximise long term profitability (return on investment) and then gives a host of checklists and charts for deriving objectives, assessing SYNERGY between different parts of the firm (functions and businesses), appraising the firm's COMPETENCE profile and deciding how to expand (how to diversify, how to assess whether entry to an industry is likely to give the desired ROI, whether to acquire or go for organic growth, and how to weight alternatives taking into account a large number of highlighted factors). He stresses the need for a 'common thread' for all a company's businesses if it is to add value to them.

Re-reading *Corporate Strategy* today is disappointing. The book has not aged well, the methodology overwhelms the substance, and it is difficult to gain much insight from the mechanistic procedures suggested. The concept of competitive advantage is not introduced systematically until page 161 (out of a total of 191 pages in my edition) and is then given only four and a half pages. On the other hand the book's checklists are useful for analysts who want to know whether they have looked at everything they should, for example in conducting an industry analysis. The ANSOFF MATRIX is definitely a useful framework for considering expansion into new areas.

In the 1970s, however, the influence of Ansoff and other strategists led to an orgy of diversification, which turned out to be mainly 'diworsification'. The dismal results of most companies' growth initiatives, even apparently close to the existing activities, has led modern strategists such as Andrew Campbell to examine rigorously the pitfalls of any move beyond the core business. As is often the case with pioneering thinkers, it may well be that Ansoff did far more harm than good.

ARGYRIS, CHRIS (b. 1923)

One of the best and longest-running examples of the humanising forces in American business academia. Since 1971 Argyris has been a Professor at Harvard Business School; before that he was at Yale. He is very much the New England preppy prof: tall, thin, mild, with a voice described as 'reedy with a slight European tinge'. He is also a formidable organisational psychologist who was banging the drum about organisational learning many decades before the theme became fashionable.

Argyris's great virtue is his extensive research into how executives and organisations learn – or fail to. He is therefore a patron saint of the 'Strategy as Learning' school. His key books are the 1957 classic *Personality and Organization*, and the two written with Donald Schön, *Theory in Practice* (1974) and *Organizational Learning* (1978).

Argyris's research highlights the extent to which most managers behave defensively and refuse to engage their emotions. 'I concluded,' he wrote about one study of senior management, 'that [they] unknowingly behaved in such a way as not to encourage risk-taking, openness, expression of feelings, and cohesive, trusting relationships.'

Argyris and Schön invented the ideas of single-loop and double-loop organisational learning. Single-loop learning detects errors and keeps the organisation on track. Double-loop learning questions whether the strategy is right and enables executives to reflect critically on what they do, and teaches them how to learn from others: how to break down the defences that block learning.

Argyris is a romantic pessimist: he insists that most people in organisations are simply not good at learning. Not surprisingly, the LEARNING ORGANISATION needs a great deal of help on its way. Argyris's work has been a good start.

BARNARD, CHESTER (1886–1961)

An industrialist who thought deeply about management. Barnard spent his entire working life with American Telephone and Telegraph. He is known for his hugely influential (and unreadable) 1938 book *The Functions of the Executive*, and for being one of the first to articulate the view that corporate leaders have to manage and inspire the values of their firm.

Barnard saw that organisations were not simply rational instruments trying to carry out defined goals. They were also communities, and 'in a community all acts of individuals and organisations are directly or indirectly interconnected and interdependent'.

Many writers claim that Barnard was ahead of his time in recognising and promoting the ethical and value-based nature of organisations. In my view this is generous and anachronistic. In reality he was an authoritarian idealist with semi-fascist leanings, the ultimate advocate (rather than satirist) of Organisation Man and conformity to the party line. Try these two chilling quotes from Barnard:

> ***'The most important single contribution required of the executive ... is loyalty, domination by the organisation personality.'***
>
> ***'Executive responsibility ... requires not merely conformance to a complex code of morals but also the creation of moral codes for others.'***

Barnard should serve as a warning for all strategists: the ethical integrity of a corporation and a distinctive culture can be great competitive strengths, but when taken to an extreme, cultural conformity can stifle debate, cut off learning, and lead to a mindless tyranny. Both the appeal and the dangers of such organisations should not be underestimated.

Rehabilitating early management writers who have been unfairly ignored (such as Mary Parker Follett) or traduced (like F.W. Taylor) is all very well; rehabilitating monsters like Chester Barnard is taking respect for those safely dead a step too far.

BOWER, MARVIN (1903–2003)

The real founder of McKinsey, who gave it its backbone and values in the 1940s and has kept watch over the firm's soul ever since. Bower was a lawyer by background and his great innovation was to think that management consulting – up to then a rather fly-by-night and *ad hoc* activity – could become a profession comparable to the law. Professionalism was partly a matter of high intelligence and codification of all useful knowledge relating to management science, but it was far more than that: it was anchored in the quality and integrity of the client-professional relationship.

Bower insisted that McKinsey should put the client's interests first, rather than those of McKinsey or of the individual consultant. Client service, client confidentiality, client responsiveness and integrity in telling the client the truth, as perceived by the professional, were all drummed into the Firm by Bower. He made McKinsey the most prestigious and envied firm in management consulting throughout the world, based on his ethic of professionalism.

CAMPBELL, ANDREW (b. 1950)

Scottish management guru, ex-McKinsey consultant and founder of the Ashridge Strategic Management Centre. Campbell is the world's leading authority on issues related to mission and has (with Michael GOOLD) been a pioneer in the area of parenting and management styles. In 1990 his book *A Sense of Mission* stressed that mission statements could be unnecessary or even counter-productive: what mattered was whether a company had a driving sense of purpose, a consistent set of values, a commercial strategy that was also aligned with the purpose and values, and a set of behaviour standards that underpinned the value system.

Along with Michael GOOLD and Marcus ALEXANDER, Campbell originated the idea of PARENTING ADVANTAGE, also discussed in Part Two. Campbell argues that the concept of parenting advantage is as key to Corporate Strategy as the idea of competitive advantage is to Business Unit Strategy. The idea of CORE COMPETENCIES, he says, implies that businesses are related if they have common know-how. 'The parenting concept, in contrast, focuses on the competencies of the parent organisation and on the value created from the relationship between the parent and its business ... The parent, we have found, is highly influential, and its impact is rarely neutral.'

Parenting advantage happens when the parent company creates more value than anyone else owning the business would do. But parenting works only in certain types of business: the heartland businesses. This is not another name for 'core businesses' but rather those businesses where parenting advantage really occurs, where the parent adds more value than anyone else could. This is a tough test, and should lead to companies becoming more selective:

> ***'Companies are coming to understand that it is often easier to change the portfolio to fit the parent organisation than to change the parent organisation to fit the businesses. That realisation accounts for the rise in de-mergers and corporate-level break-ups.'***

In 1996, Campbell co-authored (with David Sadtler and myself) *Breakup!*, a celebration of the huge trend towards SPINOFFS, whereby corporations split themselves into two or more new corporations with their own focus. In 1998 and 1999, Andrew Campbell and Michael Goold published a book called *The Collaborative Enterprise* in the US and *Synergy* elsewhere, sub-titled *Why Links Across the Corporation Often Fail and How to Make Them Work*. It contains much practical advice about whether to bother with synergy and how to make it successful but is notable for championing the common-sense view of business units rather than the ideological perspective of the Centre. 'Synergy problems, in our view,' they write, 'are more often caused by misguided parent managers than by belligerent business unit heads,' adding that 'most resistance from business managers who don't want to change' is not due to emotional or irrational parochialism but 'because they think the change will be for the worse.' They are usually right.

Andrew Campbell's latest book, written with Robert Park, is *The Growth Gamble*.[1] Another indispensable classic, the book describes why nearly all companies fail when they plan to create growth. Most companies, the authors say, have few new growth opportunities that warrant investment; and most firms spend too much, not too little, on new businesses. On the positive side, the book contains a neat new screening tool that they call TRAFFIC LIGHTS, which is outlined on pages 300–4.

One of the most salutary lessons from the book is that many firms ignore the growth potential – especially profit and cash growth potential – from their base business. Reinvestment in the core business is usually a better strategy for mature companies than seeking new sources of growth. Further, if a mature company does focus on new businesses, there are serious dangers to the core business that are entirely predictable and yet that nearly always surprise managers. 'When managers start investing in new businesses,' Campbell and Park write, 'they often underestimate both the opportunities for growth in their existing businesses and the threats these businesses face from competition.' Campbell and Park argue convincingly that the cost to the core business – particularly the diversion of the firm's best managers to the new pastures – 'can sometimes be many multiples of the benefits from the new business, even if it succeeds. Hence sponsors of new businesses ... need to make an objective assessment of the likely distraction costs as part of the proposal to proceed.'

CHANDLER, ALFRED (b. 1918)

Influential American economic historian whose book *Strategy and Structure* (1962) was based on studying major US corporations between 1850 and 1920. He is important for having made three points clearly:

1. He highlighted the close relationship between strategy and structure, and said that firms should first determine their strategy, then their structure. This was more unusual for the emphasis on strategy than the sequencing because very few writers had paid attention to strategy: it is almost completely lacking in the earlier theorists such as Taylor and Weber.
2. He believed that the role of the salaried manager and technician was vital, and talked about the 'visible hand' of management co-ordinating the flow of product to customers more efficiently than Adam Smith's 'invisible hand' of the market. This is an early recognition that corporations, in their internal dealings, favour a planned economy.
3. He was an advocate of decentralisation in large corporations, contributing to the divisionalisation and decentralisation trend of the 1960s and 1970s. He praised Alfred SLOAN's decentralisation of General Motors in the 1920s before Sloan published his book (in 1963), and was influential in the transformation of AT&T in the 1980s from a production-based bureaucracy to a marketing organisation.

Chandler provided much of the vocabulary for the subsequent management debate: it is still very much a live issue whether strategy should follow structure. Tom PETERS holds that Chandler 'got it exactly wrong': that structure inevitably determines strategy, and that the socialist principle of management must be broken down and subjected to market pressures. The truth is probably that Chandler was more right than wrong when he wrote, and that Peters is probably more right now. See PETERS.

COLLIS, DAVID (b. 1955)

David Collis well represents the modern Harvard Business School contribution to the Corporate Strategy literature. His work combines a rigorous academic underpinning with an awareness of the practical application of conceptual ideas. He has also been a prolific writer of Harvard cases so that many examples of Corporate Strategy that others use are based on his research.

David's most useful book is *Corporate Strategy: A Resource-Based Approach*, written in 1998 with co-author Cynthia Montgomery. In this weighty but wise tome, the authors are keen to distinguish their 'resource-based approach' from the simple idea of CORE COMPETENCIES, which they nicely dub 'a *feel good* exercise that no one fails'. They argue that all great corporate strategies involve the same logic of 'related' businesses – related not in the traditional sense of product market similarity, but in the sharing of a set of valuable resources that contribute to every business's competitive advantage. The application of this logic leads to a variety of effective corporate strategies that vary from the very general to the highly specific. Very general resources, like management expertise or control systems, can support conglomerate strategies, while more specialised resources, like the LCD technology of Sharp, limit the businesses the firm can enter very precisely.

Collis also argues that effective strategy implementation requires the alignment of all elements of Corporate Strategy. In particular, the organisational design and the management systems employed to administer a strategy have to be consistent with the underlying corporate resources. As a result, corporate headquarters should look very different across companies, in spite of the fact that 'most executives create plain vanilla corporate offices as if there were one best practice to follow'. There is not – yet another indication that very few corporate strategists really strive to create a central resource that fits and helps the firm's divisions.

DE GEUS, ARIE

A Dutch executive with Shell for 38 years, including stints as co-ordinator for all Shell's operations in Africa and in South Asia, and as head of planning. De Geus has recently reinvented himself as a writer and business academic. He has been credited with originating the idea of the 'learning organisation'. His 1997 book *The Learning Organisation* explored the idea that companies are really 'alive'; they are not just money-making machines, and should have their own sense of identity, purpose and self-direction.

Arie de Geus points out that most large multinational corporations live for only 40–50 years, considerably less than human lifespans. 'Companies die,' he claims, 'because their managers focus on the economic activity of producing goods and services, and they forget that their organisation's true nature is that of a community of humans.'

Here the idea of the learning organisation is taken further. The organisation should not just learn; it should also set its own priorities and perpetuate itself. 'Like all organisms,' de Geus writes, 'the living company exists primarily for its own survival and improvement: to fulfil its potential and to become as great as it can be … the real purpose of a living company is to survive and thrive in the long run …'

De Geus identifies certain characteristics of companies that live a long time, including the ability to learn, tolerance, diffusion of power, a clear self-identity, conservatism in finance, and trust between the organisation's members. 'If companies can meet those conditions, I believe that average corporate life expectancy will begin to rise, and all humanity will benefit as a result,' he concludes.

On the plus side, companies are 'alive' and are 'self-organising systems' in the same ways that cities, economies and markets are. The metaphor (and more than this, the reality) of corporations being alive is important; the machine metaphor has had its day. Yet I find De Geus's basic propositions questionable. Is it necessarily a good thing if companies live a long time and pay attention to their own perpetuation? Is it good to avoid financial risk in order to live longer? Is it bad if a company is taken over by another? The welfare of customers and society at large may be at odds with the aspirations of executives. Just because something is alive and self-organising does not mean that it is good or should be left to organise affairs for its own benefit. At root, De Geus's ideas exemplify the excesses and follies of syndicalism: the idea that the basic duty of an organisation is to itself and not to the outside world. This may be the fastest imaginable route to corporate death.

DEMING, W. EDWARDS (1900–1993)

American originator of the quality revolution: acted as a consultant to many major Japanese firms in the late 1940s and 1950s and was the single greatest external influence on Japanese industry – until Deming, Japanese goods were inferior. He became known in America only in the 1980s, when he helped to stem the tide of superior Japanese imports into the West that he had earlier contributed towards. He was a statistician who emphasised the importance of the consumer ('the consumer is the most important part of the production line') and that reducing variation was the key to superior profitability.

DRUCKER, PETER F. (1909–2005)

Defies classification: never really a strategist, it is safest to say that Drucker was a business philosopher, and the sharpest and most influential commentator that business has ever seen. His father was chief economist in the Austrian civil service. Drucker moved to England in the late 1920s and worked there as a clerk, journalist and economist, before emigrating to America in 1937. There he became a noted consultant, writer and academic.

After a prolonged flirtation with the managerialist school, Drucker came, by the 1950s, to a renewed faith in market forces and the primacy of the customer. In 1954, in *The Practice of Management*, he declared magisterially:

> ***'There is only one valid definition of business purpose: to create a customer. Markets are not created by God, nature or economic forces, but by businessmen.'***

Therefore, the purpose of business lies outside itself, it is a means to the enrichment of customers and society. From then on, Drucker's bemusedly *ex cathedra* statements proved infallible: he was the first to advocate decentralisation of large corporations; he invented the 'knowledge worker' decades before the idea became fashionable; did the same with privatisation; he was the first to insist that government should steer rather than do: and one of the first to acknowledge that the large corporation had had its day.

Drucker actually said remarkably little about strategy. His main contribution has been the idea of the 'theory of the business':

> ***'These are the assumptions that shape any organisation's behaviour, dictate its decisions about what to do and what not to do, and define what the organisation considers meaningful results. These assumptions are about markets. They are about customers and competitors, their values and behaviour. They are about technology and its dynamics, about a company's strengths and weaknesses. These assumptions are about what a company gets paid for. They are what I call a company's theory of the business.'***

I find this a compelling concept, and one very relevant to strategy. Any organisation not only has distinctive competencies but also distinctive beliefs and formulae. The way that the business looks at the world, if you like, the firm's *distinctive ideology*, is as important or more so than any explicit strategy. A firm's theory of the business may contain a tremendous amount of insight, or none at all. The fit of this theory with the business environment – that is, the degree to which the firm's theory of the business strikes a market and economic chord – may be as important to the firm's success as the strength of its core competencies or its market positions. Drucker did not exactly say this, but he would have done, had he ever deigned to write a book on strategy.

If this is true, a firm's success rests heavily on those who exercise ideological sway over it – which gives an unfashionable weight to its past and present leaders, and especially its founder. This may help to explain why, despite all the advantages of accumulated wealth and expertise, firms wane as surely as they wax. The shelf-life of ideology is generally no more than a few decades, pretty much that of the typical large company.

GHOSHAL, SUMANTRA (b. 1948)

'With his film star cheekbones, piercing eyes, hawkish intensity and intellectual brilliance, Sumantra Ghoshal is an intimidating figure,' according to Stuart Crainer. Ghoshal, who hails from India, has been at London Business School since 1994; previously he was at INSEAD and MIT. He is noted for two books written with Christopher Bartlett from Harvard Business School: *Managing Across Borders* (1989) and *The Individualized Corporation* (1997).

In the former, Bartlett and Ghoshal put forward the model of the transnational firm: one that is locally responsive but has global scale and expertise, and that can transfer that expertise effectively, cheaply, and fast.

The *Individualized Corporation* takes a justified sideswipe at many top US corporations and observes that we have not yet found a good new model to take the place of the divisionalized corporation, even though the latter has clearly had its day.

Ghoshal comments elsewhere that 'the oppressive atmosphere in most large companies resembles downtown Calcutta in summer'. His remedy is 'stretch and discipline' as at Intel, where there is both confrontation and disagreement in meetings, but common commitment at the end of meetings to the action decided. To avoid the Calcutta torpor, Ghoshal advocates the 3Ps: purpose ('the company is also a social institution'), process ('the organisation as a set of roles and institutions') and people ('helping individuals to become the best that they can be').

It is odd, but significant, that Ghoshal, who calls himself 'a plain vanilla strategy man', has come to think that the real problem with strategy is how to structure organisations and how to implement the strategy through people: 'You cannot manage third generation strategies through second generation organisations with first generation managers.'

GOOLD, MICHAEL (b. 1945)

British management writer and founding director of the Ashridge Strategic Management Centre after a career with BCG. Made his name with the excellent book *Strategies and Styles* (1987) which looked at the way in which the Centre of large, diversified firms managed their businesses. More recently he has developed a framework for corporate-level strategy built round the concept of parenting advantage described in another landmark book, *Corporate-Level Strategy: Creating Value in the Multibusiness Company* (1994). This looks at the justification for multibusiness companies and concludes that sound corporate strategies are based on the advantage created by the parent organisation. Goold's work is always original, measured, incisive and important.

See CAMPBELL, and in Part Four, PARENTING ADVANTAGE.

HAMEL, GARY (b. 1954)

An American based in California, from where he runs an international strategy consulting firm. A provocative gadfly, Hamel is best known for his work with C.K. Prahalad on STRATEGIC INTENT, CORE COMPETENCIES, and for their 1994 bestseller, *Competing for the Future*.

Hamel is the best proponent of the resource-based theory of the firm and therefore an advocate of 'opportunity share' rather than narrowly defined 'market share'. He favours creative and revolutionary strategy, with passion, imagination and emotion putting reason and analysis in the shade.

In a 1996 *Harvard Business Review* article, Hamel argued for 'strategy as revolution'. Industries divide, he says, into the rule-makers – such as

IBM, Xerox, and Coca-Cola; the rule-takers – such as Fujitsu, McDonnell Douglas and Avis, 'peasants who only keep what the Lord doesn't want'; and the rule-breakers – including IKEA, Body Shop, Swatch and Southwest Airlines. The rule-breakers are revolutionaries who overturn the 'curse of incrementalism', rewrite industry rules, and overthrow industry boundaries.

Rule-breakers have to both 'STRETCH' and 'LEVERAGE'. Stretch is 'a misfit between resources and aspirations'. But it must be accompanied by skills in leveraging limited resources, by *concentrating resources* on a limited focus, *accumulating resources* through alliances and a campaign of knowledge extraction, *complementing resources* by blending them, *conserving resources*, and *recovering resources* from the market as quickly as possible. Most fundamentally, however, rule-breakers have to do things *differently*.

It's interesting, though, that nearly all of the rule-breakers cited by Hamel were startups driven by entrepreneurs. Show me a large company that adopts revolution and I'll show you an *ancien régime* that led in erecting the barricades.

These themes are explored further in Hamel's (2000) flamboyant book *Leading the Revolution.*[2] New business models, he says, are driven by passionate and imaginative revolutionaries. Companies need to create activists and encourage radical innovation, turning their business into a revolution. 'Get off the treadmill of incrementation,' he urges. 'Make innovation your enduring capability.'

If this all sounds like empty rhetoric, be assured that the book has solid content. For instance, the section on business models and how to recreate them is creative and useful.

HAMPDEN-TURNER, CHARLES

British academic and consultant, one of the leading international experience authorities on CULTURE, both at the corporate and at the national level. Hampden-Turner has a holistic understanding of management processes and combines a refreshing, high-level view of the world with nitty-gritty examples of how to make the most out of each firm's unique culture.

He has written several highly acclaimed books, but in my opinion the two best are *Corporate Culture* (1990) and *The Seven Cultures of Capitalism* (1993, written with Fons TROMPENAARS). The first of these starts with some insights about corporate culture: cultures provide firm members with continuity and identity ('without a shared culture Volvo would not be recognisably Volvo'); cultures are patterns, where behaviour at one level (bosses to subordinates) are repeated, for good or ill, in relation to customers; cultures facilitate the sharing of experience and information; cultures are the mechanism through which organisations can learn (there is no other way); changing culture is increasingly the only way that a leader can achieve anything; culture is a stronger and cheaper way to motivate than money; cultures are deeply rooted, but can be changed by intervention from managers and consultants, provided this is skillful and does not attack the culture head-on.

Hampden-Turner believes that the key issues facing companies are *dilemmas*: safety and productivity; the need to cut staff and demonstrate a new caring view of employees; the need to exercise personal initiative and the need to maintain group solidarity; the need to raise profits and also spend money to improve infrastructure; and so on. The culture of a firm will respond to a new leader if he or she can find constructive ways to resolve these dilemmas, in a way that satisfies both its horns. Culture can be negative or positive, and the change process is seen as subtly turning what is negative (and a strong cultural belief or trait of the organisation) into something that is positive (and equally strong, using the same cultural substrate). At times Hampden-Turner comes close to making 'culture' almost the 'General Will' of an organisation, which must warm to a new task or way of doing things for it to be effective. He presents organisational dynamics as a series of either vicious circles or VIRTUOUS CIRCLES, and shows how new initiatives can use the same cultural attributes to turn a downward spiral into an upward one.

Seven detailed examples are given. One of the greatest challenges quoted was the attempt of a new Swedish manager in 1982–1986 to turn Volvo's unsuccessful and loss-making business in France into a success. The French team and Volvo dealers in the country had convinced themselves that failure was inevitable: the French people would never warm to Swedish cars, which, like the Swedes, were seen as melancholic, cold and dull. The French subsidiary talked down to the dealers, attempting to motivate them by threatening to replace them if they failed to sell more. The dealers passed this indifference on to the customers, and having a pessimistic view of their task failed to invest in their showrooms, resulting in a depressing sales picture which in turn reinforced the view that the 'hot' French would never buy 'cold' Volvos.

Instead of hitting the dealers over the head, the new manager held a series of meetings with them, listening, breaking down the hierarchy, inviting the entire French dealer network to visit Sweden, giving them pride in the company and their role, encouraging them to invest in their showrooms and treat customers differently ... and doubling sales within two years.

The case examples all stress the importance of positive 'rituals', corporate events that build on the existing culture but help to stress the desired values.

Hampden-Turner's recent works include *Riding the Waves of Culture: Understanding Diversity in Global Business* and *Mastering the Infinite Game* (1997, with Fons Trompenaars), a brilliant study suggesting the value of a synthesis between Western and Eastern ideas of business.

See also CULTURE, FLAT ORGANISATION and TROMPENAARS.

HANDY, CHARLES (b. 1932)

Delightfully civilised and quirky writer. Handy's main concerns are the philosophy of business and its place in society, and the future of work. The son of an Irish Protestant clergyman, and in former incarnations a manager for Shell in Malaysia, an economist and an academic at London Business School and MIT, Charles Handy has turned into a surprise success as an author of 'where next' books, of which the best may have been one of the earliest, *The Age of Unreason*, published in 1989.

Gary HAMEL pays appropriate tribute to Handy:

> ***'Charles is one of the few management writers who can step entirely outside the world of management and then look back in ... [yielding] an uncompromising and unorthodox perspective which will discomfort and enlighten ... Where most business authors are intent on giving you the "how", Professor Handy forces us to ask, "why?"'***

Although Handy is well worth reading, he has little to say directly about strategy. The most valuable contribution he has made here probably lies in his concept of the *federal firm*, where the Centre co-ordinates, influences and advises, but doesn't decide things. The Centre really is at the middle of things and is concerned with long term strategy, but is not a head office in disguise. Wouldn't it be nice to see quite a few such firms? Sadly, Handy does not provide a long list of examples.

Handy's most intriguing recent book is *The Elephant and the Flea.*[3] Elephants are huge organisations. Fleas are self-employed individuals. Aside from invaluable advice to anyone thinking of leaving the shelter of big organisations, the book explores and in some ways anticipates some of the 'ecological' views on strategy explored in Part Two. 'Organizations,' he says, 'are no longer seen as machines with human parts, but as communities of individuals with very individual aspirations.'

HENDERSON, BRUCE (1915–1992)

Founder of the Boston Consulting Group (BCG) and one of the most original and far-sighted American business thinkers of all time. He and a handful of colleagues invented the GROWTH/SHARE MATRIX (BCG MATRIX), as well as developing the best view of BUSINESS SEGMENTATION that exists. Bruce weaved it all together in a coherent philosophy of business that highlighted more clearly than ever before the compelling importance of market leadership, a low cost position, selectivity in business, and looking at cash flows. He was ahead of his time in seeing the threat to American business posed both by Japan and by America's (and Britain's) obsession with return on investment, which he roundly condemned.

Although a capitalist, red in tooth and claw, he understood the importance of corporate CULTURE long before it became fashionable: he was a weird but ultimately consistent mix of right wing economist and revolutionary critic of standard American corporate practice. His love of paradox, and unique style, which alternates short and shocking sentences with Gibbonesque long ones, are all of a piece with his revolutionary mind.

Bruce changed the way we think about strategy and through BCG has had a major impact on many Western companies. Yet perhaps he achieved much less than a man of his energy and vision should have. He was always a loner, and did not stamp his personality on BCG in the same way that Marvin BOWER had on McKinsey. Consultants in BCG were apprehensive about encounters with Bruce, which were challenging and often disturbing. BCG has continued his heritage of providing new ideas for management, but no-one after Bruce has had his single-minded crusading drive, and after being a tremendous hothouse of ideas in the late 1960s and early 1970s, BCG soon became (even when Bruce was still active in it) an only slightly unconventional commercial consultancy, which would often undertake work where it had little chance, and often no desire, to change the client's thinking and behaviour fundamentally. In short, BCG became domesticated, more concerned to do good professional work and to make money for its vice presidents than to change the world. Bruce realised this was happening, but lacked the practical management skills or close colleagues to stop it.

Even in terms of ideas, Bruce and BCG never fully exploited the force of the original insights, which even today are not evangelised to the extent that they should be. During his lifetime, America continued to lose global market share for the same reasons Bruce had pinpointed so well. One is tempted to conclude that, if BCG had had an organising genius interested in implementation but deeply committed to Bruce's vision, history could have been different. Bruce never developed around him a school of thought that took root in academia either: he could have done with his own Michael PORTER to develop and codify the ideas and help market them to business schools.

Bruce Henderson was a genius. That his achievements fell well short of his insights is much to be regretted.

JOHNSON, PETER (b. 1956)

An intriguing new addition to the world of strategy thinking is Peter Johnson, a don at Exeter College, Oxford and formerly a leading director of the Said Business School there. Johnson has been as responsible as anyone for developing the ECOLOGICAL THEORY of strategy (see Part Two for my version of that). According to Johnson's ecological theory, each business has a unique 'molecular formula or genetic code', which can be described by the way it competes, the ECOSYSTEMS (what we called in Part One BUSINESS SEGMENTS) where it operates, and by its relationships with customers and suppliers. Companies evolve a particular way of doing business that is unique, and the more adapted the formula is to its valuable customers, the more profitable and successful the firm will be. As Johnson puts it in his forthcoming book *Astute Competition*,

> ***'Corporations are also business model factories ... Businesses competing in a given ecosystem make better or worse returns based on the level of competitive advantage conferred by the strategies which they have embedded in their business models.'***

Corporate Strategy is the search for a formula and the places to deploy it, and the people to deepen and reinforce it. Johnson stresses the differences between different ecosystems, differences usually ignored by economists and not given due emphasis by strategists and managers.

> *'The origins of the ecosystem lie in the complex tangle of interactions between customers, competitors, intermediaries and other third parties which consumer resources, create value-added and comprise a relatively stable nexus where demand and supply rub shoulders ... One can visualize ecosystems as medieval hillside castles standing out in the flat landscape or as islands in the ocean: an enclave in which it is possible to survive for reasonable periods by living by one's wits.'*

Peter Johnson has also developed what he calls 'the economics of strategic diversity'. Business systems are more different from each other than they look, and so too are corporations. It is this diversity, and the idiosyncratic relationships between individual customers and the firm, that allow the firms to make super-normal profits. Firms are not always fully aware of the sources of their profits, however, and their business model may not be fully coherent or consistent. 'Very often,' he says, 'individuals and businesses pursue contradictory or disconnected course of action, with unsatisfactory results.'

Johnson has also given thought to the *types* of different ecosystems and corporations. Here is his introduction to such differences:

ILLUSTRATION 3.1 ◆ Businesses and contexts

Business	Ecosystem context
Natural resource businesses: minerals, oil and gas	Very high entry/exit barriers, exogenous uncertainty of demand, volatile economics, leverage, oligopolies and alliances
Manufactured commodities: textiles, chemicals, fertilisers	Medium to high entry/exit barriers, cost reduction, capacity and cycle management, process innovation
System based consumable businesses: fruit juice packing, printers	Low entry/high exit barriers, penetration marketing, maintenance of installed park, internal operational systems
Logistical businesses: containers, specialist trucking, auto delivery, airlines	High entry/exit barriers, stable demand, operational and system complexity, topology and loading, complex price and service factors

Consumer businesses: food, clothes, beverages	Medium entry/exit barriers, fluctuating demand, product development, production management, advertising, branding, promotion
Intermediary businesses: trading, broking, merchanting, investment banking	Low entry/exit barriers, rapid product service evolution, virtual markets, networks, volatility, fragmentation, spontaneity
Knowledge businesses: journals, databases	Low entry/medium exit barriers, unstructured demand, distribution plays and promotion, critical mass economics, creative knowledge
Professional businesses: lawyers, accountants, consultants	Low entry/exit, cyclical demand, HRM and operational leverage, concepts and innovation, branding, reputation, networks

Johnson advocates a taxonomic approach to business strategy rather like the classification systems which botanists use for plants, which he called 'business genomics'. 'Were we collectors of different sorts of businesses,' he comments as an aside, 'we might expect to run a sizeable business zoo.' When combined with explicit measures of strategic performance, he claims, this taxonomical approach will allow a new field of 'strategometrics' to emerge, similar to econometrics.

Johnson says 'strategy within an ecosystem is a pattern of coherent and consistent action expressed through a business model leading to the appropriation of sustained economic rents.' He has introduced the return on resources as a new gauge of competitive success, superior in several ways to traditional measures of profitability.

Peter Johnson is a refreshing and original thinker, currently almost completely unknown to the general business public but destined for a high profile. See also ECONOMIC RENTS.

JURAN, JOSEPH M. (b. 1904)

Romanian-born American electrical engineer and quality guru, who was jointly responsible (with W. Edwards DEMING) for the quality revolution in Japan after 1950. He published his *Quality Control Handbook* in 1951 and began work in Tokyo in 1953. He developed Company-Wide Quality Management (CWQM), a systematic methodology for spreading the gospel of quality throughout a firm. He insisted that quality could not be delegated and was an early exponent of what has come to be known as empowerment: for him quality had to be the goal of each employee, individually and in teams, through self-supervision. He was less mechanistic than Deming and placed greater stress on human relations. In 1988 he published *Juran on Planning for Quality* which included his quality trilogy of quality planning, quality management and quality improvement. A firm and all its people must commit to and be obsessive about quality: it must become a way of life built into the firm's CULTURE. Well worth looking at, though not the lightest of reads.

KANTER, ROSABETH MOSS (b. 1943)

US sociologist, Harvard Business School professor and editor of the *Harvard Business Review* and the driving force behind empowerment as a change management crusade. Three of her books are important.

Men and Women of the Corporation (1977) criticised the way that human talent was cramped within bureaucratic structures, hurting both the corporation and the individuals. Kanter proposed career development mechanisms to move more women (and some other 'powerless' groups) into more senior jobs, and also urged empowering strategies leading to flatter structures and autonomous work groups.

The Change Masters (1983) profiled companies that were good at innovation and identified their underlying characteristics. The most significant finding was that such firms have an 'integrative' view of the world and were iconoclastic; firms poor at innovation were analytical, compartmentalised, 'segmentalist' and conservative. The book developed the theme that individuals should be made more powerful, but within a framework of common corporate purpose.

When Giants Learn to Dance (1989) stresses the need for even giant corporations to become 'post-entrepreneurial': demonstrating all the attributes of an entrepreneur such as flexibility, responsiveness and personal initiative, but combining this with the discipline of a large firm and the realisation of SYNERGY between different parts of the firm by having a vision of the firm overall and where it can go. In a striking metaphor, Kanter talks about the dancing elephant: 'the power of an elephant with the agility of a dancer'. Another useful phrase is 'the corporation as a switchboard, where a small centre helps to direct other parts of the organisation to realise synergies'. She also invents PAL, not a type of dog food but rather '*pool* resources with others, *ally* to exploit an opportunity, or *link* systems in a partnership'. The wise corporation becomes PALs with customers, suppliers, joint venture partners and outside contractors. The company of the future will be lean but not mean, able to do more with less (fewer layers), but operating within a framework of shared values.

Kanter is right about all of this, though to me she misses (or chooses not to stress) the key role that an individual leader has in transforming a corporation.

During the 1990s, Kanter wrote three books, *The Challenge of Organizational Change* (with B. Stein and T.D. Jick, 1992); *World Class: Thriving locally in the global economy* (1995); and *Rosabeth Moss Kanter on the Frontiers of Management* (1997). None of these contains strikingly new insights, although *World Class* is a good read.

See also STRATEGIC ALLIANCE, SYNERGY and KEIRETSU.

KAY, JOHN (b. 1948)

An English economist and strategy professor, former head of the new business school at Oxford University. Kay's excellent 1993 book, *Foundations of Corporate Success*, is a very useful statement of the 'resource-based' view of strategy and is particularly forceful in its denunciation of 'wish-driven' aspirational strategy.

Kay gives the example of the French computer company Groupe Bull, set up to become 'a European IBM'. For 30 years Groupe Bull aspired to become the 'major European supplier of global information systems'. Great, but it didn't have the corporate ability to do so. Following huge losses in the early 1990s, it wisely gave up and formed an alliance with IBM.

Kay advocates that 'the rationalist approach in which strategy is devised for the organisation gives way to a view of strategy which sees it as derived from the organisation'. An organisation must therefore have a solid and realistic view of its 'distinctive capabilities', or what others call 'core competencies'. Successful strategy is often opportunistic and adaptive rather than calculating. The organisation moves forward crab-wise, as organisations comprise changing coalitions of differing interests, so that all change is normally incremental.

But Kay parts company with some resource-based strategists – one thinks of HAMEL and PRAHALAD's views of strategic intent and stretch goals – who advocate the development of new core competencies. He says this can lead to wish-fulfilment in another form. He refers to Komatsu's strategic intent of 'encircle Caterpillar' and its success, apparently against the odds, in eroding Cat's market share in earth-moving equipment. The success, Kay insists, was because of Komatsu's superior products and their value, not because of the strength of Komatsu's will.

He highlights three types of distinctive corporate capabilities exhibited by successful firms:

- innovation
- architecture
- reputation.

Architecture he defines as the combination of relationships that a firm may have with outside forces: suppliers, customers, collaborators, competitors or governments. He usefully draws attention to the value of reputation, which may have arisen as a result of innovation or architecture, but which may sustain the success of the firm even after others have copied the innovation, or the architectural advantage has faded.

A firm may also have 'strategic assets', such as high market share and a low cost position, that are valid bases of strategy, even though they are not distinctive capabilities. And firms must not only have distinctive capabilities: they must be in the right place at the right time, and they must be steered and managed appropriately.

LEAVITT, HAROLD J.

American management psychologist who is one of the most stimulating and original thinkers in the field. His 1978 book, *Managerial Psychology*, is one of the best texts on the subject, and in particular on the interactions and communication patterns of groups, and the distortions that arise from links in a chain. But Leavitt's most interesting, landmark work is *Corporate Pathfinders*, which examines the characteristic personalities of leaders. In particular, he introduces a very useful categorisation into TYPE 1, TYPE 2 and TYPE 3 executives.

LEVITT, THEODORE (b. 1925)

German-born American marketing guru, professor at Harvard Business School. Wrote the legendary *Harvard Business Review* article on 'Marketing

Myopia' in 1960: it has since sold half a million reprints. The article said that firms and industries should be 'customer-satisfying' rather than 'goods-producing' in their orientation: marketing-led not production-led. Levitt said it was not good enough to meet customer demand with a new product and then believe that the key to continued success was low cost production. He criticised 'Fordism' for giving the customer what was thought to be good for him, rather than continually being alert to what the customer wants. Hence Ford's decline in the face of General Motors' policy of offering cars in any colour and later in the face of the compact car from Japan and Europe. He also castigated the myopia of the US railroad industry in thinking that it was in the railroad business (a production-led view) rather than consumer transport: if it had had the latter view it would have diversified into airlines and not seen its business wither.

Levitt was wholly right and partly wrong. He was well ahead of his time in telling firms to be customer-obsessed. But his railroads example and others he gave were simplistic and possibly wrong. What expertise or cost sharing did the railroads have for entering the airline business? Perhaps they should have been experts at marketing transport to passengers, expertise that would have been transferable. But they weren't, and if Penn Central had bought an airline it would have gone bust much quicker than it did. The criticism was right, the remedy wrong.

More recently, Levitt has become a prophet of global BRANDS. His work is fun to read, stimulating and bursting with ideas – we should not complain if some of them are flawed.

MAGAZINER, IRA C.

Important American writer and consultant who has written on industrial policy in Japan, Sweden and Ireland and whose 1982 book, *Minding America's Business* (co-authored with Robert B. Reich), is still the best account of how and why the US has lost market share to Japan. It stresses the need for the US Government and industrialists to focus on competitive productivity and to develop industrial policy for specific industries in a discrete and precise way. In 1989 Magaziner wrote *The Silent War* (with Mark Patinkin), providing new examples of how American firms had lost out to Europe (Airbus Industrie), Korea (Samsung, the world's largest maker of microwave ovens), and Japan (many examples), but also how

Corning Glass beat the Japanese in fibre optics. The book advocated an American fightback and outlined measures for both companies and corporations to follow in dealing with foreign competition.

Magaziner is iconoclastic, populist and was an early adviser on healthcare to President Clinton. He clearly has a future in Democratic party politics, despite swimming firmly against the prevailing tide of economic liberalism. Meanwhile, America's relative industrial decline is being reversed, although in the main not by the means Magaziner advocates. Yet his work is fresh, stimulating and worth a quick read.

MINTZBERG, HENRY (b. 1939)

According to Tom PETERS, 'perhaps the world's premier management thinker'. Professor Henry Mintzberg of McGill University in Montreal, and of INSEAD, is certainly one of the world's foremost experts on strategy and is highly respected for his willingness to engage in detailed empirical research and also his keen and sceptical intellect. He is, however, a little bit of an elusive butterfly: his exact position on many issues is hard to pin down, even though he is an avid collector, classifier and debunker of the views of others.

Mintzberg made his name as early as 1973 with *The Nature of Managerial Work*, which noted the messy reality in which managers were immersed, and destroyed the idea that they were principally planners or rational analysts. Strategy emerged on the run; it was rarely planned.

Mintzberg deserves great thanks for helping to destroy the theory and practice of strategic planning, and substituting the idea, which he published in the *Harvard Business Review* in 1987, that strategy should be 'crafted'. A potter at her wheel mixes thought and action, guiding the clay, responding to how it shapes itself, sensing rather than analysing. If strategy should be crafted, there can be no hard distinction between developing it and implementing it. Crafting requires those who are closest to the material to be involved in strategy development, ensuring that the strategy is flexible and responds to events and market needs as they unfold.

In 1998, Mintzberg (with co-authors Bruce Ahlstrand and Joseph Lampel) published *Strategy Safari*, an elaboration of the ten schools of strategy Mintzberg had described earlier (and which are summarised in Part Two of this book). It is a detailed and scholarly review (it certainly belies its racy title), rather along the lines of *Everything you could possibly want to know about strategy and strategy professors*. For the academically-inclined, there is a tremendous amount of useful meat in this book, but do not attempt to swallow it all in one sitting.

Gary HAMEL has given five reasons why he likes Mintzberg: 'He is a world class iconoclast. He loves the messy world of real companies. He is a master story-teller. He is conceptual *and* pragmatic. He doesn't believe in easy answers.' Both Hamel and Mintzberg are anti-establishment characters, colourful revolutionaries in a sea of grey. More power to them.

OHMAE, KENICHI (b. 1943)

Brilliant, un-Japanese, Japanese, whose book *The Mind of the Strategist* (published in Japan in 1975, but not in the US until 1982) remains one of the best on strategy, and who contributed towards the development of Toyota's JUST-IN-TIME system. An analyst who gives a higher place to intuition and insight, Ohmae was among the first to drive everything from the customer, and place the customer at the heart of the firm's value system: 'customer-based strategies are the basis of all strategy'. *The Mind of the Strategist* is an eloquent plea for creative, customer-based strategies, while giving a large number of hints and prompts in the form of analytical diagnoses and examples of unconventional strategies successfully pursued by Japanese companies. See also KEY FACTORS FOR SUCCESS (KFS) and STRATEGIC DEGREES OF FREEDOM (SDF).

In recent years, notably in his landmark 1990 book, *The Borderless World*, and in *The End of the Nation State* (1995), Ohmae has turned his attention to the way that the world's largest companies are creating what he calls the ILE (Inter-Linked Economy) of the US, Europe and Japan/Asia, based largely on the need to meet the requirements of demanding consumers in all important economies. He argues persuasively the case for inevitable GLOBALISATION, albeit based on LOCAL GLOBALISATION rather than UNIVERSAL PRODUCTS, a process being slowed down but not stopped by the rearguard actions of protectionists, bureaucrats and governments around the world. The companies forcing the change are becoming multilocals rather than multinationals. According to Ohmae, 'nothing is "overseas" any longer'; the word is banned from Honda's vocabulary, for example, 'because [Honda] sees itself as equidistant from all customers'. Multilocals must become 'insiders' to each important market (a process he describes usefully as INSIDERISATION) and be driven by a determination to serve customers better wherever they are: 'Global players must have the engine and knowledge to propel themselves. They must be directly familiar with the key markets. That knowledge is the secret of success in the borderless world.' See GLOBALISATION (definition 2), GLOBAL LOCALISATION and ILE.

PARETO, VILFREDO (1848–1923)

A distinguished Italian economist, Pareto is important for business strategists because of his discovery in 1897 that there economic inputs and outputs are reliably related to each other in a topsy-turvy, unbalanced way. In looking at wealth statistics, he found that not only was most wealth owned by a few people, but also that the shape of the statistical distribution was nearly always the same, whatever data he was looking at. It didn't matter what country or what century – the shape was always the same.

Pareto reasoned that in any distribution of economic causes and effects, there would be a few causes which were hugely important, and the large majority of causes, which made little difference. Pareto never expressed his theory very concisely or elegantly, and his work never reached a wide audience, although academic economists took his work very seriously and empirical research always vindicated Pareto's 'rule' that most results flow from a small minority of causes. In the 1940s and 1950s, however, Pareto's work attracted the attention of Harvard Professor George Zipf and quality control guru Joseph JURAN. Now renamed the EIGHTY/TWENTY RULE, Pareto's discovery came to be summarised with the approximation that '20 per cent of causes lead to 80 per cent of results'.

Every executive – and arguably every person interested at all in achievement in any sphere – needs to know that most causes don't matter, but that a few causes matter a stupendous amount. In business, the three most important '80/20' things to know are:

- 80 per cent of any firm's profits are likely to come from only 20 per cent or fewer of its products.
- 80 per cent of any firm's profits probably come from 20 per cent or fewer of its customers.

- 80 per cent of any executive's economic value or impact on profits come from 20 per cent or less of his or her time.

Whenever empirical studies are made, the relationship is found to hold, sometimes in a much more extreme way. For example, one recent published study showed that 93 per cent of profits at the Royal Bank of Canada came from 17 per cent of its customers.

I wrote a reinterpretation of Pareto's finding in 1997 and called it *The 80/20 Principle*, because it seemed to me that it is the *principle* that few things really matter that is essential, not reliance on a 'rule'.[4] The book struck a chord and at the time of writing has sold over 700,000 copies.

It is quite stunning to realise that most of your turnover and most of your time is largely irrelevant to results!

PASCALE, RICHARD T. (b. 1938)

Consultant and professor at Stanford Business School. Pascale first made a mark as the co-author (with Anthony Athos, then of Harvard Business School, and the then McKinsey consultants, Tom PETERS, and Bob WATERMAN) of the SEVEN SS framework in the early 1980s, and for his 1981 bestseller, written with Anthony Athos, *The Art of Japanese Management.* The common theme was the integration of strategy with 'softer stuff' and the importance of internal consensus – the Seven Ss are strategy, structure, staff, skills, shared values, systems and style – and the way that Japanese management in particular 'goes with the flow' of events in evolving strategy.

Pascale and Athos quote Takeo Fujisawa, co-founder of Honda: 'Japanese and American management is 95 per cent the same and differs in all important respects.' They comment on the different way that Japanese managers make decisions:

> ***'Whereas Western management beliefs tend to portray a decision as fixed and final, Eastern philosophical tradition emphasises individual accommodation to a continuously unfolding set of events.'***

Pascale and Athos were influential in drawing attention to the importance of 'vision' to Japanese management and in getting Western executives to pay attention to this idea. The result was the renewed emphasis on MISSION in the later 1980s and 1990s, although inevitably many Western companies ended up with more form than substance.

Just at the time that the Japanese miracle was beginning to seem less miraculous, in 1990 Pascale published the highly acclaimed *Managing on the Edge*, which starts with the great and true line, 'Nothing fails like success'. The book is about how great companies go astray and stagnate unless they make deliberate and subtle efforts to transform themselves. The danger is that existing mental models will prove resistant to change, particularly if dissent and conflict are sidelined. Here the task of leaders is presented as creating and destroying paradigms.

TRANSFORMATION will not work unless all employees are involved and believe that they have power to influence events. Different opinions and conflict should be harnessed rather than suppressed. If necessary, the organisation should be split into smaller units where everyone can have a strong sense of identity and ownership.

Most recently, Pascale has stressed 'agility' as the way to move organisations forward. They are 'agile' if their employees feel powerful, if they identify with the organisation, if they 'contend' (meaning the constructive use of conflict), and learn to deal with new ideas. How many large organisations could pass this test of agility?

PETERS, TOM (b. 1942)

Probably the world's foremost management guru and the one who has made most money out of the profession. His achievements are real: a McKinsey consultant until after he and Bob WATERMAN wrote *In Search of Excellence* (1982), which now has sales exceeding 6 million (unprecedented for a business book), when he left to publish, lecture and evangelise for passionate management. He has built up a massive and highly profitable business in merchandising himself and his artefacts: books, videos, cassettes, TV series, consultancy and personal appearances. He is the Billy Graham of management, though in his case the profits go back to The Tom Peters Group.

The Excellence project had prosaic origins in a McKinsey business development exercise that started in 1977. The simple and relatively uninspired idea was to isolate the best performing US companies over the previous 20 years, looking at the top decile of the *Fortune 500*. In the end, Peters and Waterman chose 43 companies and tried to describe what common characteristics had led to their success.

The methodology was sensible, if rather loose; the conclusions questionable; and the glorification of some of the companies naive, the product of hindsight and corporate propaganda as much as a real understanding of what had gone on. Within five years of the book's publication, two thirds of the 'excellent' companies celebrated had hit trouble, and one, People Express, had gone bust. Yet the success of the book was well deserved. It was an inspiring read, quite unlike any previous book on management – it made readers want to go out there and do great deeds, like those celebrated in the book. It put passion, leadership, values, and the customer at the centre of excellence, and in these respects was 100 per cent correct, even if the particulars it used to celebrate excellence were often flawed. The Gospels and other great religious writings do not depend for their meaning on literal truth – simply because people can respond to them, and achieve miracles, is testimony enough. So it was, and is, with Excellence.

Peters wrote a sequel (with Nancy Austin), *A Passion for Excellence* (1985), then changed tack significantly by writing *Thriving on Chaos* (1987), demonstrating enormous chutzpa by starting with the sentence, '*There are no excellent companies*'. Clearly true, but not many opinion formers would have demonstrated such bravado, and fewer still would have emerged with their reputation enhanced rather than tarnished by such a u-turn two years after another book celebrating more excellent companies. *Thriving on Chaos* is about change, whether it is possible to manage it, and if so, how. In the book Peters took a relatively optimistic view about change management, broadly advocating a move from hierarchical bureaucracies to customer-centred adhocracies. In classic Anglo-Saxon style he provided a checklist of 45 precepts for managers, of which the most important are:

- specialise/create niches/differentiate
- provide top quality
- become a service addict
- make manufacturing the prime marketing tool
- over-invest in people, front line sales, service, distribution – make these the company heroes
- become customer-obsessed
- support failures by publicly rewarding well thought-out mistakes

- make innovation a way of life for everyone
- guarantee continuous employment for the core workforce
- radically reduce layers of management
- become a compulsive listener
- demand total integrity in all dealings, both inside and outside the firm.

Not many of these are original, but the synthesis is good and the way in which they are urged is, well, excellent.

Since then Peters has moved on, and become much more 'pessimistic about planned change'. It is true that 75 per cent of such efforts at TRANSFORMATION fail, but should he not say that the cup is a quarter full rather than three quarters empty. Concentrating on the 25 per cent and trying to move that to, say, 50 per cent, might be a better use of Peters' talents than defeatism.

His 1992 book, *Liberation Management*, is important but difficult to handle: long, rambling, poorly organised, easy to put down and full of American jargon. It reads more like *Bonfire of the Vanities* than *In Search of Excellence*, though without the plot of either. There are five main points being made in *Liberation Management*:

1 All business is becoming fashion.
2 Create mini-SBUs everywhere.
3 Organise everything and everyone around projects.
4 Destroy functional departments.
5 Use partners outside the formal organisation.

The book is very concerned with structure because Peters believes that without changing the structure of organisations, very little can be achieved. He is probably right, but the message in *Liberation Management* is not put across as eloquently as in his previous books. In my opinion, Peters' recent books are not as interesting as their predecessors. For the record, these are: *The Tom Peters Seminar* (1994); *The Pursuit of Wow!* (1994); and *The Circle of Innovation* (1997). See WATERMAN; FASHION.

PORTER, MICHAEL (b. 1947)

The second highest paid management lecturer after Tom PETERS: Harvard Business School professor, consultant, and the star of Corporate Strategy worldwide. Porter even talks about the 'Porter brand'. In two books, *Competitive Strategy: Techniques for Analysing Industries and Competitors* (1980) and *Competitive Advantage* (1985), Porter summarises and builds on the main concepts of Corporate Strategy. A brilliant synthesizer, formulator and packager, Porter defines two kinds of competitive advantage: low cost, or differentiation. He places a firm in the context of its industry (see PORTER'S FIVE COMPETITIVE FORCES) and identifies the firm's value chain (all the ways it adds value from start to finish by activity) systematically.

Since the mid 1980s he has looked at global competition and the comparative advantage of nations, building on work done earlier by Ira MAGAZINER. He stresses the need for clusters of mutually supporting industries (see also KEIRETSU) and comes as close as a mainstream American could to recommending industrial policy: *The Competitive Advantage of Nations* (1990) should be compulsory reading for all politicians. Like Peters, Porter has come up with some useful and insightful strategic prescriptions, including:

- Sell to the most demanding buyers, as they will set standards for your people.
- Seek buyers with the most difficult needs, so they become your R&D lab.
- Establish norms exceeding the world's toughest regulations.
- Source from the world's best suppliers: scour the world for them.
- Treat employees as permanent partners.
- Use outstanding competitors as motivators.

Precisely.

Porter's *Competitive Strategy* (1980) codified how to gain competitive advantage. His analysis suggests four diagnostic components of looking at any specific competitor:

1 *Future goals*: What are they trying to achieve, including their ambitions in terms of market leadership and technology?

2 *Assumptions*: How does the competitor perceive himself, and what assumptions does he make about the industry and his competition?

3 *Current Strategy*.

4 *Opportunities*: What do they think they have?

Armed with this framework, one can then construct scenarios about competitors' possible reactions to any action by one's firm.

PRAHALAD, C.K. (b. 1941)

Best known for his collaboration with Gary HAMEL and the idea of CORE COMPETENCY, STRATEGIC INTENT and STRETCH AND LEVERAGE. C.K. Prahalad is a long-serving professor at the University of Michigan's business school, and a consultant to many international corporations, including AT&T, Motorola and Philips. Prahalad became Hamel's mentor after Hamel quit his hospital administration job to take a PhD in International Business at Michigan in 1978. 'We shared a deep dissatisfaction with the mechanistic way strategy was carried out,' Hamel recalls.

Hamel and Prahalad's most important collaboration was their 1994 bestseller, *Competing for the Future*. The book is a plea for multi-faceted strategy, going beyond analysis and searching for purpose, both emotional and passionate. They caution against excessive simplicity:

> ***'We like to believe we can break strategy down to Five Forces or Seven Ss. But you can't. Strategy is extraordinarily emotional and demanding. It is not a ritual or a once-a-year exercise, though that is what it has become. We have set the bar too low.'***

They denounce downsizing as 'corporate anorexia', commenting that 'a company surrenders today's business when it gets smaller faster than it gets better. A company surrenders tomorrow's business when it gets better without getting different.'

Prahalad has also collaborated with Yves Dox, an INSEAD professor, resulting in their influential 1987 book, *The Multinational Mission: Balancing Local Responsiveness and Global Vision*.

QUINN, JAMES BRIAN

A former strategy consultant, long associated with the Amos Tuck School of Management, who started in the 1960s by advocating a formal systems planning approach. Quinn changed his mind, however, as a result of extensive research he undertook in the late 1970s, when he went into Chrysler, Exxon, Pilkington and Xerox to observe how strategy really was developed and implemented. The results, published in 1980, came in his important book, *Strategies for Change: Logical Incrementalism.*

'Logical incrementalism' is a useful concept, and not just a euphemism for 'muddling through'. According to Quinn:

> ***'The real strategy tends to evolve as internal decisions and external events flow together to create a new, widely shared consensus for action ... in well-run organisations, managers pro-actively guide these streams of actions and events incrementally toward conscious strategies.'***

Quinn's model is sort-of-top-down, but in a loose and semi-political, semi-learning way. The chief executive and other senior managers work towards a picture of where they want to go, even before they can describe it; they nudge their people towards the goal, but will shift the targets along the way, experimenting, holding off irrevocable decisions until more information is available, corralling and cajoling support for new ideas, and defining an increasing precise strategy. This process – what MINTZBERG has characterised as 'strategy on the run' – 'allows executives to blend analysis, organisational politics and individual needs into a cohesive new direction'.

In the firms Quinn researched, financial analysis and quantitative modelling were not useful, and the process of strategy formulation merged with that of implementation into one 'continuous, pulsing dynamic ... successful managers who operate with logical incrementalism build the seeds of understanding, identity, and commitment into the very processes that create their strategies. By the time the strategy begins to crystallise in focus, pieces of it are already being implemented. Through their strategic formulation processes, they have built a momentum and psychological commitment to the strategy, which causes it to flow toward flexible implementation.'

REICHHELD, FREDERICK F.

Fred Reichheld is Director Emeritus of strategy consulting firm Bain & Company and the inventor of the concept of LOYALTY as a major strategic weapon. In his excellent classic, *The Loyalty Effect*,[5] he describes 'the power of loyalty-based management as a highly profitable alternative to the economics of perpetual churn'.

See LOYALTY and CUSTOMER RETENTION.

RIES, AL (b. 1947)

A non-academic consultant and writer, who has made his name as a marketing expert. Yet, though his name does not appear in Mintzberg *et al.*'s comprehensive *Strategy Safari*, Ries is one of the best exponents of business strategy. His 1996 book, *Focus*, is a formidable polemic in favour of keeping whole corporations, as well as individual business units, focused on one special market and approach to business.

Ries documents the 'unfocusing' of corporate America in the 1980s and early 1990s. Companies, driven by managerial hubris, extended their product lines, entered new businesses, and often made disastrous acquisitions: 'diworsification'. But now managers are reaping the whirlwind, and those who have offended the gods of focus are being eased out of the executive suite.

GLOBALISATION implies specialisation. 'The larger the market, the more specialisation that takes place,' Ries argues. 'Like amoebas dividing in a petri dish, business can be viewed as an ever-dividing sea of categories.' Cars used to be cars; now there are a large number of specialist producers. As in evolution by natural selection, species divide to form new species. 'The surge of SPINOFFS and sell-offs is proof positive that the age of diversification and the age of conglomerisation are finally over. We have entered the age of focus.'

I strongly recommend anyone devising strategy, especially at the corporate level, to read *Focus*, and its sequel, *Future Focus* (2000). Ries is a joy to read and, what is more, he is right.

Ries's latest book – co-authored with his daughter Laura Ries – is *The Origin of Brands*.[6] Although the title is misleading, this is another excellent book and required reading for the serious strategist. The book would have been far better called *Divergence*, since it is about the process whereby product and service categories diverge over time and how a firm can create a new category – in my terms a new ECOSYSTEM – and dominate it for ever by associating the category with an appropriate new brand:

In the 'great tree of products and service,' Al and Laura Ries ask, 'how do new categories arise?' By divergence of existing categories.

> *'First, there was a branch called computer. Today that computer branch has diverged and now we have mainframe computers, midrange computers, network computers, personal computers, laptop computers, and handheld computers. The computer didn't converge with another technology. It diverged ...*
>
> *If you want to build a successful brand, you have to understand divergence. You have to look for opportunities to create new categories by divergence of existing categories. And then you have to become the first brand in this emerging new category.'*

See VALUE INNOVATION and especially 'Create a New Ecosystem' in Part Two.

RUMELT, RICHARD (b. 1942)

A professor from the Harvard General Management group. In 1997 Rumelt proposed a useful framework for choosing between possible strategies:

- *Consistency*: the strategy must be internally consistent and coherent
- *Consonance*: the strategy must be consonant with the environment and changes in it
- *Advantage*: the strategy must create and maintain competitive advantage in the area of focus
- *Feasibility*: the strategy must not be too ambitious or unrealistic for the organisation.

Rumelt has also provided one of my favourite quotes about strategy. In commenting on the controversy over how Honda wiped out the British motor cycle industry and the exact nature of its strategy, he makes a valuable point:

> *'I believe that strategic thinking is a necessary but greatly overrated element of business success. If you know how to design great motorcycle engines, I can teach you all you need to know*

about strategy in a few days. If you have a PhD in strategy, years of labour are unlikely to give you the ability to design great new motorcycle engines.'

Strategists should remember that strategy alone does not guarantee success, nor even failure!

SCHEIN, EDGAR H. (b. 1928)

A distinguished and commercially astute American social psychologist based at MIT. Schein is 'well networked', having worked with and been influenced by Doug McGregor, as well as having close links with Warren Bennis, Chris ARGYRIS and Charles HANDY, whom he taught. Schein was one of the first to focus on process consulting, the title of his 1969 book, which involves looking at how a firm operates and its CULTURE and helping it be more effective, rather than supplying expert content-oriented consulting. Schein has been influential for the past 20 years, and has added three concepts to management language: Process Consulting, the Psychological Contract and the Career Anchor.

The 'psychological contract' is the bargain struck between employees and the firm, covering not only the normal economic contractual terms but more broadly what each expects of the other. Unless the terms of the psychological contract are understood (at least intuitively) by each side, the basis for a long term relationship does not exist, and there may be unexpected friction in the short term. The psychological contract relates to trust and expected patterns of behaviour.

The 'career anchor' is the self-image of an individual in an organisation that holds him or her in place. Early on in a career the individual may develop (or fail to develop) a sense of worth, satisfaction and confidence in his or her role in the organisation. Without the anchor, the individual may strive for a new role inside or outside the organisation.

Schein was an early writer on corporate culture, which he defines as 'what [an organisation] has learned as a total social unit over the course of its history'. He stressed the importance of VALUES, modes of behaviour, and artefacts (the external manifestations of a firm's culture, such as Mars' white coats and clocking-in, IBM's white shirts, open-plan or compartmentalised offices, the way that people in the firm talk to each other, and so on). Schein emphasises also the role of leadership in change management. His best books are: *Process Consultation* (1969); *Organizational Culture and Leadership* (1985, 1992); and *Career Anchors: Discovering your real values* (1990). See MISSION.

SCHONBERGER, RICHARD J. (b. 1937)

Interesting and creative American industrial engineer and the author of the two bestselling books on manufacturing: *Japanese Manufacturing Techniques* (1982) and *World Class Manufacturing* (1986). Introduced just-in-time and other techniques used in Japan to the US market in the early 1980s. But Schonberger's most interesting book is *Building a Chain of Customers* (1990), which argues boldly that world class business can be built only if each function in a business is viewed as the customer of the preceding stage, all the way to the final customer. Each part of the corporation must satisfy its (internal or external) customers' four needs: 'ever-better quality, ever-lower costs, ever-increasing flexibility, and ever-quicker response.' Schonberger packaged the idea of cellular manufacturing as the way to meet these needs: clusters of employees and the operations are deployed according to the work flow rather than on artificial functional or departmental lines. He thus laid the foundations for BUSINESS PROCESS RE-ENGINEERING and for the recent theories of Tom PETERS and other prophets of customer obsession.

SELZNICK, PHILIP

Way back in 1955, Philip Selznick coined the term 'distinctive competence' to mean what a firm was particularly and unusually adept at doing. He drew attention to the peculiarities of each firm's history, which resulted in its 'special limitations and capabilities ... an emergent pattern that decisively affects the competence of an organization to frame and execute desired policies.'

He told the story of a master boat-builder, a firm with outstanding craftsmen and a dedication to high quality above all else. Because the market for such top-end boats was fairly small, the firm decided to make low-cost speed boats, which represented a much bigger market. The move was a fiasco. The craftsmen would not and could not cut corners and make boats cheaply.

That firm, Selznick said, not only had a distinctive competence in crafting high-quality boats, but also a 'distinctive incompetence' the production of cheaper boats. All firms, he said, should realise that the flipside of being very good at something was that they would probably not be any good at something quite different. The size and attractiveness of the market was irrelevant.

In 1990, PRAHALAD and HAMEL revived and popularised Selznick's point, talking about a firm's CORE COMPETENCE. Sadly, they did not place quite equal emphasis on what may be called 'core incompetencies'.

Selznick was well ahead of his time. His work fits snugly and brilliantly into the concept of evolving the genetic code of firms discussed in this book. See also CORE COMPETENCE, GENETIC CODE.

SENGE, PETER M. (b. 1947)

Originally an engineer, studies social systems at MIT and is director of the Center for Organizational Learning there. Senge is best known for his 1990 work, *The Fifth Discipline*, subtitled *The Art and Practice of the Learning Organization*, and its sequel, *The Fifth Discipline Fieldbook: Strategies and Tools for Building a Learning Organization* (1994), which he co-authored with C. Roberts, R. Ross, B. Smith and A. Kleiner. He is responsible more than anyone else for adapting the ideas of 'systems thinking', particularly the idea of Jay Forrester from MIT, into management thinking. The five disciplines are: personal mastery; mental models; building shared vision; team learning; and systems thinking. 'Systems thinking,' Senge writes, 'is the fifth discipline. It is the discipline that integrates the disciplines, fusing them into a coherent body of theory and practice.'

Senge has popularised the idea that organisations need to learn collectively, forming a collective VISION that takes account of how everything is connected to everything else. But defining the learning organisation is tough: Senge offers not so much a product or a concept as a process, reminiscent of the much older 'process consulting' model championed by Ed SCHEIN. This makes it difficult to assess how successful Senge's work has been, and whether the 'learning organisation' is more than a nice aspiration or a consulting fad.

The idea that organisations' success is dependent on their ability to learn collectively must be substantially correct, but helping an organisation learn is difficult to describe and even more difficult to do. I feel there is a real danger, in the Senge approach, of ignoring content and structure. *What* the organisation learns may be more important than how it does so; the learning needs to be steered according to a clear rationale. And making the corporation simpler and smaller may dramatically multiply the chances of functional learning. See Arie DE GEUS.

SLOAN, ALFRED P. (1875–1966)

One of the very few industrialists to be referred to as an authority on management; head of General Motors from 1923 to 1955; author of *My Years with General Motors* (1963); and notable for three reasons. First, he virtually invented the decentralised, divisionalised firm, establishing what he called federal decentralisation, when he transformed General Motors in the early 1920s from a mass of untidy and overlapping entities, with sporadic and ineffective central control, into eight separate divisions (five car divisions and three component divisions) which were treated as though they were separate businesses, but which were subject to professional controls on finance and policy from the Centre.

Second, Sloan changed the structure of the car industry and its SEGMENTATION, and provided a model for how other firms could do the same. When he took over, there were just two car segments in the US: the mass market, dominated by the black Ford Model T, which had 60 per cent of the total car market volume; and the very low-volume, high-class market. Sloan aimed to plug the gap between these two markets by creating five price and performance segments, with the aim that these five markets should be dominated by one of the new five GM car ranges: the Chevrolet, Oldsmobile, Pontiac, Buick and Cadillac (this represented a range rationalisation for GM from eight competing models). He turned Ford's no-choice policy on its head by introducing a range of colours and features so that cars could be 'customised' at relatively little extra cost, and he introduced new models each year to encourage trading up.

The segmentation fitted neatly with the divisionalisation: each of the five car segments and models had its own division, thus inventing the idea of the Strategic Business Unit (SBU) about 50 years before GE actually articulated it.

Sloan's third innovation was to establish the three component divisions as separate profit centres that supplied not only the five car divisions but also outside customers. Again, this concept had to wait 50–70 years before its virtues became fully appreciated.

Sloan is fascinating because he had a foot in the old management camp of scientific management, drawing on many of the nineteenth century ideas of Henri Fayol, as well as anticipating some of the tenets of very contemporary theory, including decentralisation, segmentation as a basis for organisation, and the value of creative dissent. The latter side can, however, be exaggerated. Sloan was at heart a mechanistic autocrat who was also a marketing genius, and to expect him to be a liberation manager into the bargain is to expect too much. MIT named its business school after him, a fitting tribute for both. See DIVISIONALISATION in Part Four.

TROMPENAARS, FONS (b. 1952)

Dutch expert on international cultural differences between managers. Co-author with Charles HAMPDEN-TURNER of the excellent *Seven Cultures of Capitalism* (1993), and author of *Riding the Waves of Culture* (1993) that covers some of the same ground but focuses particularly on how the transnational corporation should maximise effective co-operation between operations in different countries and between these and the Centre. Trompenaars insists that cultural diversity must be recognised and that the transnational corporation is 'polycentric' rather than a hub and spoke from the Centre. The transnational corporation must synthesise the advantages of all the national cultures and facilitate communication, but leave local operations free to reward their people in the way most effective for their culture. An important message from an increasingly prominent guru. Trompenaars is also co-author, with Charles Hampden-Turner, of the unjustly neglected *Mastering the Infinite Game* (1997), a thoughtful comparison of Western and Eastern ways of doing business.

See GLOBAL LOCALISATION, CULTURE, FLAT ORGANISATION, HAMPDEN-TURNER and COMPETITIVE ADVANTAGE.

WATERMAN, ROBERT H. JR (b. 1936)

A laid-back Californian, forever linked with Tom PETERS as joint author of *In Search of Excellence* (1982). Waterman is the older, more reflective and, many would say, more original of the two. He has written two outstanding books since: *The Renewal Factor* (1987) and *The Frontiers of Excellence* (1994). Both are concerned with how organisations learn, manage change and chaos, use taskforces and develop their distinctive roles in life. Waterman has pointed out that most managers still live in the shadow of TAYLOR, and practise the opposite of what they preach.

Waterman's 1994 book, called *What America Does Right* in the US edition, and *The Frontiers of Excellence* in the UK, looks at ten US organisations that 'put people first', including Federal Express, Levi Strauss, Motorola, Procter & Gamble and Rubbermaid. It is a useful and enjoyable read that asserts that the most successful companies do not put shareholders first, paying primary attention to customers and employees. A side-effect is excellent stock market performance. The case examples are fresh, but a little rose-tinted; the general argument is not original, but well debated, inspirational and broadly correct.

See PETERS.

ZOOK, CHRIS (b. 1968)

Chris Zook of Bain & Company has written two books of interest to strategists – *Profit from the Core*[7] and *Beyond the Core*.[8] The former book notes that while 90 per cent of firms aim to grow twice as fast as the economy, only 10 per cent of them succeed for any period of time. Rather than have unrealistic growth aims, as most firms do, *all* firms could benefit from maximising the growth and profit from their core business. Paradoxically, it is often the best businesses that are underperforming the most. Because they are the strongest, they should be showing by far the highest returns on capital. But usually firms 'average profit', that is, tend to have similar profit expectations from all their businesses, they often accept profits from the best businesses that are far lower than they could be. There are normally neglected opportunities to cut costs, raise price, and/or raise sales. Zook & Allen advocate a full potential analysis of the core, including new geographies, new value chain steps, new channels, new customer segments, and new products.

In *Beyond the Core*, Zook suggests that once firms have put their existing businesses into winning positions and extracted their profit potential, it may be time to look at growth from ADJACENT SEGMENTS. An adjacency (good) is different from diversification (bad) to 'the extent to which it draws on the customer relationships, technologies or skills in the core business to build advantage.'

Zook says there are six dimensions of adjacency:

- customers
- competitors
- channels
- geographies
- cost structures
- core competencies.

If the customers (or competitors) are different in a proposed new business from the customers (or competitors) in the core business, that is 'one step away'. If the customers and competitors are both different from those in the core business, but the other four dimensions are identical, that is 'two steps away'. And so on. Zook's finding is that new businesses that were just one step away succeeded in 37 per cent of cases. But when the new business was two steps away, the success rate was only 28 per cent, and when it was 3 steps away, under 10 per cent. The message is clear: unless the case is highly compelling, don't invest in a new business that is more than one adjacency step away – and even then realise that the odds against success are nearly two to one.

PART 4

Strategic concepts, tools and techniques

ADHOCRACY

Invented by Warren Bennis in 1968 and popularised by Alvin Toffler. Crudely the opposite of bureaucracy, an adhocracy is an organisation that disregards the classical principles of management where everyone has a defined and permanent role. Adhocracies are usually fun to work in, chaotic, task and project team based, disrespectful of authority if not accompanied by expertise, and fast changing. Adhocracy suits cultures and individuals used to thinking for themselves and willing to tolerate ambiguity. Adhocracy is most suited to workforces that are highly educated and motivated and where the work requires creativity and responsiveness to unpredictable and volatile customer needs. Most car plants are not adhocracies, most advertising agencies are.

MINTZBERG supplies a more formal definition: 'Highly organic structure, with little formalisation of behaviour, high horizontal job specialisation, based on formal training; a tendency to group the specialists in functional units for housekeeping purposes, but to deploy them in small market-based teams to do their work' (*Structure in Fives: Designing effective organizations* (1983)).

ADJACENT SEGMENT

A product or product-customer combination that is 'close' or similar to another one and that could be served by a company with relatively little extra effort. Marketing executives often list their adjacent segments as a prelude to deciding which new customers to target or new business areas to enter. For example, a local newspaper serving one area may decide to enter another area (the adjacent segment) either by extending the coverage of its existing paper or by bringing out an additional edition. Entering an adjacent segment is normally a more sensible step than going after a more distant segment (in this case, a distant newspaper area).

The skill in describing and evaluating adjacent segments lies in thinking about dimensions of the adjacency that may not be obvious. It is easy to think of a geographically adjacent market, but the newspaper may also be adjacent to other segments if it can use its skills, cost base or market franchise to enter that market. In this case, local radio, local magazines, or even the promotion of concerts may be adjacent segments for the newspaper.

In choosing adjacent segments it is important to avoid potential segments that are already dominated by existing competitors, or that are themselves adjacent to other segments controlled by powerful players. For instance, a pet-accessory maker may think that pet food is an adjacent segment, but if it is already dominated by a large and well run pet food manufacturer he should steer clear. A better bet may be to enter an adjacent segment unrelated to pets, for example the manufacture of leather belts (if these have high cost sharing with making cat and dog collars) or other accessories that have high cost sharing with existing operations. See also ANSOFF MATRIX.

ALIEN TERRITORY

In the Ashridge Strategic Management Centre's theory of PARENTING ADVANTAGE, this is business where the centre of the company has nothing to contribute and nobody in the company has the necessary management skills. For American Airlines (or any other airline), the manufacture of ice cream would be alien territory. It is also likely that for British Airways the budget airline business was alien territory, explaining why they sold the GO airline and should probably never have owned it.

ANSOFF MATRIX

As shown in Illustration 4.1, this gives four options for increasing sales.

Box 1, selling more of existing products in existing markets, is a low risk, market share gain strategy. To be useful, this must specify how this objective is to be attained, for example by enlarging the salesforce, increasing advertising or cutting price.

Box 2 implies product development to sell new (or modified) products to existing customers: fine as long as the firm has a good track record of new product development and provided the new products share enough costs and skills with the existing products, and do not face a very strong incumbent competitor (see also ADJACENT SEGMENT).

Box 3 takes existing products and sells them to new markets or customers. This is clearly sensible if the new markets can be cultivated at relatively little extra cost, but can be risky if a new market requires investment in fixed cost (for example, a new salesforce), if the customers have different requirements, or if there are entrenched competitors.

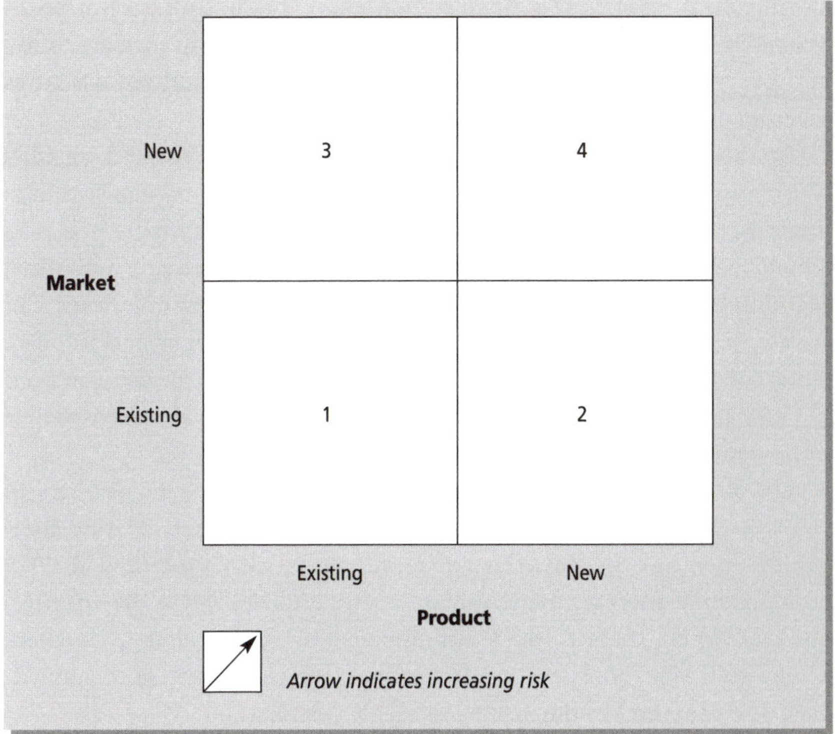

ILLUSTRATION 4.1 ◆ The Ansoff Matrix for business development

Box 4 – new products to new markets – is the highest risk strategy: the segments being entered are not adjacent to the existing business and it is almost like starting a new business from scratch. The presumption is that Box 4 strategies are inherently unsound and should only be taken either in desperation or because there is a compelling short term opportunity not being exploited by others.

APOLLO

One of Charles HANDY's four GODS OF MANAGEMENT. In 1978 Handy made a breakthrough in thinking about organisational styles by gracing four typical ways of running companies with the names of Greek gods. Apollo represents 'role culture', being the god of order and rules. This CULTURE assumes that reason should prevail and that tasks can be parcelled out logically. An organisation chart that has a series of boxes describing jobs and that is a classic pyramid represents 'Apollonian' thinking. Everyone knows their role and works on their delegated activities according to their job description.

Apollo represents bureaucracy in the pure sense invented by Max Weber rather than the modern pejorative sense. The Apollo style can be the most efficient way of running firms operating in a stable and predictable environment. Everyone can be given their individual accountabilities and a system such as management by objectives can ensure that individuals are treated fairly according to their performance rather than the personal opinion or liking of their bosses. Because responsibilities are clear and fixed, many people find the Apollo style easy to deal with, secure and stress-free.

Life insurance companies, monopolies, state industries, the civil service and local government are good examples of Apollo cultures. Private companies operating in slow-changing industries with protected market positions may also exemplify Apollo. This style is unlikely to be effective, however, where there is rapid technological or market change or where teamwork is vital. Nor does it suit creative, restless or questioning individuals, or those who like the firm to be highly personal.

ATHENA

One of Charles HANDY's four GODS OF MANAGEMENT, representing a task-oriented way of running companies. Athena was a young warrior goddess, the patron saint of craftsmen and explorers. Athena firms have a problem-solving CULTURE, are not hierarchical, respect professional expertise and encourage teamwork, creativity and energy. They tend to work in project teams which may be dismantled once a problem is solved and be re-assembled, perhaps with different members, to attack a new challenge. The teams are like guerilla commando units rather than massed armies.

Athena firms are most appropriate to 'knowledge industries' and professional firms, to times of expansion, and to people who think for themselves and can tolerate ambiguity and rapid change. The Athena culture may fit badly and be vulnerable if a firm hits a crisis or stops growing, or if the work becomes more routine.

AVERAGE COSTING

A term coined by the Boston Consulting Group to indicate inadequately accurate costing systems that average costs across products or services which really cause quite different amounts of cost, especially indirect and overhead costs. For example, a special or one-off product for a particular customer may cause unusual levels of cost in terms of specification, selling, quality control and so forth, yet when the costing is done be charged no more for these elements of cost than for standard products. It is almost always true that traditional cost-centre based methods of costing understate the cost of top-of-the-line and special products and services and overstate the cost of high volume standard products. This can be very damaging if (as usual) it leads to AVERAGE PRICING. The way in which average costing and pricing works is demonstrated in Illustration 4.2.

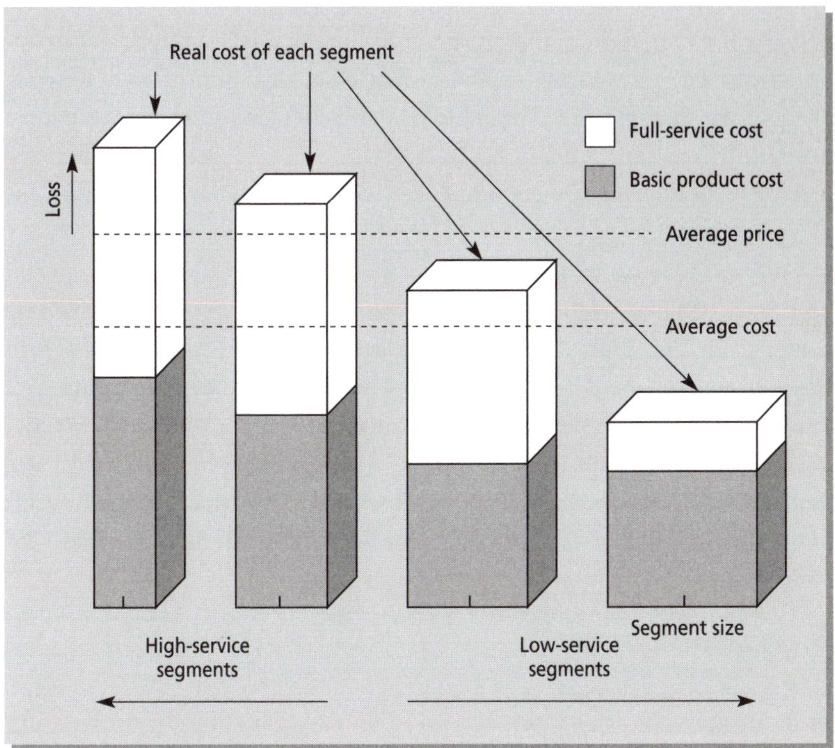

ILLUSTRATION 4.2 ◆ Average costing and pricing

AVERAGE PRICING

Traditional costing systems understate the cost of producing special or one-off products. This AVERAGE COSTING leads to average pricing, which as the name suggests means failing to charge enough of a premium for top-of-the-line or special products, and conversely charging too much for standard products (because the prices of the two types of product are averaged rather than sharply differentiated).

Average pricing is still rife, to a much greater extent than most managers realise. They may charge more for higher specification products, but rarely enough to reflect the real (but hidden) extra cost. For example, a firm making coin mechanisms for vending machines made a special one for the London Tube (metro/subway) system. In tendering for the business the firm put in what it considered to be a very high price, so that the managers believed the work would be highly profitable. After the contract had been completed, a consulting study using ABC analysis (activity-based costing) showed that it had in fact been very unprofitable because of the extra time required for engineers and the additional service people needed. 'If we had understood then about average costing and average pricing,' the managers concluded, 'we would have charged 30 per cent more for the work.'

Average pricing is dangerous, not just because of losses on special products, but because it can lead to loss of market share through over-pricing on the high volume, standard products. A producer who concentrates on the latter, 'commodity' business may be able to afford a much lower overhead structure, lower prices and higher profits. Over time, the specialist may gain market share of this profitable business and leave the high-overhead, broad-line producer with a higher share of the unprofitable business. If costs are not correctly allocated and prices set accordingly, the commercial consequences can be dire.

BALLAST

In Ashridge's theory of PARENTING ADVANTAGE, ballast businesses are those that parent managers know well, but are able to add little to, since they are already well run (by managers at the subsidiary). For example, the oil exploration business at Exxon or the detergent business at Procter & Gamble.

BARRIERS TO ENTRY

Obstacles making it difficult or impossible for competitors to enter a particular business segment. Barriers sometimes exist naturally but astute managers will try to raise these barriers and introduce new ones in order to restrict competition among their customers. It is worth reflecting from time to time on what can be done to raise barriers by examining a checklist of potential barriers (Illustration 4.3).

BARRIERS TO EXIT

Exit barriers are undesirable forces that keep too many competitors in a market, and lead to over-capacity and low profitability, because firms believe it is too expensive to leave the business. Barriers to exit may be real or imagined, economic or illusory, as Illustration 4.4 shows.

In general, too much thought is given to barriers to exit and too little to barriers to entry.

BCG MATRIX

The popular name for the GROWTH/SHARE MATRIX, an abused but powerful tool encapsulating the most important insights into business of the past 50 years. See GROWTH/SHARE MATRIX.

ILLUSTRATION 4.3 ◆ Barriers to entry

Barrier to entry	Comment
1 Investment scale	**Building a bigger or better plant, service network or retail outlet** can discourage competitors from trying to compete with you, especially if your installed customer base means it would take longer for them to get the scale of business to cover the cost of the initial investment, or if your investment gives you a lower cost base than existing competitors

▶

ILLUSTRATION 4.3 ◆ continued

Barrier to entry	Comment
2 **Branding**	**Making your product or service synonymous with superior and consistent quality,** whether or not a 'brand' in the conventional sense is used
3 **Service**	**Providing such a high level of service** that customers will be naturally loyal and not want to switch to competitors
4 **Building in 'cost to switch'**	**Locking customers in,** for example by promotional schemes such as 'Air Miles' where customers are saving up for incentives and will not want to switch to another supplier, or by giving over-riding discounts once a level of sales has been triggered, or even by supplying equipment (such as freezer cabinets for newsagents selling ice cream) which can be withdrawn if a competitor's product is bought, or in professional services by knowing so much about a client's business that it would take another supplier too long to 'come up to speed'
5 **Locking up distribution channels**	**Buying or having a special relationship with distributors** that makes it difficult or impossible for a new supplier to get his product to the ultimate consumer: a policy followed for many years with great success, for example, in petrol retailing, where the superior siting of major oil companies' service stations helped them sell their oil
6 **Locking up sources of raw material supply**	**Obtaining the best (or all) the product from its source** either by owning the raw material (as with many large dairy companies) or by having a special relationship with suppliers, or by paying them more
7 **Property/location**	**Obtaining the best sites** can be crucial in businesses as diverse as oil production and retailing. It is worth asking from time to time whether the desired location might change in the future and then moving to lock up suitable new sites, as for example in edge of town/out of town superstores
8 **Expertise/hiring the best people**	**Knowing how best to do something that is important to customers** is an under-rated barrier. The key thing is to locate the functional expertise that is most important and then make sure that your firm is better than any other at this. For example, in mass market retailing the buying and merchandising function is crucial. Wal-Mart, the leading US retailer, has a huge advantage because it has the best buyers and best relationships with suppliers. Hiring in the best people available to an industry can be a winning tactic, although only if the people can fit into

	the culture or the culture can be adapted to make best use of the newcomers
9 **Proprietary expertise/patents**	**The logical extension to 8 above** in many businesses is a patent and in some businesses such as pharmaceuticals patents are hugely important in leading to much higher margins than would otherwise apply. Intellectual property can apply to a surprising range of businesses and it is worth checking whether anything your firm possesses can be patented
10 **Lowest cost producer**	**One of the very best barriers is to be able to produce a product or service for a particular market at a lower cost than competitors,** usually by having larger scale in that SEGMENT than competitors and defending that relative advantage ferociously. To be most effective the cost advantage should be passed through in the form of lower prices, although spending more than competitors can match in terms of advertising, sales force or research can also be an effective way of using a cost (and margin) advantage to build barriers
11 **Competitive response**	**Making it clear to competitors that you will defend 'your patch',** if necessary by 'crazy' actions, is a very effective barrier to entry. If a competitor ignores the warnings and enters, the response must be immediate and crushing, for example by dropping prices to its potential customers
12 **Secrecy**	**Sometimes a profitable market is relatively small** and its existence or profitability may not be known by competitors. **Keeping these segments well hidden from competitors** can be very important, if necessary by obscuring or playing down their importance to your firm. Conversely, someone seeking to enter a new market should invest properly in information about all potential customers.

ILLUSTRATION 4.4 ◆ Barriers to exit

Barrier to exit	Comment
1 **Redundancy costs**	**The cost of paying off employees** may be very heavy and much larger than the annual loss in a business. If a company is strapped for cash, it may find it easier to carry on in the short term and hope that others in the business will remove capacity first, thus postponing and perhaps removing the need to spend cash laying off the workforce. More of a problem in the US than most developing countries, more in the UK than the US, and more in most Continental countries than the UK, because of higher statutory pay-off provisions

▶

ILLUSTRATION 4.4 ◆ continued

Barrier to exit	Comment
2 Investment write-offs	**Exiting from a business may cause a write-off of expensive plant and machinery that can only be used in that business.** This leads to a feeling that the investment is being wasted and to a large one-time loss going through the profit and loss statement and a reduction of net assets in the balance sheet. This reason is, however, usually a very bad one for not exiting from a loss-making business, since it refers to paper entries and not to industrial reality. A business which ought to have a write-off but does not is no more valuable, and probably less valuable, than a business that bites the bullet. The stock market understands this, and often large losses and write-offs from exiting a business lead to an increase in share price, as investors are relieved by management's realism and look forward to the elimination of losses in the business
3 Real disengagement costs	**Leaving a business may sometimes lead to real, one-off costs** other than labour ones. For example, a quarry may have to pay to restore the countryside to its previous glory, or a shop may have to carry out improvements before leaving. One of the most serious disengagement costs has been long leases on property which cannot be re-let at rates as high as the business is paying, and which would still need to be paid once the business has closed
4 Shared costs	**Often leaving one loss-making business is difficult because it would leave another profit-making business with higher costs, where these are shared between the two.** For example, a factory may make two products and have shared overhead (and sometimes labour) costs, or a sales force may sell two products to the same customers. Very often, however, shared costs are an excuse for inaction. The proper answer, wherever possible (and however painful), is to slim down the overheads for the profitable business to what is necessary for that business after exiting the unprofitable one
5 Customers require a 'package'	**Customers sometimes value the provision of multiple products by the same supplier** and would be reluctant or unwilling to buy from one that merely supplied the profitable products. For instance, a supermarket that refused to sell loss leaders such as baked beans or milk might find itself short of customers. Very often, however, this claim is a spurious excuse, and customers would continue to buy a narrower product range provided this had a real advantage to them
6 Non-economic reasons	**Barriers to exit are very often openly non-economic**, as when a government or trade union requires the business to be kept open and has the power to enforce this. More

covert non-economic reasons include management ego or emotional attachment to a business, fear (normally unfounded or exaggerated) that it will affect a business's image and relationships in the trade, or simply opting for the line of least resistance. Non-economic reasons are increasingly becoming discredited, although they can work to your advantage when you are less sentimental than your competitors or when they face less economically numerate governments.

BLUE OCEAN STRATEGY

The more recent term used to describe VALUE INNOVATION – that is, how to create uncontested market space and make competition irrelevant. See VALUE INNOVATION.

BPR (BUSINESS PROCESS RE-ENGINEERING)

A theory devised in the early 1990s for rethinking what a company does and redesigning its processes from first principles in order to produce dramatic improvements in cost, quality, speed and service. Some view BPR as just a 1990s management fad, but it deserves to be taken seriously. Many leading US companies (such as Eastman Kodak, Ford and Texas Instruments) have used BPR to change their way of doing business, leading to cost reductions in excess of 25 per cent, and in some specific areas of up to 90 per cent.

BPR reinvents the way that companies do business, from first principles, by throwing out the view that firms should be organised into functions and departments to perform tasks, and paying attention instead to processes. A process here is a set of activities that in total produce a result of value to a customer, for example, developing a new product. Who is in charge of this? In the non BPR-ed company the answer is 'no-one', despite the involvement of a large number of traditional functions such as R&D and marketing.

The essence of BPR is reversing the task specialisation built into most management thinking since Adam Smith's 1776 pin factory, and focusing instead on completing a total process with value to customers in one fell swoop. A good example is IBM Credit, which used to take seven days to process applications for credit for people wishing to buy computers. Before BPR, there were five separate specialist stages through which an application progressed: logging the credit request; credit checking; modifying the standard loan covenant; pricing the loan; and compiling a quote letter. Experiments then proved that the actual work involved took only 90 minutes; the real delay was caused by having different departments that did the work in stages and had to pass it on to each other. The solution was to replace the specialists with generalists called deal structurers who handled all the steps in the process. The average turnaround time was reduced from seven days to four hours, and productivity was increased 100 times.

'Doing' BPR means taking a fresh page and asking fundamental questions such as why do we do this at all? How does it help to meet customer needs? Could we eliminate the task or process if we changed something else? How can we get away from specialisation so that several jobs are combined into one?

'BPR-ed' companies have thrown away their 'assembly lines', particularly in respect of clerical and overhead functions. One person, such as a customer service representative, may, for example, act as the single point of contact for a customer, taking care of selling, order taking, finding the equipment to be purchased, and delivering it personally. Performance improvement comes from eliminating the expense and misunderstandings implicit in 'handoffs' from one part of the organisation to another, as well as eliminating internal overheads necessary to manage the complexity brought on by task specialisation.

The process claims several benefits:

1 Customers can deal with a single point of contact (the 'case manager').

2 Several jobs can be combined into one, where the primary need to satisfy the customer is not lost in organisational complexity.

3 Workers make decisions, compressing work horizontally (that is, doing without supervisors and other overhead functions that are necessary as a result of specialisation), resulting in fewer delays, lower overhead costs, better customer response, and greater motivation of staff through empowerment.

4 The steps in the process are performed in a sensible order, and removing specialisation enables many more jobs to be done in parallel, as well as cutting down the need for rework.

5 Processes can be easily adapted to cope with work of greater or lesser complexity, instead of forcing everything to go through the same lengthy steps.

6 Work can be performed where it makes most sense, which is often not by specialists.

7 Checks and controls and reconciliations can be reduced without loss of quality.

Like all forms of radical change, BPR often fails – objective estimates are that this is so in almost 75 per cent of cases. The most frequent causes of failure are lack of top management commitment, an insufficiently broad canvass on which to operate (as when parts of the organisation refuse to take the effort seriously), and lack of readiness to adapt corporate CULTURE. Nevertheless, BPR has achieved such stunning results in many documented cases that it cannot be ignored. In the most successful cases it is clear that BPR as a technique was the catalyst for more far-reaching changes in culture and standards.

Two points about BPR are not sufficiently well made by its protagonists. One is that certain types of company and business are more likely to benefit from BPR than others. The most susceptible companies are those where manufacturing is a relatively small part of the cost structure, where overheads are a large part, where customer needs have been neglected, and where the potential benefits of information technology have not yet been exploited.

The other point is that BPR is not a Do-It-Yourself technique: serious attempts at BPR nearly always involve help from consultants. As BPR has boomed, so too has the supply of consultant help, but often at the expense of quality. See also Part One, pages 83–6.

BRAND

A visual design and/or name that is given to a product or service by an organisation in order to differentiate it from competing products and which assures consumers that the product will be of high and consistent quality. Examples include manufacturers' brands such as Coca-Cola and Ford, retailers' brands such as Gap Kids or Sainsbury's, and even a brand which is synonymous with a whole company such as British Airways or Air Canada. Firms often create 'sub-brands' or new brands within a particular category, such as Diet Coke or Club Europe.

Branding goes back to the time when medieval guilds required tradesmen to put trademarks on their products to protect themselves and buyers against inferior imitations. Nowadays virtually everything has been branded. Consumers prefer brands because they dislike uncertainty and need quick reference points. A brand is particularly powerful if it can gain a slot in the brain and be identified either with whole product categories ('hoovers' for vacuum cleaners or 'filofax' for personal organiser) or with particular attributes (a Rolls-Royce will always be high quality, a Mars bar will supply energy, Avis will always try harder). Many brands have helped companies remain market leaders in particular products throughout the past 60 years, including Bird's in custard, Heinz in soup and tomato ketchup, Kellogg's in cornflakes, McVitie's in digestive biscuits, Schweppes in mixers, Colgate in toothpaste, Kodak in film, Gillette in razors, and Johnson's in floor polish.

Despite the longevity of brands, it is always possible to develop new, powerful brands, although this requires a real new product advantage and usually very heavy investment in advertising and other marketing (there are exceptions to the latter requirement, such as Filofax, Laura Ashley and Walkers Crisps, where a cult develops almost spontaneously, but they are few and far between). Examples of strong new brands include Flora, Ariel, Canon, Sony, Heineken, Diamond White cider, Mr Kipling and *The Sun* newspaper.

Brands have seven major advantages for suppliers:

1 They can help to build *consumer loyalty* and thus give a higher and more enduring market share.

2 Most brands involve a *price premium* which can be very substantial and which greatly exceeds the extra cost in terms of superior ingredients and marketing. The most profitable food companies in the UK in terms of return on sales are Kellogg's and Walkers Crisps, whose sales are exclusively branded. Cider is another UK industry where clever branding and product innovation turned a low-price industry into one with high prices. Market research has often asked consumers what they would pay for a particular new product, both unnamed and with a trusted brand name, and it is not unusual for the latter to attract a 30 per cent price premium in the research.

3 By virtue of their premium price (which widens margins for wholesalers and retailers as well as for the manufacturer) and consumer pull, brands can make it easier for manufacturers to gain *vital distribution*. This is particularly crucial for new products and for smaller suppliers.

4 Brands can sometimes *change the balance of power* between different parts of an industry. The development of manufacturers' grocery brands between 1918 and 1960 helped to put manufacturers in the driving seat and give them higher margins than retailers. In the past 25 years consolidation in food retailing and the development of retailers' (own label) brands has handed higher margins to retailers and enabled them to introduce new products from smaller suppliers, including some high margin innovations such as chilled ready meals.

5 Brands can make it easier to *introduce new products* and get consumers to try them, so that often a new product will use some of the brand equity in an existing brand while adding a differentiating sub-brand, such as Miller Lite or Guinness Draught Bitter.

6 Closely associated with point 5, branding facilitates the *creation of new market segments* within an established product category. For instance, low-calorie or low-fat versions of almost any food or drink product, the creation of at least three classes of airline travel, or longer-lasting products such as Duracell batteries.

7 Finally, the combination of trust and razzmatazz that brands carry can enable whole industries to defy the market maturity stage of the alleged product life cycle, taking a fusty and declining market and injecting *new growth into an industry*. Besides the cider and stout examples, successful branding has helped to revive markets as diverse as shampoo, hand razors, bicycles and newspapers, all of which once seemed stuck in steady decline.

Some observers believe that the Internet will reduce the power and price premiums that brands command, and this may be true to a degree, but when brands – such as amazon.com – connote high service and warm feelings, and consistently deliver what they promise, then the value of brands will endure.

BRAND STRETCHING

The popular process whereby an existing well-known brand name is used on new products that compete in a different market from the brand's existing core product(s). Some examples from the UK are given in Illustration 4.5.

ILLUSTRATION 4.5 ◆ Examples of brand stretching in the UK

Brand	Core Market Category	New Market Category
Bisto	Gravy	Casserole sauces
Bowyers	Meat products	Chilled salads
Flora	Margarine/spreads	Salad dressings
KP	Crisps and peanuts	Peanut butter spread
Mars	Confectionery	Ice cream & milk drinks
Mr Kipling	Cakes	Frozen puddings
Quaker	Cereals	Bread
Ryvita	Crispbread	Cereals

Source: OC&C Strategy Consultants

The basic reason for brand stretching is the increased probability of success using an established brand. Of new product launches examined by OC&C Strategy Consultants from 1984 to 1993, only 30 per cent of new brands survived at least four years, but brand extensions had more than double the survival rate, at 65 per cent. It is easier to get brand stretches into the trade and consumers are more likely to experiment with, and purchase repeatedly the brand extensions. Moreover, the cost of launching new products is much lower using existing brands.

We appear to be moving into a new era where brands are positioned as having emotional and lifestyle benefits that are transferable across several products, rather than being narrowly identified with a particular product.

The benefits of brand stretching are clear, but there are also risks, principally the danger of diluting the core brand image. These risks can, however, be contained to acceptable limits by (1) providing an excellent new product, at least comparable in quality to the current brand leader, and (2) by *not* putting a lot of advertising support behind the stretched product, so that if consumers give it the thumbs down it can be allowed to die a decent death without contaminating the core branded product.

Brand stretching is here to stay and is an accelerating trend. It increases both the rewards and the risks for established brands, in whatever market.

BREAKUP

When a firm splits itself into two or more new corporations in order to remove VALUE DESTRUCTION and allow each new business to focus on what it does best. Breakup is the generic word popularised in the 1996 book *Breakup!* by David Sadtler, Andrew CAMPBELL and Richard Koch; the Americans use the term SPINOFF, the British use DEMERGER, and South Africans talk of UNBUNDLING.

By the late 1990s, breakups had become more important in value terms in the US than Leveraged Buy Outs at the peak of their popularity in the late 1980s; one third of all disposals, measured by value, now take the form of breakups. This is a hugely important phenomenon that is changing the face of capitalism. According to a study by J.P. Morgan, when spinoffs of small and highly focused new corporations take place, their value increases by an average of 45 per cent within 18 months of the spinoff.

BUILD

One of the Ashridge Strategic Management Centre's five generic ways in which the Centre of multibusiness corporations can add value. 'Building' implies that the Centre enlarges the businesses and improves their positioning; lying behind the 'build' strategy there should be a value creation insight, such as the consolidation of a fragmented industry or the opportunity to go global.

BUSINESS ATTRACTIVENESS

An assessment of how attractive a business or market is, based on a number of criteria. Often a distinction is made between the attractiveness of the market, on the one hand, based on desiderata such as market growth, average industry profitability, BARRIERS TO ENTRY (which should be high), BARRIERS TO EXIT (preferably low), the bargaining power of customers and suppliers (ideally low), the predictability of technological change, the protection against substitutes, and on the other hand, the strength of the individual company's business within the market, based on relative market share, brand strength, cost position, technological expertise and other such assessments. One can then produce a matrix such as that shown in Illustration 4.6 and plot all a firm's businesses on the matrix to see where scarce corporate resources such as cash and good management should be allocated.

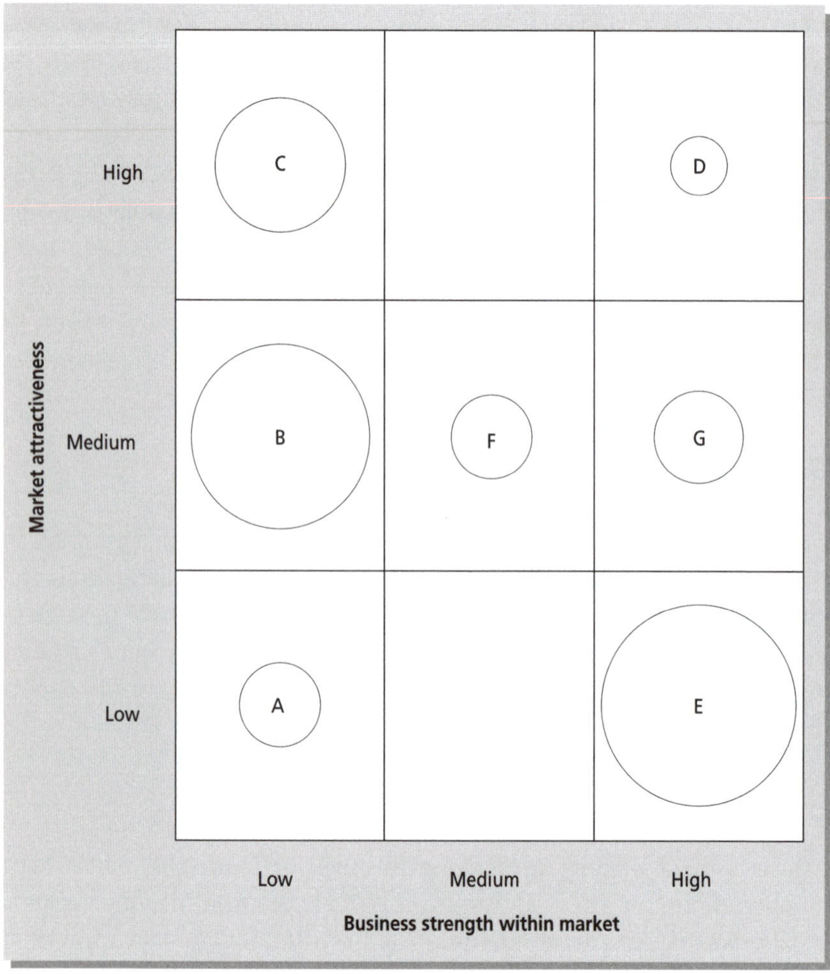

ILLUSTRATION 4.6 ◆ Business attractiveness matrix

In this case, the most obviously attractive businesses for investment would be D, followed by G, and then probably C or F. Business C could be a very good investment target, but only if the investment could drive it to a very strong position within the market (i.e. move it from the top left to the top right). If this does not seem likely, it may be best to sell C for a high price. Businesses B and A are also disposal candidates if a reasonable price could be obtained.

The matrix is an alternative to the BCG MATRIX and has the advantage that it can take into account several factors in evaluating the attractiveness of both business and market. On the other hand the lack of quantification of the axes can be a subjective trap, with management unwilling to admit that businesses are not attractive. For any overall corporate plan it is useful to position all businesses on both matrices, and see whether the prescriptions are at all different. If they are, you should carefully examine the assumptions leading to the difference.

BUSINESS MODEL

The unique formula used by each firm to conduct its business and seek COMPETITIVE ADVANTAGE. The business model is strong and will lead to returns above the required rate of return on capital only if it is in some way innovative, different from the model used by any competitor, and delivers attractive products or services to customers at high margins to the firm. See also Peter JOHNSON and Part Two.

BUSINESS SEGMENT

A defensible competitive arena within which market leadership is valuable. Contrast market segment, which is usually defined by market researchers' pre-ordained categorisations of the population into social class or psychologically defined groups, and much less useful. A business segment is an area within which a firm can specialise and gain COMPETITIVE ADVANTAGE. An example of a business segment would be high performance sports cars, which is a defensible market against mass market cars (at least for the time being). Thus Ferrari does not have to worry about its share of the overall car market if it can be the leader in its own segment. On the other hand, companies cannot define the market in a way that gives them market leadership and *ipso facto* call that a business segment. For example, red cars are not a separate segment from black cars, because specialising in red cars would not result in either extra consumer appeal or lower cost for producing red cars, and would therefore not be a defensible segmentation. See also SEGMENTATION for a much fuller discussion.

CANNIBALISATION

When a new product or service is introduced in the knowledge that it will eat into the market for an existing product or service already being provided by the supplier. Diet Coke, for example, cannibalised the existing market for Coke, or turkey flavoured Whiskas cannibalised the demand for existing Whiskas variants. Suppliers know that these goods will to some extent reduce existing product demand, but expect this to be more than compensated for by the extra demand created by the product introduction (and in some cases higher prices too, as when Whiskas was originally introduced and cannibalised Kit-e-Kat). Moreover, if one supplier does not introduce a product to cater for a potential product category, the competitor might, thus causing loss of market share, which is always a greater evil than cannibalisation.

CASH COW

A business that is highly cash positive as a result of being a market leader in a low growth market. Such a business typically requires only moderate investment in physical assets or working capital, so that high profits result in high cash flow.

Cash cows are one of the four positions on the BCG MATRIX. In the BCG theory, cash from cash cows can be used to support other businesses that are leaders or potential leaders in high growth markets and that need cash to improve or maintain their market share positions.

The BCG theory has often been misinterpreted, partly as a result of the tag 'cash cow'. Cows need to be milked, so the natural (but incorrect) inference is that the main role of cash cows is to give cash to the rest of the portfolio. Yet the original BCG theory stressed the key point that cash cows should have the first call on their own cash: whatever investment was necessary to support and reinforce the cash cows' position should come first. This common-sense prescription is often overlooked. Cash cows are not glamorous, and generally require only moderate amounts of grass, but they should still be allowed to graze on the most verdant pastures. It would have saved us all a great deal of trouble if BCG had stuck to the alternative name for cash cows, namely gold mines. Nobody would dream of denying a gold mine its required share of the maintenance budget.

CASH TRAP

Useful jargon invented by the Boston Consulting Group to describe businesses that absorb cash but will never repay it fully, if at all. BCG even went so far as to say in 1972 that 'the majority of the products in most companies are cash traps. They will absorb more money for ever than they will generate. This is true even though they may show a profit in the books'. Typically, QUESTION MARK businesses (poor market share positions in high growth businesses) are the worst cash traps, although some dogs may also be. BCG crusaded against cash traps, urging managers to cut their losses in these businesses and focus cash on businesses that were or could become market leaders. The crusade has had real impact in the past two decades or so, partly through the action of managers but even more through hostile acquisitions that have led to unbundling, which is often little more than the sale or closure of cash traps. Are you sure you know what your cash traps are?

CATEGORY KILLER

Retailer that specialises in a particular type of product, such as toys, baby products or furniture, and offers both the widest range and the greatest value, usually by means of very large and 'fun' out-of-town stores. See DESTINATION RETAILING.

CAUSE

Pioneering work on change management has stressed the need for all companies to have an overall medium term objective that can unite everyone's efforts and focus on what the company as a whole is trying to achieve. Causes should be snappy phrases that encapsulate the company's forward momentum and help to guide individual behaviour. Examples of good Causes include 'Putting People First' (British Airways), 'Encircle Caterpillar' (Komatsu), 'Number One and Pulling Ahead' (Coca-Cola Schweppes Beverages) and 'Become larger than BCG' (Bain & Company).

CHAOS THEORY

Important inter-disciplinary science elaborated between about 1965 and 1990 which has considerable relevance to business. The concept of chaos is that most phenomena in the world do not have a linear relationship between cause and effect; relationships are non-linear. 'Chaos' is a bad name because there is an underlying coherence behind non-linear relationships. There *are* persistent and often remarkably similar non-linear patterns that can be identified and modelled mathematically.

One of the most important ideas of chaos is *sensitive dependence on initial conditions*. Sometimes known as the *butterfly effect* – the idea that the flapping of a butterfly's wings in Brazil may lead to a hurricane in Miami – sensitive dependence on initial conditions says that very small and often undetectable influences can have very large effects. Weather is probably the best example, which is why attempts to forecast it over periods of more than a few days are doomed to disappointment.

Therefore: expect the unexpected. Build flexibility into your plans. When something goes wrong, do not search for wrong-doers to punish. When something goes right, do not think it is because you are a genius.

Chance is also important in leading to the FIRST MOVER ADVANTAGE. Since most complex systems are very sensitive to initial conditions, it makes sense to be in on the ground floor of any significant new development, and *lock in* standards that are tilted in your favour.

Another key idea from chaos is *fractal similarities*: things such as trees, clouds, snowflakes or coastlines, which are very similar to each other, but where the patterns also exhibit infinite variety. Business is also fractal – full of recurring patterns that can be recognised only by those who are experienced in observing precisely *that* kind of business. This explains the frequent triumph of experience and intuition over analysis and raw intelligence. It also explains why apparently similar markets – hotels and restaurants, for example, or even luxury versus budget hotels – can have very different key factors for success: the patterns are subtly different. The rules of thumb that work in one area may not work in another, even slightly different, market.

CHERRY-PICKING

Specialising in parts of a product range that are most profitable and/or easiest to access rather than providing a full line of product. Large, full-line suppliers are often vulnerable to smaller cherry-pickers, especially if the larger player has made the mistake of AVERAGE COSTING and AVERAGE PRICING.

COMB ANALYSIS

A very useful and simple technique for comparing customers' purchase criteria with their rating of suppliers. Let us assume that you are a textile manufacturer producing women's clothes and selling them to retailers who are fashion specialists. You want to find out what the most important reasons are for them to choose one manufacturer rather than another. You also want to find out what the retailers think about you and your competitors on each of these purchase criteria.

You should engage independent researchers to interview the retailers and ask them two questions. First, on a 1–5 scale, the importance of various purchase criteria. Let us assume that the average results are as shown in Illustration 4.7.

ILLUSTRATION 4.7 ◆ Example of comb analysis

Criterion	Importance Score
Fashion appeal of garments	4.9
Strength of brand name	4.6
Service & speed of delivery	4.5
Willingness to deliver small orders	3.5
Price from manufacturer to them	3.0
Durability of garments	2.3

These results can now be displayed on the first part of the 'comb' chart (Illustration 4.8).

The second question is how each of the competing suppliers rates on each of these criteria, again on a 1–5 scale. Let us start by overlaying on the previous results (the retailers' purchase criteria) their rating of the company sponsoring the research, which we will call Gertrude Textiles (Illustration 4.9).

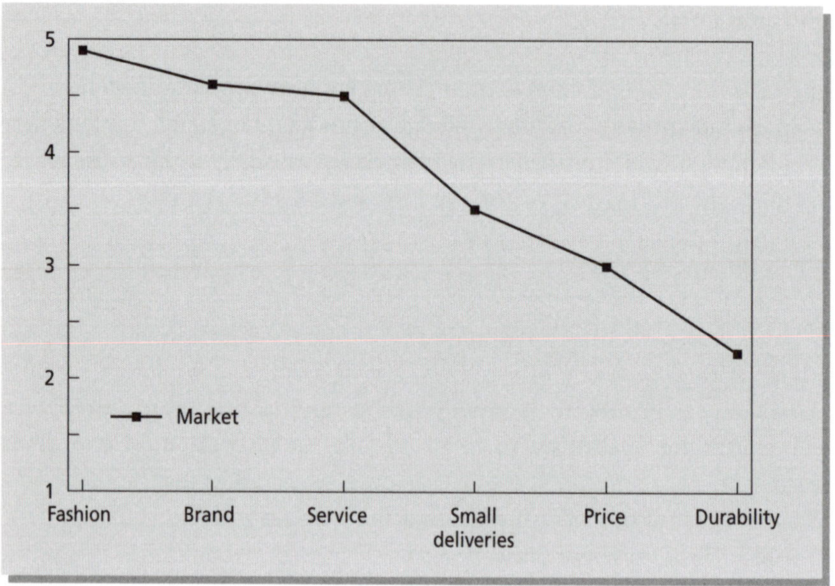

ILLUSTRATION 4.8 ◆ Comb chart: retailers' purchase criteria

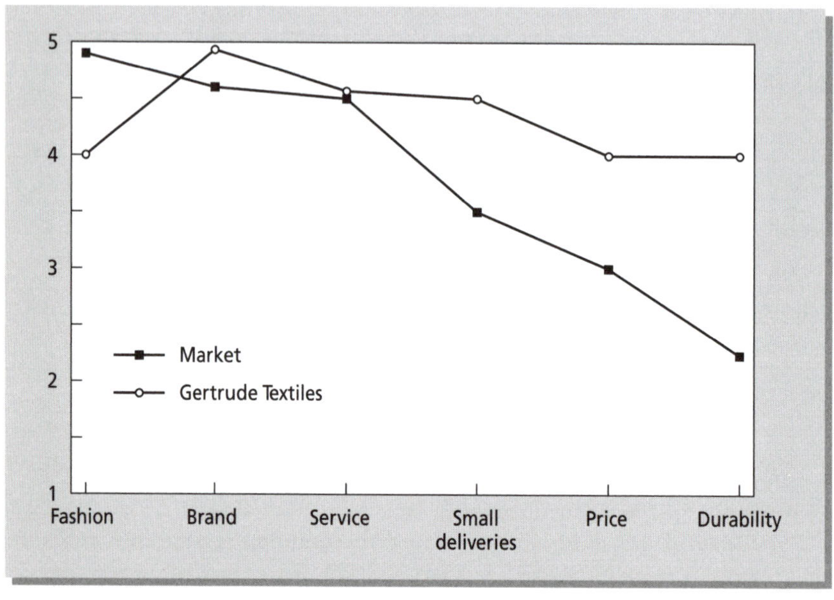

ILLUSTRATION 4.9 ◆ Comb chart: retailers' purchase criteria and their rating of Gertrude Textiles on these criteria

These results should be of great interest to Gertrude Textiles. Except on one criterion, Gertrude manages to score above the importance of the criteria to the retailer. Unfortunately, the one criterion on which Gertrude scores below market expectations is the most important one: the fashion appeal of its clothes. To increase market share, Gertrude Textiles must focus on improving its garments' fashion appeal. Of interest too is that on the last three criteria – willingness to deliver small quantities, price and the durability of its clothes – Gertrude scores *above* what the market requires. No doubt this is costing Gertrude a lot of money. This comb profile suggests that Gertrude could afford to not be so accommodating on small deliveries, could raise prices, and could stop building in long life to its clothes. The money saved should be invested in doing whatever is necessary to improve perceptions of its fashion appeal – perhaps by luring the top designer team from a rival.

Then we come to the rating of competitors. We can now overlay on the previous picture the ratings given by retailers to two of Gertrude's rivals: Fast Fashions and Sandy's Styles (Illustration 4.10).

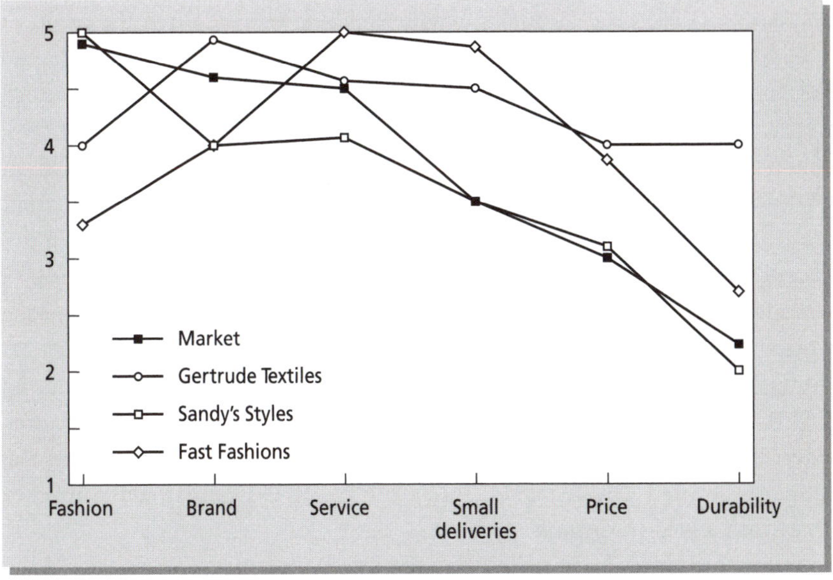

ILLUSTRATION 4.10 ◆ Comb chart: rating of three competitors against market criteria

From this we can make three important observations:

1 The only competitor that meets the market's very high fashion requirements is Sandy's Styles. This is the team for Gertrude Textiles to poach or beat.

2 Gertrude has the best brand name, according to the retailers, and can meet all the other purchase criteria apart from fashion. If this criterion can be met, Gertrude will be in a very strong position to increase market share.

3 Only Gertrude is significantly over-performing on the price requirements of retailers. This helps to confirm that Gertrude may be able to afford some price increases to retailers, particularly if the fashion element improves.

COMMODITY

Undifferentiated product, where suppliers are doomed to compete on price, branding has no value, and the low-cost competitor will be able to earn higher returns and/or gain market share at the expense of his weaker (higher cost) brethren. Actually, commodity markets are often the result of a lack of imagination and marketing flair on the part of the participants. Almost anything can be successfully branded, and a price premium extracted. Take baked beans as an example: easy to produce and, you might think, a classic commodity market. Yet brilliant advertising based on brand identity – 'Beanz Meanz Heinz' – enabled Heinz to become market leader and extract a high price premium at the same time. Or take a more recent example where a commodity market has been transformed into a branded market: flour. This is a large market where the competing products are almost indistinguishable in functional performance. So competition used to be based on fierce price discounting. Until, that is, RHM turned the market upside down with its branded marketing campaign for Homepride based on the bowler-hatted flour-grader and the slogan: 'Graded Grains make Finer Flour.' RHM gained both market share and a price premium.

Many industrial companies have discovered also that markets previously thought to be 'commodity' bear gardens can be turned into higher margin ones where one competitor gains an advantage based on service, technical excellence, industrial branding, or some other attribute of value to buyers.

COMPETENCES, COMPETENCIES

Skills that an organisation has, what it is good at. Much recent thinking has stressed that an organisation's operating skills relative to competition are at least as important to its success as its strategy is. To be successful an organisation must be at least as good as its competition in certain core competencies. For example, in retailing, one of the most important skills is Buying and Merchandising, that is, procuring goods that consumers will want to buy and displaying them attractively. This very obvious statement explains in large part why some retailers, such as The Gap or Wal-Mart, are consistently more successful than their market rivals. Assessing and improving competencies (relative to competition) has rightly become the top priority for many managements.

COMPETITIVE ADVANTAGE

One of the most enduring and valuable catchwords of strategy. Competitive advantage obtains when one player has identified a market or market niche where it is possible to have a price advantage, or a cost advantage, or both, over competitors.

Price advantage means that the product or service is thought sufficiently superior by its buyers to make a price premium (for equivalent quality and cost to produce) possible. Brand leaders usually command a price premium over secondary brands or own label products, sometimes as much as 20–40 per cent, which far exceeds the additional cost of advertising and superior product formulation.

Cost advantage can come from superior scale (and therefore greater spreading of fixed costs), from having lower factor costs (for example, by using cheap labour), from superior technology, or simply having workers who perform their tasks more intelligently or quickly.

Competitive advantage is usually, although not invariably, related to superior market share in a defined segment. Even if not caused by competitive advantage, market leadership should be the result of competitive advantage – otherwise it is being under-exploited.

COMPLEXITY THEORY

An important outgrowth from chaos theory that added three new themes:

1 *Complexity focuses on complicated feedback systems*, showing that they often have surprising results

2 *Complexity is about 'emergence'*: how the whole of each system behaves differently from the aggregation of its parts. Individual customers emerge as a market, water molecules into steam, body cells into a butterfly wing, business units into a corporation, birds into a flock

3 *Complexity is above all interested in* SELF-ORGANISING SYSTEMS which start in a random or unordered state and somehow organise themselves spontaneously into a large-scale and recognisable pattern. Examples include cities, markets, a brain, a stock market crash, a hurricane, an earthquake, a meteorite, a human embryo – or a corporation!

There are two important implications I draw for business from complexity:

- Small changes can transform the whole competitive system. Therefore, when something goes wrong, don't assume you know why. Above all, don't invent a large cause when a small one will do, particularly if you can influence the small cause. For example, Filofax assumed in the late 1980s and early 1990s that the catastrophic decline in its sales was due to the death of the yuppie. Filofax became fatalistic because clearly it could not resurrect yuppies. Yet the truth was that it had lost its market share to cheaper rivals: something that it could, and eventually did, reverse
- Look for and practise emergence. Do not plan, but do steer the process in the direction you want. Self-organisation will not necessarily (or even often) lead to what you want. You may have to compromise with what would emerge anyway, but do not accept the emergent pattern as inevitable or immutable.

Chaos, complexity and other important scientific advances, and their implications for business, are covered much more extensively in my book *The Power Laws of Business*.

CONCENTRATION

The extent to which a few suppliers cover the market. The UK grocery retailing market is highly concentrated, with 75 per cent of it being dominated by five supermarket chains; the American grocery retailing market is much less concentrated. Concentration is often measured by the market share controlled by the largest four or five suppliers, known respectively as the C4 ratio and the C5 ratio. Another measure is the Herfindahl Index.

Most markets have the potential to be concentrated and a fragmented market should be a challenge for suppliers to undertake the process of concentration. In the absence of misguided anti-trust constraints, it is economically logical to have up to 80 per cent of a market controlled by three competitors, with perhaps 40 per cent, 25 per cent and 15 per cent of the market for the number one, two and three respectively.

CONTINUOUS IMPROVEMENT

A Japanese concept holding that a company's COMPETITIVE ADVANTAGE accrues from the persistent search for improvement and a series of tiny steps made continuously, rather than from great leaps forward. The latter are more consistent with Anglo-Saxon cultures, which helps to explain the popularity of BPR (BUSINESS PROCESS RE-ENGINEERING). The evidence is that the Japanese approach works very effectively for Asian cultures, while more revolutionary techniques are both more necessary and more acceptable for Anglo-Saxons.

CONTRACTING-OUT aka OUTSOURCING

Process of using outside suppliers of services to a corporation or public authority rather than using an internal department. There is a strong and increasing trend towards contracting-out in both business and government, largely to cut costs, but also motivated partly by the belief that organisations should concentrate on their core competencies and leave other specialists to fulfil other roles. Some astute observers, such as Charles HANDY, believe that contracting-out will eventually transform our economic landscape, leading most organisations to employ far fewer people, the CORE WORKERS, while using armies of contractors from several smaller, specialist firms. One result will be that many people will leave larger organisations halfway through their working lives to found or join contracting organisations. See also SHAMROCK ORGANISATION.

CORE COMPETENCY, CORE COMPETENCIES

Similar to the idea of a corporation's 'distinctive competence' (the phrase coined by Philip Selznick in 1955) or 'distinctive capabilities', the idea of core competencies was put forward by C.K. PRAHALAD and Gary HAMEL in a renowned 1990 *Harvard Business Review* article. Prahalad and Hamel defined core competencies as:

> ***'the collective learning in the organisation, especially how to co-ordinate diverse production skills and integrate multiple streams of technology ... unlike physical assets, competencies do not deteriorate as they are applied and shared. They grow.'***

To be valuable, core competencies must add something really substantial to customers; they must be unique or at least rare; they must be difficult to imitate, and they must be able to be used effectively by the organisation.

The concept of core competencies became extremely fashionable in the 1990s, and it does have a great deal to commend it. Still, it is remarkably difficult for organisations to decide what their core competencies are, while at the same time avoiding wishful thinking. One problem is that if core competencies are defined in a sufficiently rigorous and precise way, they may prove not to be relevant to many businesses within the corporation. These businesses should be divested. But since managers tend to like to hang on to what they've got, they often fudge the issue and define the core competencies in too inclusive a way. The danger then is that the core competencies become meaningless; they do not realistically describe any competitive advantage.

Another problem (see CAMPBELL in Part Three) is that core competency theory starts with the characteristics of the operating businesses rather than those of the parent organisation (the Centre); the latter may be a better approach to corporate strategy.

Therefore it may be that, like BCG's GROWTH/SHARE MATRIX, the idea of core competencies is more valuable at the business unit level than at the corporate level, despite having been designed for the latter. See section 5 of Part One, where I have used core competency theory in this way.

CORE WORKERS

Those people who are central to an organisation's success and who need to be nurtured and rewarded accordingly. This professional core, increasingly made up of qualified professionals, technicians and managers, comprises the knowledge and skills that explain an organisation's success (or lack thereof). Core workers are precious, hard to replace, expensive and increasingly footloose. Because they are expensive, organisations are tending to be more discriminating in defining what functions and which people should be regarded as core workers, resulting both in downsizing, and also in contracting-out functions that used to be performed by core workers. Core workers are coming to be a privileged but hard-working élite, who in return for high pay, rewarding work and a CAUSE they can believe in, are willing to dedicate themselves to the success of their firms. See SHAMROCK ORGANISATION.

COSTS OF COMPLEXITY

Very important idea that the more complex a business, the higher the costs, for any given level of scale. Complexity can mitigate the advantages of additional scale or even overturn them altogether. Complexity arises when a firm extends its product line, customers, areas of expertise and/or use of different technologies in order to expand. The wise firm seeks extra scale without extra complexity, or reduces complexity without sacrificing scale.

Complexity cannot be totally avoided, and is often market-driven. What separates the operationally skilful firm from others is very often its ability to manage customer-demanded complexity simply: providing CUSTOMISED or preferably CUSTOMERISED products with little added internal complexity.

But very often complexity is self-inflicted rather than market-driven. Customers may say they want a special product or service but be unwilling to pay for the real extra cost: they do not want it badly enough. And in many cases complexity is nothing to do with the customer but merely reflects bad management, and is often against the interests of both the firm and the customer. Production systems that resemble spaghetti, poor factory layouts, unnecessary stages in the production process, quality control departments (instead of building quality in on the line), excess staff numbers and too many functional boundaries, insistence on doing everything within the firm rather than outsourcing wherever possible, interfering head office functions – all of these are complexity own-goals.

Waging war on complexity can lead simultaneously to stunning cost reductions and improvements in customer value. About half of all the value-added costs in the average firm are complexity-related, and half of these provide opportunities for radical cost reduction. Some tips for reducing the costs of complexity are reducing the number of suppliers and entering more collaborative relationships with them; buying in components and services wherever possible rather than 'making' them yourself; avoiding products or customers where added complexity is not fully compensated; eliminating complexity from product design and making product families modular; reducing the number of process steps; improving factory layout; creating small business units within the firm that take charge of a whole product/process from design to customer delivery; decimating head office; abolishing management hierarchy; reducing the information collected and disseminated; and generally not doing anything that is not essential to making customers happy. See BPR, AVERAGE COSTING and VALUE CHAIN.

COST STRUCTURE

The total cost elements of a company broken down into key elements and often shown in the form of a bar, which can then be compared to the cost structure of a competitor making the same product, or to the cost structure of other products in the same firm, as in Illustration 4.11.

Cost structures have changed over time, as the 'typical' cost structures in Illustration 4.12 show.

The major change has been the decrease in direct labour, due to greater automation, and the increases in indirect labour and other overheads. This makes the allocation of fixed costs to products much more important than previously. In fact, 'fixed' cost very often increases as turnover goes up, particularly if the firm is adding product lines or product variants, or customer service and after-sales support in an effort to appeal to a new customer group or to gain more market share. Product proliferation and more demanding customers have increased the proportion of overhead costs, and the latter, if not carefully controlled, can negate or overturn the advantage of increased turnover. See AVERAGE COSTING, AVERAGE PRICING and COSTS OF COMPLEXITY.

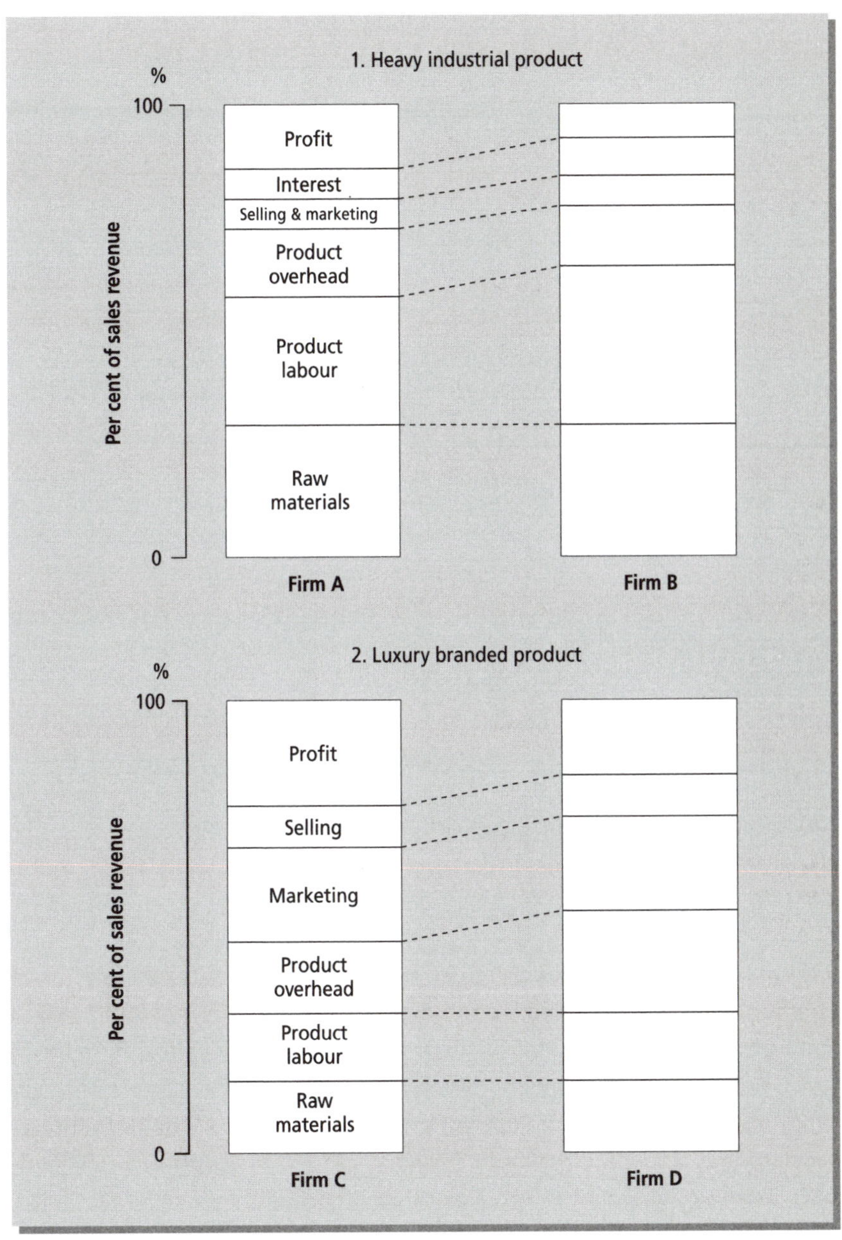

ILLUSTRATION 4.11 ◆ Competitive cost structures

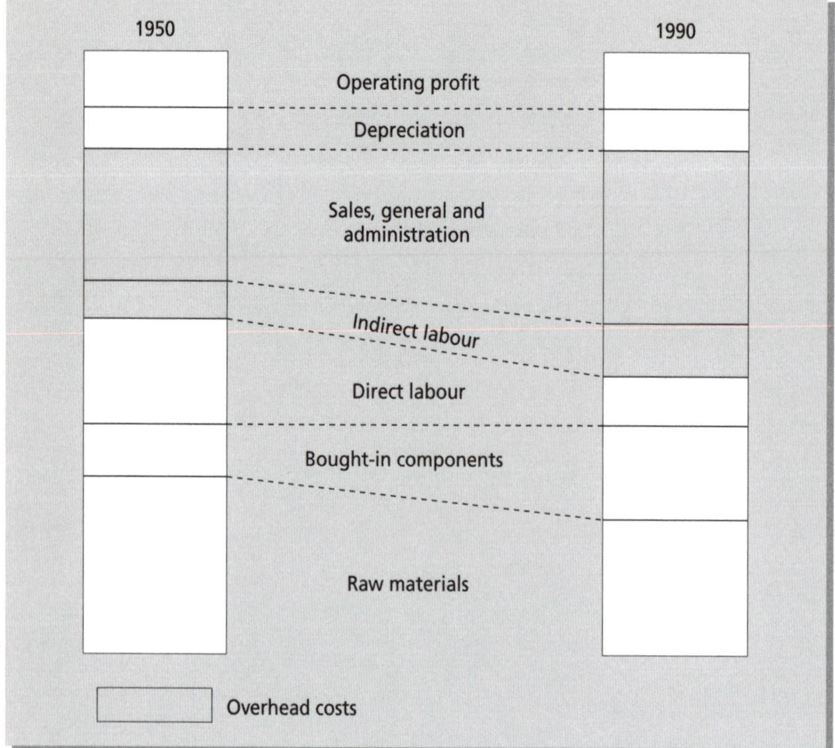

ILLUSTRATION 4.12 ◆ Typical cost structures in 1950 and 1990

COST TO SWITCH, COSTS TO SWITCH

The psychological and/or financial cost to move from one supplier to another. Classical micro-economic theory held that buyers would switch from one supplier to another if there was even a very slight difference in price, provided product quality was equivalent. In practice, there are very often high costs to switch suppliers, even if they are of equal quality. A supplier may know a customer's business well and educating a new supplier may take time and effort. This is an often hidden BARRIER TO ENTRY that can make market shares 'sticky' and make it difficult to gain share. Consultants who know a company well can often rely on the cost to switch to keep out competitors.

CULTURE

The personality and character of a company, derived from generations of people and experience and leading people inside a firm to behave in certain characteristic ways without thinking about it. Firms in the same country and industry may have radically different cultures, and the difference may be far more important in determining relative success than any other factor, including variations in strategy, which may themselves be explained partly by the culture. Increasing but still insufficient attention is being paid to creating and sustaining winning cultures within firms. It is impossible to succeed in a corporate TRANSFORMATION without such radical culture change, though this takes many years and single-minded determination by a firm's leader. See also Charles HANDY's useful description of four GODS OF MANAGEMENT – APOLLO, ATHENA, DIONYSUS and ZEUS, which describe four broad cultural groups. Other useful dimensions of culture are:

- by class/background of senior staff
- open and collaborative versus 'dinosaur' and backbiting culture
- traditional/clubby versus professional
- forgiving/low standards versus relentless/high standards
- marketing and customer-led versus production/internal orientation
- personal versus bureaucratic
- intellectual versus street-smart
- 'learning' versus know-it-all
- 'believed in' by staff versus 'not believed in'.

Such categorisations can be thought-provoking but cannot fully capture the richness of each company's unique culture. Nothing is more important for management than understanding culture and how to change it. See *Wake Up and Shake Up Your Company* by Richard Koch and Andrew Campbell and *The Seven Cultures of Capitalism* by Charles HAMPDEN-TURNER and Fons TROMPENAARS.

CUSTOMER RETENTION

The extent to which customers repeat-purchase. Customers defect at average rates of 10–30 per cent, and far more in some businesses such as car dealing. Losing customers is expensive because the marketing costs to win them over in the first place are so high. Differential customer retention can often explain a significant part of profit differences between firms. More and more attention is being given to monitoring and increasing customer retention, since it has been discovered that a 5 per cent shift in customer retention can result in 25–100 per cent profit swings. Customer retention arises from customer loyalty, which arises when superior value has been delivered. Loyalty in turn leads to higher market share of the chosen customer base, which is often the most value-conscious and least price-conscious part of the market, and therefore the most desirable. High share of value-conscious customers leads to lower costs, both directly through added volume, and indirectly through referrals and word-of-mouth appreciation, which lowers marketing and selling costs. The effect can carry through to employees, who are proud to be offering such good value to customers, and who in turn reinforce the value proposition by particularly good service. With turnover going up and costs going down, profits increase, which allows further investment in product quality and service and in hiring and retaining the best employees. These effects further reinforce the competitive advantage of customer value and loyalty. This VIRTUOUS CIRCLE can carry on *ad infinitum*, until competitors with inferior value and loyalty go out of business, or are contained to unprofitable commodity segments.

The most besotted adherents of customer retention claim that relative customer retention (RCR) explains differential competitor profitability much better than RELATIVE MARKET SHARE (RMS), RELATIVE COST POSITION (RCP) or any other variable. Whether this is true or not, providing customers with the best product and service is clearly one of the best ways to engender loyalty, customer retention and high relative market share, and it therefore makes sense to monitor both absolute and relative customer retention. It is clearly also true that the way to deliver SHAREHOLDER VALUE in the long term is to provide the best value to customers in the short, medium and long term, so that the debate about whether to put customers or shareholders 'first' is largely sterile. A good starting point for creating trust between the firm and its customers, employees and shareholders alike is to provide the best possible customer value and obtain the highest relative retention rates.

CUSTOMERIZED, CUSTOMERIZING

Allowing customers to adapt products themselves. In Tom PETERS' words: 'Produced by, directed by and starring our customers.' The customer, not the firm, is the initiator. Why does Peters have a penchant for coining useful but ugly words?

DECISION TREE

A flow chart that sets out possible future events and highlights the effects of decisions or chance occurrences in a sequential order. Can be very useful in estimating the probability that any event may happen, or simply in pinpointing the critical decisions that have to be made. For some peculiar reason decision trees are nearly always drawn from left to right, although I much prefer to draw them from top to bottom. Two examples are given in Illustrations 4.13 and 4.14. In Illustration 4.13, a manufacturer is trying to decide whether to open a new factory, in the face of uncertainty about whether his main rival will decide to do the same thing and whether the economy will move into recession or boom. The decision tree helps him to lay out the possibilities and calculate the returns under all eight possible outcomes.

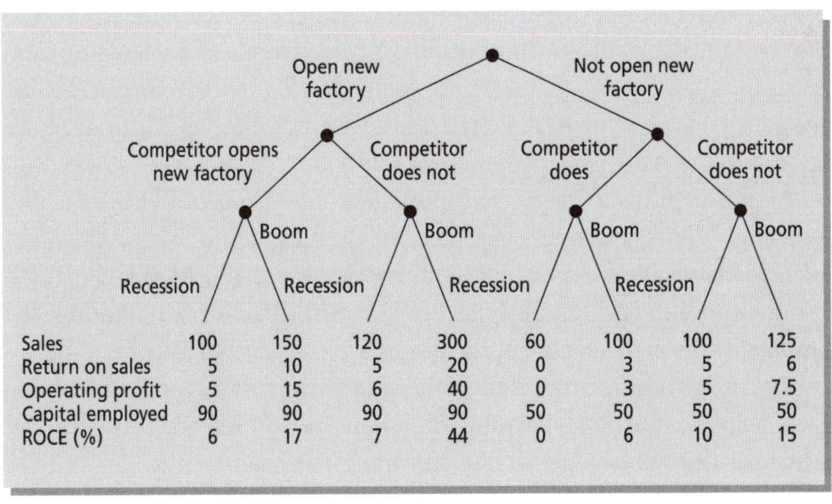

Sales	100	150	120	300	60	100	100	125
Return on sales	5	10	5	20	0	3	5	6
Operating profit	5	15	6	40	0	3	5	7.5
Capital employed	90	90	90	90	50	50	50	50
ROCE (%)	6	17	7	44	0	6	10	15

ILLUSTRATION 4.13 ◆ Decision tree for Superior Sprogetts Limited

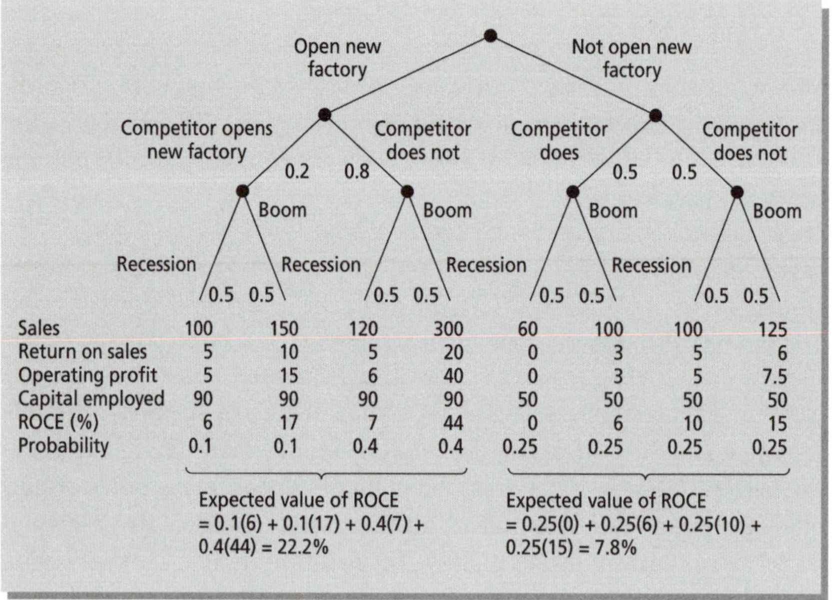

ILLUSTRATION 4.14 ◆ Decision tree with probabilities and expected values

The decision tree has helped by laying out the possibilities, although it does not yet tell Superior Sproggetts Limited (SSL) what to do. For this we need to overlay on the decision tree the *probabilities* of each of the four possible outcomes arising from (a) an investment by SSL and (b) a decision by SSL not to invest. Illustration 4.14 overlays these probabilities and therefore allows a calculation of the EXPECTED VALUE (the weighted average value) in terms of ROCE (Return on Capital Employed) under both (a) and (b).

From this it can be seen that investment has a much higher expected return on capital, at 22 per cent, than the decision not to invest, which has an expected value of 8 per cent. One important reason for this is that the competitor is much less likely to invest if SSL does so first. Adding the probabilities helps to highlight the importance of this judgment.

Decision trees can be used for a wide variety of purposes and are a great help in clarifying what should be done when events are unclear and outcomes depend to some degree on earlier uncertain events.

DECLINING INDUSTRY

One where demand is falling and expected to continue to do so. Two comments can be made about declining industries. One is that there is no inevitability about secular decline in many cases. An industry may continue declining solely because of lack of investment and imagination. Railroads in the US are an example, where poor service, lack of investment and industry fatalism wrecked the industry before more recent initiatives reversed the decline. Similarly, newspapers suffered in most countries as TV gained ground, but the growth of segmented titles and freesheets has turned markets upwards once again. Cider in the UK is another instance, as is 'real ale', while an example from Japan is the way that Yamaha has revived the piano industry by creating a PC-based retrofit and a new digital electronic piano, turning a market declining at 10 per cent annually into an explosive growth market.

The second comment is that even if a market continues to decline, the last one or two players can end up with a very profitable, extremely cash positive business. Often there is a greater payoff to gaining market share in declining than in growing markets, particularly if a position of dominance can be attained. Decline can be a mirage or an opportunity.

DELAYERING

Removing whole layers of management, resulting in a more FLAT ORGANISATION, lower costs, less bureaucracy and greater accountability of executives. Very often, a high proportion (often in the range of 30–50 per cent, sometimes even as high as 90 per cent) of overhead and head office staff can be removed by delayering. A typical example is removing two whole tiers of management from a firm that starts with five. This is not just cost reduction in response to crisis or recession, but a secular trend.

DELIVERY SYSTEM

The activities a firm performs in delivering a product and/or service to the customer. The concept of the delivery system far transcends physical distribution and can be used to think about new ways of delivering value to the customer, as for example, with the Internet. IKEA, the Swedish furniture and home furnishing company, has grabbed global leadership in an industry previously characterised by local suppliers. IKEA achieved this by rethinking the structure, processes and skills across the entire supply chain, from timber to customer, to develop a totally new delivery system. The company offers customers a new division of labour: in return for high design and low prices the customer takes on key tasks previously performed by manufacturers or retailers, such as assembly of products and delivery to the home. Every aspect of the IKEA business system facilitates customers taking on this new role, from the time that customers at the front door are given catalogues, tape measures, pens and paper, to the time that they leave with a loaned roof rack.

DELPHI TECHNIQUE

Forecasting technique using a number of experts (or managers) who each make estimates in round one, then receive everyone else's estimates and re-estimate in round two, and so on until consensus is reached.

DEMERGER

Split of one company into two (or very rarely, more than two) new companies. Most common where a company already has two divisions engaged in different businesses. It is a word used in the UK that is equivalent to the US words 'SPINOFF' or 'spinout' (see BREAKUP). Generally involves shareholders in the original company being given shares in both the new companies, with the new shares being quoted separately. An alternative is where a company demerges one division by selling it and pays out a one-time dividend to shareholders.

Demergers are increasingly common but not common enough. Where two businesses have different CULTURES and little SYNERGY they should be separated, both to allow management in each business to focus and have full control, and to enable investors to have a 'purer play'.

DESTINATION, DESTINATION RETAILING

The practice of running large, out-of-town or edge-of-town superstores that are themselves a 'destination' rather than just part of the high street or a shopping mall. The retailer therefore needs to offer a sense of excitement, fun and facilities for the whole family in order to attract people. IKEA, the Swedish furniture retailer, is a classic example (see DELIVERY SYSTEM); so too is Toys 'Я' Us. Increasingly, retailing is polarising between the high street, which is still economic for frequent and generally low ticket items, and destination retailers out of town, for infrequent and high ticket items. Destination retailing is increasing its share of total retailing in the UK and many other countries, particularly when associated with CATEGORY KILLERS, that is, specialists in a particular product range such as toys, baby products, CDs or furniture.

DEVELOP

The second of the methods for the Centre to add value in multibusiness corporations, according to the Ashridge Strategic Management Centre. 'Develop' means that the Centre injects expertise into the developing business. Technology-based expansion falls naturally into the 'develop' category: a new project is supported by resources from the Centre and the other businesses, and, if successful, eventually becomes a new business unit. Most core competency-based corporate strategies are 'develop' propositions.

DIONYSUS

In Charles HANDY'S GODS OF MANAGEMENT, Dionysus is the god of existential culture, and Dionysians are the most individualistic and anarchic of those found in organisations. The Dionysian culture is found in universities, research institutions, some professions, and some 'way out' professional service firms, especially small ones, as well as in many self-employed businesses, the arts, and crafts. Dionysians often comprise outposts within large firms, notably in R&D or any other rarefied, highly qualified technical post. Dionysians are difficult to manage and often impossible to motivate: they are self-motivated, inwardly directed, self-contained, and concerned about the quality of their work, not what anyone else thinks about it or them. It is difficult to make Dionysians behave as team players, unless they have strong personal bonds with the rest of the team. They are most effective in very small firms or as one-person units.

DIVERGENCE

Al RIES says that Divergence is 'the least understood, most powerful force in the universe'. New species arise by divergence from existing species. In business, new products and new ECOSYSTEMS arise when a competitor creates a product or service that splits an existing category into two, creating a new arena appealing to a subset of existing customers. Competitors who create such ecosystems can create a lasting and very profitable niche for themselves provided they create a distinctive brand in the ecosystem and continue to innovate so that their product and way of delivering it is always better adapted to customers than product from any competitor. See also VALUE INNOVATION.

DIVERSIFICATION (1)

Being in or moving towards being a group of companies engaged in several different products and markets. Diversification is usually driven by the wish (or financial ability) to expand beyond the apparent limits of existing markets, and/or by the wish to reduce business risk by developing new 'legs'.

Many forests have been destroyed by writers praising and damning diversification. The balance of recent opinion has been against diversification (as in 'stick to the knitting'), although this has not stopped conglomerates (diversified companies) gaining a larger and larger share of corporate activity throughout the world, and especially in Britain.

The main justifications behind diversification are:

1 *Financial.* The BCG MATRIX developed a theory in the late 1960s/early 1970s that central management of successful firms can and should shovel cash around the corporation in order to move it away from businesses that would always consume cash and into those few businesses that have the potential for market leadership and thus for long term cash generation. This was a rather selective theory of diversification, but Bruce HENDERSON became an apostle of conglomerates, convinced that the strategically directed conglomerate could continually compound its cash generation capability and expand the scope of its operations. Modern financial theorists counter that shareholders, not managers, should diversify their holdings and that it is better for shareholders to be offered a selection of 'pure plays' of non-diversified companies.

2 *Management skills.* Several diversified companies such as Hanson and BTR are highly skilled at identifying under-performing companies and at changing management structures and behaviour in order to improve performance. Diversification of this type involves buying, fixing, and at the right time selling, such companies.

3 *Core skills or COMPETENCIES.* A company's expertise may not really reside in knowing a particular market, but in certain skills that are applicable across several markets. This is well illustrated in Illustration 4.15, a list of examples of successful diversification compiled by Charles Coates.

Companies must not fool themselves about whether they have competencies that are applicable in new areas. But a moment's thought is usually all that is necessary to dismiss many instances of clear wishful thinking. The most notorious instances of unsuccessful diversification could not have been justified by the principle of core skills. Had this principle been the touchstone, Cummins, the world leader in diesel engines, would not have gone into ski resort development; Letraset, the world specialist in dry transfers, would not have bought stamp dealer Stanley Gibbons; General Mills would not have ventured from its core area of food manufacturing into toys; Coca-Cola would not have gone into the film industry by buying Columbia Pictures; and Lex Service, the car dealer and importer, would not have gone into the specialist world of electronic distribution.

ILLUSTRATION 4.15 ◆ Diversification using core competencies

Company	Country of origin	Original core business	Key skills	Growth path
Honda	Japan	Motorcycles	Piston engine design and development	Cars, lawnmowers, small generators
Gillette	USA	Shaving products	Advertising effectiveness	Other toiletries, e.g. deodorants
Hanson	UK	Textiles	Financial control; acquisition evaluation	Post-acquisition cash maximisation in low technology businesses
McDonald's	USA	Hamburger restaurants	Site selection; quality standardisation	Extension of opening hours to include breakfast; product innovation (fish, pizza, salads)

ILLUSTRATION 4.15 ◆ continued

Company	Country of origin	Original core business	Key skills	Growth path
Marks & Spencer	UK	Clothes retailing	Supplier management; value-for-money branding	Diversification into food, furniture, flowers
Sony	Japan	Transistor radios	Production innovation; evaluation of future customer desires	Broad consumer electronics; TV cameras; computer components
NEC	Japan	PABX; Semiconductors	Semiconductor technology	Telecommunications products (mobile phones, faxes, etc). Lap-top computers; office automation
Toyota	Japan	Cars	Flexible manufacturing; quality control	Geographical expansion

Source: Coates, Charles (1994) *The Total Manager*

All good diversification builds on competitive advantage in core businesses and reinforces rather than detracts from that by strengthening still further the competencies that drive success in the existing businesses. This is true even though the product areas may seem only tangentially related, as in Marks & Spencer's inspired move from clothes retailing to selling a narrow line of up-market foods. The core competencies of buying and merchandising, branding, stock management and customer care were reinforced by the diversification, even though at the time it seemed to many observers an odd move. See also ANSOFF MATRIX.

DIVERSIFICATION (2)

Investment diversification is the process of spreading risk by buying a number of different assets. Analysis of share diversification suggests that this sort of risk reduction can be achieved by buying as few as 15 shares (provided they have a reasonably low beta coefficient).

DIVISIONALISATION

Divisionalisation is dividing up a firm into several somewhat autonomous subfirms or 'divisions'. Divisionalisation was invented in the 1920s by

Alfred P. SLOAN as a way of structuring General Motors. In part it was a defensive measure, since too many decisions were rising to the top and paralysing the corporation's ability to act decisively. By constituting GM into five separate divisions, each with its own CEO and management team, it was possible to avoid excessive centralisation and allow more executives the freedom to act creatively. It was Sloan's genius to combine this partial decentralisation with an entirely new marketing focus on five new market segments, inventing 'a car for every purpose and purse', that was synonymous with the new divisions – Chevrolet, Pontiac, Oldsmobile, Buick, and Cadillac. Du Pont, also influenced by Sloan, and other large corporations soon followed suit by creating their own separate divisions.

Divisionalisation enjoyed great vogue from the 1920s through to the 1980s, but in retrospect it was a revolution stopped halfway. It would have been better to bite the bullet and divide up General Motors not into five divisions but into *five entirely separate and autonomous companies*, with initially common owners. Instead of divisionalisation, there could have been the true 'division' or BREAKUP of over-centralised corporations. This would have enabled each new company to develop fully its own GENETIC CODE or way of working, unconstrained by corporate shibboleths and the needs of 'sister' divisions. See also Part Two, pages 106, 126–9, and SLOAN, BREAKUP and GENETIC CODE.

DOG

1 Bad business, candidate for disposal.

2 Term invented by BCG to describe a company's low relative market share businesses (i.e. those that are not market leaders) in low-growth markets (those growing at less than 10 per cent per annum). BCG originally said that dogs (which it called 'pets' in the early days) were unlikely to be very cash positive or to be capable of being driven to market leadership; dogs should therefore be sold or closed. Since a majority of nearly all firms' businesses are dogs, this advice is draconian indeed, and was later soft-pedalled by BCG. Dogs are in fact often quite cash positive, especially if they are STRONG FOLLOWERS (i.e. not very much smaller than the market leader). It is also untrue that dogs cannot be driven to market leadership (i.e. become CASH COWS), though this is less usual than for followers in high growth markets (QUESTION MARKS). See GROWTH/SHARE MATRIX and MARKET CHALLENGER.

DOMINANT FIRM

One that has a RELATIVE MARKET SHARE well above that of competitors in a particular market. There is no accepted definition of how much larger a firm should be to be considered dominant, but it should be at least double the size of the next largest competitor (i.e. have a relative market share of at least two), and probably be at least four times as large. A dominant firm should be highly profitable.

DOOM LOOP

Consultantese for vicious circle. A doom loop is a self-reinforcing downward spiral that follows from inadequate response to competitor initiatives. Illustration 4.16 shows a typical doom loop. Doom loops are easier to describe than to correct, so the first priority must be to avoid getting into one in the first place, which requires continual effort to upgrade the customer product proposition and service and to improve the efficiency of the DELIVERY SYSTEM. Once in a doom loop, the only way out is to do something quite radical, usually involving a major re-focus of the firm on a smaller number of businesses and a fundamental change in the firm's CULTURE and way of conducting itself. Existing top management can almost never escape from a doom loop if it affects the firm's most important business.

ECOLOGICAL THEORY

The view developed by Bruce HENDERSON, Peter JOHNSON and myself that businesses are living entities that devise unique ways to create and serve particular ECOSYSTEMS – market niches or groups of customers with needs and characteristics different from other markets and customers. Every successful firm has a unique GENETIC CODE – a way of acting and organising itself, based on the knowledge, skills, attitudes and actions of people, both employees and outside collaborators – which enables the firm to serve its most profitable and important ecosystems better than any other firm. See Part Two, pages 103–110. See also ECOSYSTEM and GENETIC CODE.

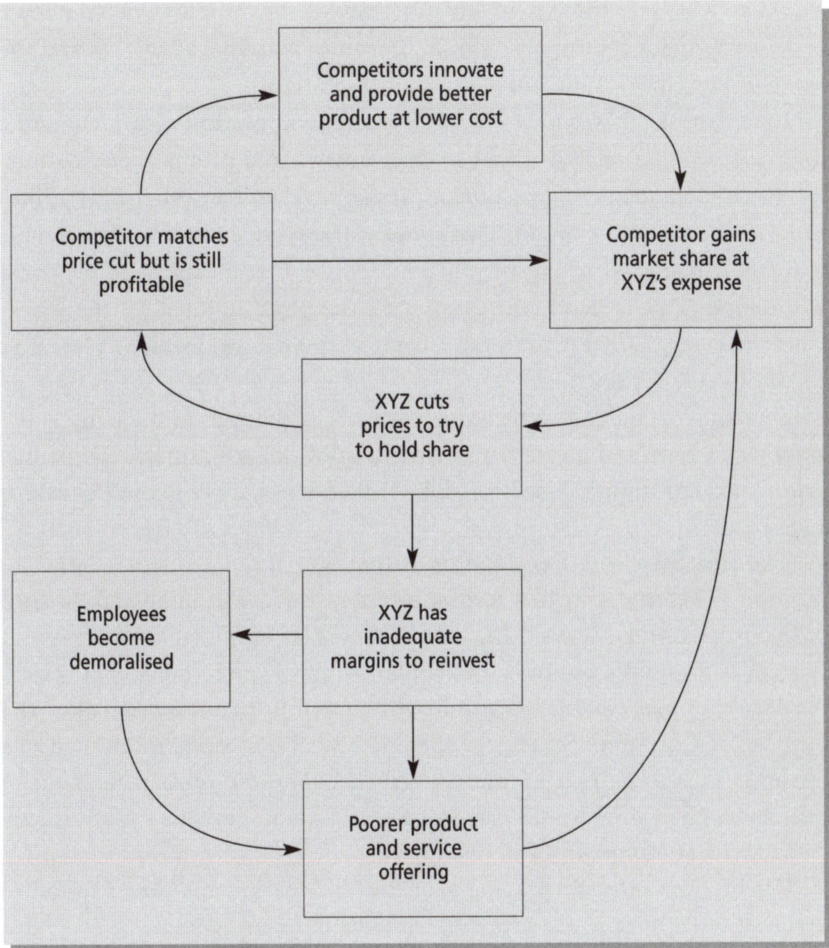

ILLUSTRATION 4.16 ◆ Example of doom loop for firm XYZ

ECONOMIC RENTS

This is quite an exciting concept, both ancient and modern, which explains how companies can earn returns above the normal cost of capital. The idea originally came from the brilliant early nineteenth-century economist, David Ricardo. He explained how a particularly desirable property – for example, a corner site in the centre of a town – could provide exceptional returns. Originally, before the town was built, the land would be worth no more than any other site of similar size. Once the town becomes a major metropolis, the site becomes extremely valuable and the lucky owner enjoys 'rent', an abnormally high return.

In business, this type of 'rent' goes to companies who have some unique asset that enables them to earn exceptional profits. For example, the Coca-Cola drink enjoys a price premium relative to other fizzy drinks simply because of the brand. The brand is therefore exceptionally valuable – in fact it is the world's most valuable, said by brand experts to be worth $70 billion. This is nearly three times all the physical assets of the Coca-Cola company, and yet the brand costs very little to develop. The extra profit or value is pure 'rent'.

One way of looking at business is that it is the pursuit of 'rent' – the extra profit over and above the normal cost of doing business. Rents only occur through unique assets or skills. Business strategy is the pursuit of such rents.

The strategist who has done most thinking about rents in relation to business is Peter JOHNSON, a former business partner of mine and director of Oxford University's Said Business School. He says that the purpose of strategy is to build a business model that will give rise to the highest possible levels of sustainable economic rent from a business, and that the purpose of Corporate Strategy – running a firm that owns more than one business – 'is to extract greater sustained economic rents from a set of businesses than they would earn on a stand-alone basis or when directly owned by a common set of shareholders.'

For me, the most interesting aspect of his work is his classification of different types of rent. He says there are five different types:

- First, there are the rents that most economists focus on, those derived from a company having a *monopoly*, giving higher prices than would be justified by the cost of production and a normal profit.
- Second, rents that are similar but not normally so high, deriving from an *oligopoly*, that is, when two or three competitors control a market.
- Third, there are *Ricardian rents*, named for David Ricardo, the type we've just been discussing, comprising not just brands but any type of asset that is unique and valuable – for example, the location of the Plaza Hotel in New York, or a massive copper and gold field in Peru that has just been discovered by an exploration company.

- Fourth, there are *Schumpeterian rents*. This mouthful relates to the intriguing Austrian-American economist, Joseph Schumpeter, active in the first half of the twentieth century. Schumpeter was the patron saint of entrepreneurs and innovation, and he pointed out that most exceptional business profits (rents) did not derive from monopoly or oligopoly, but from innovation – being ahead of the competition with a technology or product, despite all players having access to the same raw materials of competition. Innovative companies derive Schumpeterian rents because no other firm can do what they do, or maybe no other firm can do what the innovator does as well, or as cheaply, or as quickly. To keep these rents rolling, of course, the innovative firm must stay ahead of the competition. Economists can have a field day, verging perhaps on orgasm, trying to decide whether Microsoft's rents – its exceptional returns – are mainly monopoly rents or Schumpeterian rents. That's too difficult for me. All I know is that innovation is a great way to make super returns, but that an innovative firm that comes to rely upon its market position rather than renewed innovation will sooner or later run out of rent.
- But the most interesting type of rent highlighted by Peter Johnson is his fifth category, which he calls *opportunity rents*. These are those that relate to particularities in the exchange between a firm and its customers, allowing the firm to charge more (or have lower costs) than a competitor. 'Typically,' he says, 'business–customer exchange is deeply specific and idiosyncratic (on both sides)', creating the opportunity for the firm to earn opportunity rents. The customer does not know what all suppliers would charge for any product, and maybe doesn't care. For some reason the customer prefers to go to a particular supplier, who is able to charge more than the going rate because he supplies something that is slightly different that the customer likes – maybe it's the location, maybe the service, maybe it's the range of products available, maybe it's something that neither supplier nor customer could define but that still binds them together.

Opportunity rents exist because business is not homogeneous and each competitor is able to create its own unique ECOSYSTEM. As Johnson says:

> ***'Heterogeneity is the source of value in exchange and the source of opportunity rents and profits. "The price", "the cost", and "the product" are generalized idealizations on the part of econo-***

> ***mists that do not arise in actual exchanges. Rather, we have fuzzy, extended notions of price, product, and cost in business. Out of the fuzziness arises the possibility of valued idiosyncratic exchange.'***

Johnson says that opportunity rents are probably a bigger source of profits than the other four categories of rent that economists have focused on. This fits my experience of how business really works.

ECONOMIES OF SCALE

Reduction in unit costs through having greater scale. One of the main reasons why the high market share competitor has lower costs than the smaller player. Economies of scale can cease to operate (or more precisely, are thought incorrectly to exist) when additional revenue is not exactly of the same type, that is, requires additional cost. See COSTS OF COMPLEXITY.

ECONOMIES OF SCOPE

Economies that come from having a broad product line that can utilise the same skills or cost infrastructure. Relies upon cost sharing between two different lines of business. Even if such sharing is not perfect, i.e. only part of the costs can be shared, the importance of economies of scope may outweigh economies of scale. For example, one supplier of product A may have 100 units and an average cost of $10, and a smaller supplier of product A may have only 50 units and an average cost of $12. This means that the larger supplier has economies of scale, the smaller supplier suffers diseconomies of scale. But assume that the smaller supplier enters two other markets, producing 100 units of product B and 100 units of product C. Assume also that products B and C each manage to share half of their costs with product A. The smaller supplier of product A now has economies of scope, and his unit costs for producing A will effectively be based on 150 units equivalent of A (the 50 actual units of A, and half of the 200 units of B and C, giving a total scale for cost sharing purposes equivalent to 150 units of A). The economies of scope mean that the smaller player in the A market can have lower costs even in that market – in the example above, the economies of scope may reduce the unit cost from $12 to $9.

Economies of scope exist only if there is genuine cost sharing and if there are no additional, hidden costs (such as additional supervision or overheads) required by having a broader product line. See COSTS OF COMPLEXITY.

ECOSYSTEM, STRATEGIC ECOSYSTEM

The place where competition occurs, where there are different customer needs and different competitor positions. 'Ecosystem' is therefore the same as 'segment' or 'business segment' as defined in Part One. 'Ecosystem' is the preferred term in Part Two, however, to emphasise that each ecosystem is a unique, living and changing entity defined by the interactions of customers and firms selling to them, and influenced also by technology, suppliers to the firms, other intermediaries active in the ecosystem, and by events in adjacent ecosystems. Each ecosystem is a niche where a competitor can make its living and, if it is better adapted to the needs of the ecosystem than any other competitor, can make returns above the cost of capital. The ecosystem is characterised above all by the interactions and idiosyncrasies of the *people* active in it. The ecological theory of strategy is presented in Part Two. See also BUSINESS SEGMENT, Peter JOHNSON, and the whole of Part Two.

EIGHTY/TWENTY RULE, 80/20 RULE, 80/20 PRINCIPLE

The Pareto rule, that 80 per cent of sales or profits or any other variable may come from 20 per cent of the products. Can clearly be looked at empirically in any case, and usually one of the most valuable simple steps to understanding any business. Invented by Vilfredo Pareto, the nineteenth-century economist. Looked at in retrospect, many of the major insights of business in the last half century are derived from the Pareto principle, including BCG's focus on those few high relative market share businesses that generate most of the cash for a company, the insight that COSTS OF COMPLEXITY derive from too extensive a product range, and that therefore maximum use should be made of outsourcing, as well as the movement to rationalise stock-holding, restrict the numbers of SKUs (Stock Holding Units), and conduct ABC analysis of true profitability.

The 80/20 rule applies to individuals as well: 80 per cent of the value you provide in your job may come from 20 per cent of your time, so if you delegated the activities that take the remaining 80 per cent of your time to a lower cost or less experienced person (or stopped doing them altogether), you could multiply your impact up to five times. For both firms and individuals, some of the low-value 80 per cent may actually have negative value. Perhaps firms should legislate that all of their people spend at least 15 minutes a week contemplating the 80/20 rule. Or alternatively, that they should all buy my bestseller *The 80/20 Principle* (1997)!

EXPECTED VALUE

The weighted average expectation as to what an investment will be worth or what any other outcome (revenues, profits, etc.) will be. Usually calculated by constructing various scenarios and weighting them according to probability. For example, if I think there is a 10 per cent chance of selling an asset (usually at a specified future date) for £3m, a 50 per cent chance of selling it for £4m, and a 40 per cent chance of selling it for £5m, its expected value is £4.3m (0.1 × £3m + 0.5 × £4m + 0.4 × £5m). The expected value is not necessarily or even normally the most probable outcome (£4m in this case) but is the weighted average expectation. Expected value is sometimes guestimated without resorting to a formal calculation.

EXPERIENCE CURVE

Along with the BCG MATRIX, the greatest discovery of Bruce HENDERSON, although it started life in 1926 as the 'learning curve'. Briefly it states that when the accumulated production of any good or service doubles, unit costs in real terms (i.e. adjusted for inflation) have the potential to fall by 20–30 per cent. Accumulated production is not a concept much used, nor is it usually very easy to calculate: it is the total number of units of a product that have ever been made by a firm, or the total number of units of a product ever made by all participants in the market. It is not related to time, because accumulated production can double within one year for a new or very fast growth product, or take centuries for a very old or slow growth one.

BCG found and documented many exciting instances in the late 1960s and 1970s where accumulated production had increased rapidly and deflated (inflation adjusted) costs had fallen to 70–80 per cent of their previous level each time this happened. One of the most important examples is the decline in the cost of integrated circuits (ICs), which explains why the cost of calculators was able to plummet so dramatically. A typical example of a cost experience curve is shown in Illustration 4.17.

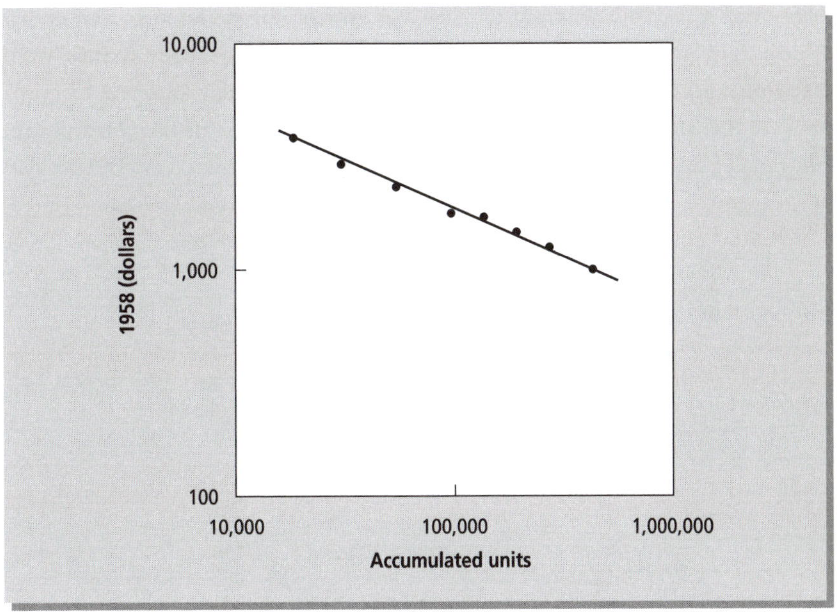

ILLUSTRATION 4.17 ◆ Cost experience curve

BCG used the experience tool both to identify cost reduction opportunities and as a dynamic tool for describing and influencing the battle between competitors in a particular product. If a particular firm was found *not* to have cut costs in line with the experience curve, this was held to be a cost reduction opportunity. The beauty of the method was that it described precisely the point that costs should have reached (although not how to get there), and therefore set a firm and seemingly objective target for management to meet. A great deal of cost reduction was actually achieved this way.

In terms of competitive strategy, BCG invented a second type of experience curve: related not to costs but to prices. For any market as a whole, but particularly for an individual firm, BCG would chart how real prices (after adjusting for inflation) had behaved in relation to accumulated production of the product. The price experience curve might or might not follow the shape of the cost experience curve. In Illustration 4.18 we show a cost experience curve of 80 per cent (that is, costs behaved as they should, reducing by 20 per cent each time accumulated production doubled), but different cost behaviour in three phases. In the first phase, prices did not come down at all: in other words, the deflated price experience curve was 100 per cent (or prices were increased in line with inflation). In the second phase, prices came down very sharply, to compensate for the earlier failure to match cost reductions. In the third phase, prices fell in parallel with costs, that is, the price experience curve was also 80 per cent.

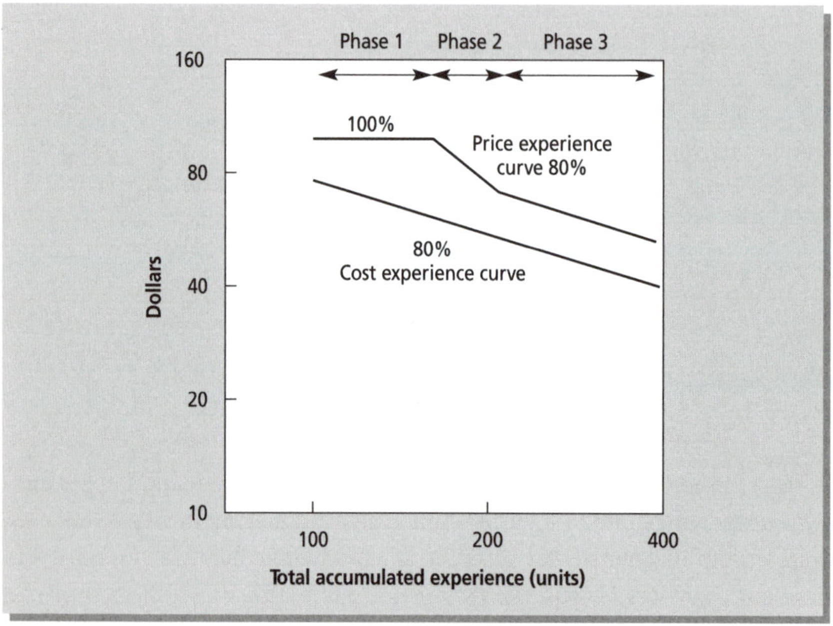

ILLUSTRATION 4.18 ◆ Price experience curve in three phases compared to cost experience curve

BCG explained the first phase as one of complacency and excess profits, where consumers are willing to continue paying a high price and where competitors all enjoy higher margins by not passing cost savings on to customers. Eventually, however, these high profits encourage new players into the marketplace, and at least one of these new players cuts costs to try to gain market share. The other players have to respond, and prices are therefore reduced until 'normal' margins prevail again.

BCG preached that it was doubly foolish to have a flatter price experience curve than cost experience curve (i.e. to widen margins in the first phase), firstly, because it would lead to loss of market share initially, and secondly because the player with the greater market share would have lower costs, so that a market leader who held market share (by having competitive prices, so that his price might be below new entrants' cost) would continually compound his competitive advantage of low cost and make it impossible for new players to enter unless they were willing to lose money initially. Prices should therefore be reduced by the market leader at least as fast as costs, in order to keep competitors out or unprofitable, and thus consolidate market leadership and compound the low cost position.

BCG was able to explain the success of Japanese companies such as Honda in motorcycles by reference to 'experience curve cost reduction' and 'experience curve pricing'. Ultimately the experience curve effect was used to explain the incidence of short-termism in Western industry up to around 1985 and the consequent loss of global market share.

The concepts behind the experience curve are wholly correct. It must be admitted that calculating accumulated volume was often a black art, and that BCG sometimes exaggerated the scientific and empirical nature of the experience curve. Since the late 1970s the experience curve as a practical management tool has fallen into disuse, though lone adherents persist (and use it effectively). Experience curve thinking, even if no experience curves are drawn (and one suspects that very few Japanese executives ever drew such curves), should be an integral part of good management. The mysterious disappearance of the experience curve from Western boardrooms is much to be deplored, even though experience curve thinking is in part imbedded in the Quality Revolution of the 1980s and the BPR Revolution of the 1990s.

FASHIONIZE

To pursue a 'fashionizing' strategy, launching many new products and getting them to market quickly, segmenting the customer base repeatedly, and moulding the organisation so that it can respond quickly to customers, by DELAYERING, using taskforces, partnering with outside firms, and pushing down decision-making to small, entrepreneurial units positioned as close to the customer as possible.

FIRST MOVER ADVANTAGE

The (usually correct) idea that the first into a market, the innovator, has an opportunity to stay ahead of competition, provided that the first mover builds in as much customer value as possible, lowers costs aggressively, and pursues a low-price policy rather than maximising short term profits. See PRICE UMBRELLA for an explanation of how the opposite often happens.

FLAT ORGANISATION

One with relatively few levels, such as the Roman Catholic Church (which has only five). Work by HAMPDEN-TURNER and TROMPENAARS has shown that managers from different countries describe their organisations with varying degrees of flatness, as shown in Illustration 4.19.

This display should make one pause before asserting that flatter is better: it may be in many Western countries, but Japan, Hong Kong and Singapore have hierarchical structures that work well. Hampden-Turner and Trompenaars explain the paradox by these countries having 'Organic Ordering' mechanisms: they are hierarchical, but they are also 'integrating', where knowledge flows *up* the hierarchy and where each level is harmonised effectively with the layer immediately above and immediately below. Western hierarchies operate in reverse, where orders and initiatives flow from top to bottom. Organic ordering allows the organisation to be close to the customer and may actually speed up the process of operating effectively in knowledge-intensive industries such as electronics. Flatter may only be better, therefore, in the Western paradigm, where knowledge has difficulty percolating up a steep structure. See *The Seven Cultures of Capitalism* by the two authors referred to: a brilliantly original and thought-provoking work.

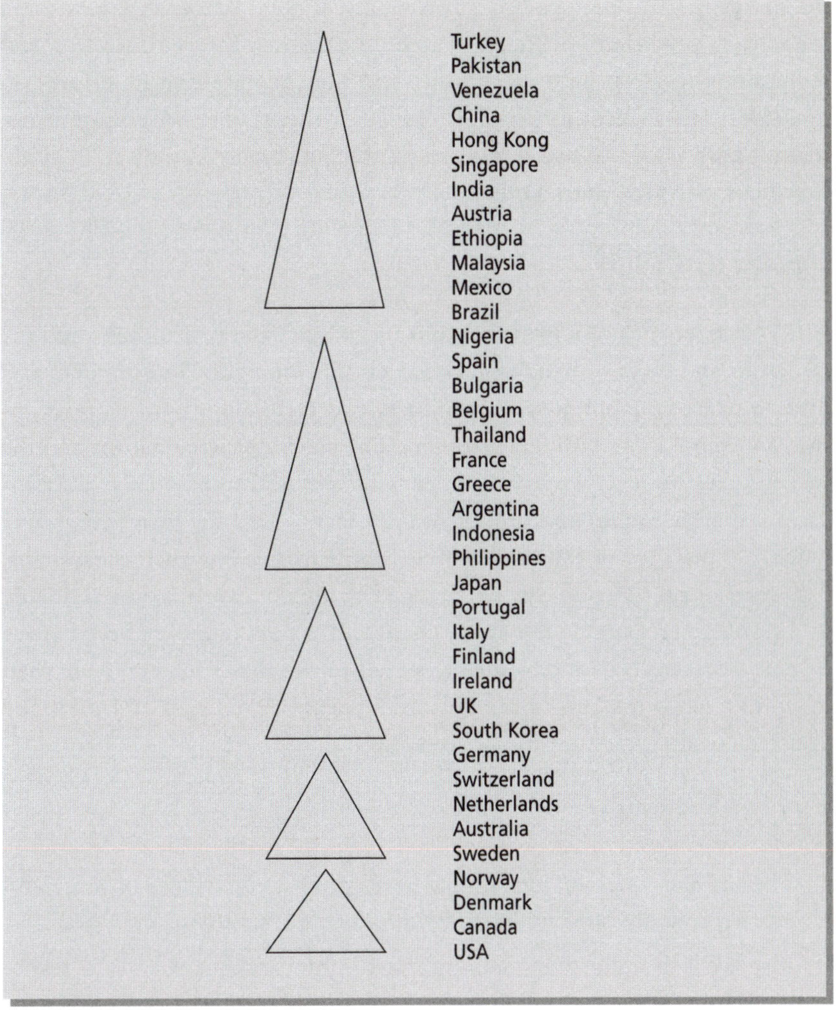

ILLUSTRATION 4.19 ◆ Company triangles

FOCUS

One of the fundamental principles of strategy, preached with passion by Bruce HENDERSON since 1964, no less relevant today, and only a little less neglected. Smaller firms in particular must focus on a small number of BUSINESS SEGMENTS where they can be the largest. Even most large companies could raise their profits and market value by a tighter focus on the things they do best and most profitably. A good example of focus and tenacity is provided by Sharp, which stuck to exploiting liquid crystal technology in electronic calculators and concentrated all its efforts on making them as slim as possible. In 1975 there were 45 competitors; today, Sharp is one of two dominant producers, largely as a result of superior focus. See RIES (Part Three).

GENETIC CODE

The characteristics of a firm that make it unique. Every firm has a unique structure and ways of behaving, based on its employees, its suppliers and other outside collaborators, its products and technology, and its relationship and reputation with its customers. The character of each firm and the way it goes about its work will be peculiarly suited to particular ECOSYSTEMS – market niches and groups of customers – and the firm will usually make 100 per cent or even more of its profits from a few such ecosystems. The firm's genetic code can be changed gradually over time or suddenly as a result of crisis and wrenching change. It generally makes better sense to find or create ecosystems ideally suited to the firm's genetic code than to try to change the latter dramatically. See Part Two, pages 104–119. See also ECOLOGICAL THEORY and ECOSYSTEM.

GLOBALISATION

1 The process whereby global tastes and product offerings converge and are increasingly satisfied by global products rather than local ones.

2 Also used to indicate something much more significant and far reaching. Few real global products exist, but globalisation is a reality for most of the world's largest companies, in the sense that they think and operate with a global perspective on customers, technology, costs, sourcing, strategic alliances and competitors. The market for these firms' products is wherever there are affluent consumers or significant industrial customers; the firms must appeal to their customers wherever they are, regardless of borders, the firm's nationality (an increasingly tenuous concept) or where its factories are.

   Globalisation is driven by hard economics: to compete effectively firms have to incur high fixed costs (for R&D, development of technology, sales and distribution networks, brand building and so on), forcing executives to spread these costs over higher volumes, which means trying to gain market share in all important world economies. New technologies also get dispersed globally very quickly, so that innovators must exploit their property on a global scale, if necessary by means of strategic alliances, or see it adopted and adapted by competitors. Global competition has accelerated sharply. Between 1987 and 1992, US direct investment outside the US rose 35 per cent to $776 billion, while the value of foreign direct investment into the US more than doubled, to $692 billion.

These trends do not require product universalism: product localisation is necessary for global success in most businesses. Some observers, such as Kenichi Ohmae, believe that the economic thrust of globalisation is irresistible and will cast aside conventional views of national politics, macro-economics, trade and citizenship. See also GLOBAL LOCALISATION, GLOCALISATION, MULTILOCALS, OHMAE and ILE.

3 Ability to carry out financial transactions on an international basis (in London, New York, Tokyo, etc.) around the clock.

GLOBAL LOCALISATION

Sony catch-phrase where a global product is adapted to local tastes by low cost customisation. Has the advantages of low cost but somewhat differentiated product. May also involve use or creation of a local distribution network peculiar to one country or region. For example, Coca-Cola's success in Japan was due both to setting up its own route sales forces and to the rapid introduction of many products sold only in Japan. For most markets, the quest for the holy grail of a global product will fail; global localisation is a much surer route to success.

GLOCALISATION OF ORGANISATIONS

Contraction of 'global localisation' and a very useful word, describing an escalating process. Glocalisation aims at making the organisation everywhere responsive to customers, who may themselves be global, and insists that the organisation be structured in the way that makes it as easy as possible for the global customer to deal with. An important by-product of this approach is elimination of operational duplication and often dramatic reductions in management numbers and cost.

The opportunity for standardisation worldwide in large organisations is enormous. Standardisation alone usually reduces overheads by 20 per cent by eliminating administrative confusion on an international scale. Chief executives need to insist on the standardisation of organisations and roles worldwide in order to remove the heavy, hidden costs of complexity and confusion. European companies find this both harder to achieve and more rewarding when accomplished than US or Japanese companies, because the European firms are more likely to exhibit corporate federalism and feudalism and therefore huge local autonomy and diversity.

GODS OF MANAGEMENT

Four cultural types defined by Charles HANDY in the book of the same name. Strikingly original formulation of truths immediately recognisable by those who have worked in organisations. For a description of each god, see APOLLO (role culture), ATHENA (task culture), DIONYSUS (professional culture) and ZEUS (patron culture).

GROWTH/GROWTH MATRIX

Useful two-by-two chart (invented by BCG) which compares the growth of a firm's business in one product or BUSINESS SEGMENT to the growth of the market as a whole, thus enabling one to see whether market share was being won or lost and by whom (Illustration 4.20).

Illustration 4.20 shows an example, using imaginary data, of three competitors in a particular market at a particular time (three, five or ten years are generally used). According to the (made up) data, the largest competitor is McKinsey, which is growing more slowly than the market as a whole (and therefore losing share); the next largest is BCG, which is growing at the same rate as the market; and the smallest but fastest growing competitor is Bain & Company. Note that companies on a Growth/growth chart are always at the same vertical height, since this represents the overall market growth and must by definition be common for all.

Growth/growth charts are not much used nowadays but are very useful, especially if used in conjunction with the main BCG MATRIX (the GROWTH/ SHARE MATRIX).

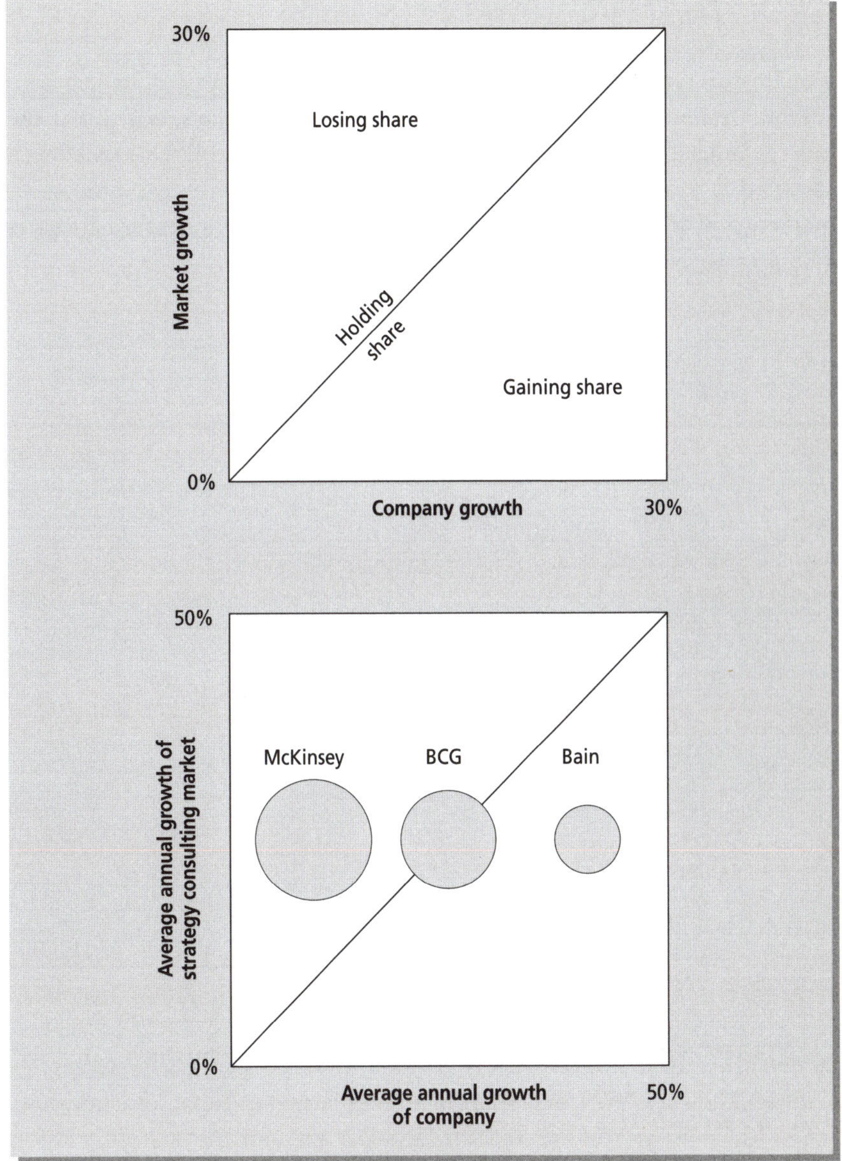

ILLUSTRATION 4.20 ◆ Examples of Growth/growth matrix with competitors arrayed

GROWTH/SHARE MATRIX

The Boston Consulting Group has invented several matrices, having consultants trained to think in terms of two-by-two displays, but this is the most famous and useful one (it is also sometimes called the BCG MATRIX). Invented in the late 1960s and still of great importance today, it measures market growth and relative market share for all the business a particular firm has. An example is shown in Illustration 4.21.

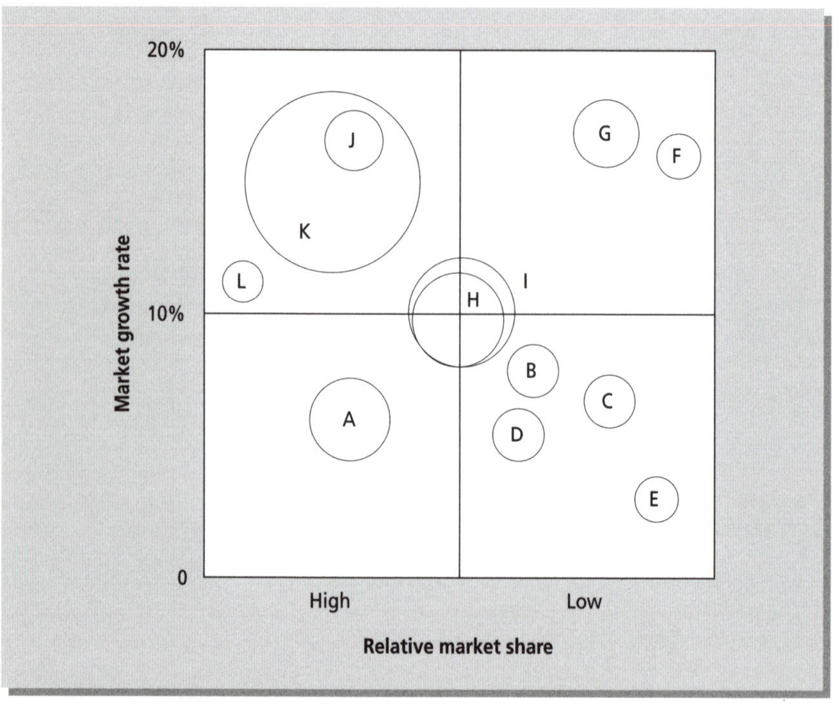

ILLUSTRATION 4.21 ◆ Engulf & Devour Plc, Growth/share matrix

It is important to define the axes properly. The horizontal axis is of fundamental importance and measures the market share that a firm has in a particular business *relative to the share enjoyed in that business by its largest competitor*. Thus if Engulf & Devour Plc has a 40 per cent market share in Business A and its nearest competitor has a 10 per cent market share, its relative market share ('RMS') is 400 per cent or 4 times (written as

4.0×). In Business B, Engulf & Devour may have a 5 per cent share and the leading competitor 10 per cent, in which case Engulf & Devour's relative market share is 50 per cent or 0.5×. Note that absolute market share (for example, 20 per cent of a market) means little, because it could mean a relative market share of 0.33 per cent (if the dominant competitor has 60 per cent market share), or of 10.0× (if the rest of the market is very fragmented and the next largest player has only 2 per cent).

The vertical axis is the growth rate of the market in which the business competes. Much confusion surrounds the precise definition of this market growth rate. The correct definition is the *expected future annual growth rate* (over the next five years) *in volume* (units of production) *of the market as a whole*, not of the particular Engulf & Devour business.

Before going on, it is important to understand the reasons why BCG and I think that the axes are significant. The relative market share is key because a business that is larger than its competitors (has a high relative market share, more than 1.0×) *ought to have lower costs, or higher prices, or both, and therefore higher profitability* than a competitor in that business with a lower share. This is generally true, although not always, as confirmed by databases such as the PIMS studies.

It is also logical – a business with higher volume ought to be able to spread its fixed costs over more units, and therefore have lower fixed and overhead costs, as well as make better use of any expensive machinery or people that are the best for that particular business. The higher share business may also be able to charge a higher price, either because it has the best brand or because it has the best distribution or simply because it is the preferred choice of most people. Since price minus cost equals profit, the higher share competitor should have the highest margins, or be ploughing back his advantage in the form of extra customer benefits that will reinforce his market share advantage.

Note that we say that the higher share competitor *ought* to have lower costs or higher prices. It does not necessarily follow, since he may squander his potential advantage by inefficiency, sharing costs with unprofitable products, or by having poorer customer service than a rival. Where the higher share player does not have profits higher than competitors there is usually an unstable competitive relationship which can create both opportunity and vulnerability in that market (see the OPPORTUNITY/VULNERABILITY MATRIX).

In some cases having a higher share of a business does not confer any benefit or potential benefit, for example where a one-man plumbing business faces a ten-man plumbing business, and the costs of labour are the same for everyone. Many people have claimed that the importance of market share, and the value of the Growth/share matrix, have been greatly overstated, and produce examples of cases where larger businesses are *less* profitable than smaller businesses, or where there is no systematic difference in profitability according to scale. On detailed examination, however, there are few individual business segments where it is not or cannot be a real advantage to be larger, all other things being equal. The qualification in the last phrase is absolutely crucial: relative market share is not the only influence on profitability, and it may be overwhelmed by different competitors' operating skills or strategies, or random influences on profitability.

One of the major causes of confusion is that businesses are often not defined properly, in a sufficiently disaggregated way, before measuring market share. The niche player who focuses on a limited product range or customer base may be playing in just one segment. The broad line supplier will be present in several segments and may actually not be very large in any one segment despite appearing to have a high overall market share. For example, a national supermarket chain may be bigger than competitors which have regional chains, but the relevant basis of competition may be local scale and customer awareness. See BUSINESS SEGMENT and SEGMENTATION for the importance of correct business definition and some hints on how to do it.

If businesses are defined properly, the higher share competitor should have an advantage at least nine times out of ten. It therefore follows that the further to the left a business is on the BCG MATRIX, the stronger it should be.

What about the vertical axis: the growth rate of the market? BCG claimed that there was a real difference between high growth businesses (where demand is growing at 10 per cent or more) and lower growth ones, because of greater fluidity in the former: that is, if the market is growing fast, there is more opportunity to gain market share. This is logical, both because more new business is up for grabs, and because competitors will react much more vigorously to defend their absolute share (to avoid a loss of turnover) than to defend loss of relative share, which they do not even notice in a fast changing market.

Having understood these points, we can go on to characterise the four quadrants of the BCG MATRIX (see Illustration 4.22).

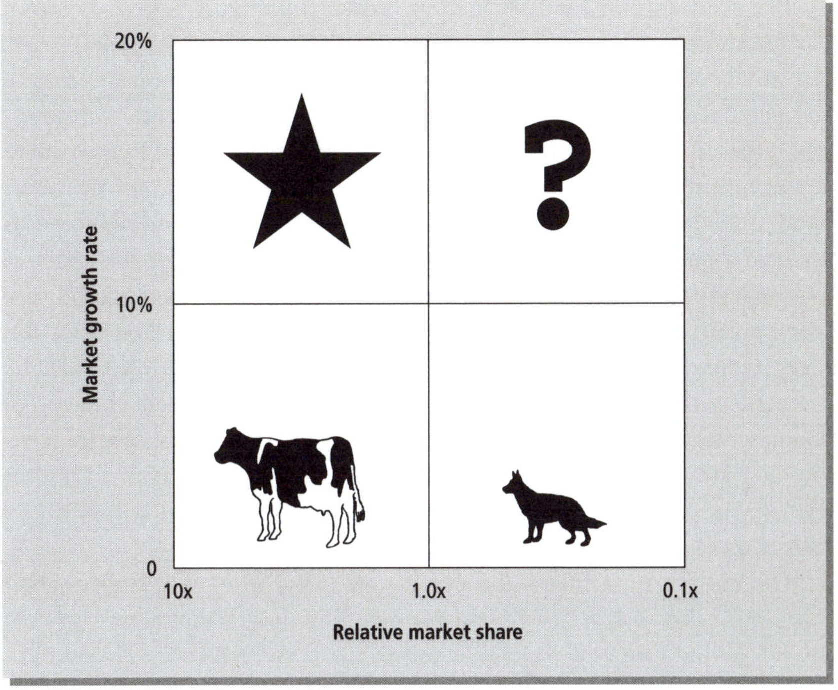

ILLUSTRATION 4.22 ◆ The Growth/share matrix four quadrants

The bottom left box contains the CASH COWS (also called gold mines in some early versions of the matrix: in many ways a better name). These businesses have high relative market share (they are by definition market leaders) and therefore ought to be profitable. They are very valuable and should be protected at all costs. They throw off a lot of cash, which can be reinvested in the business, used elsewhere in the business portfolio, used to buy other businesses, or paid out to shareholders.

The top left box comprises STARS: high relative market share businesses in high growth markets. These are very profitable but may need a lot of cash to maintain their position. This cash should be made available. Whatever it takes to hold or gain share in star businesses should be undertaken. If they hold RMS, star businesses will become cash cows when the market growth slows down, and will therefore be hugely valuable over a long time. But if star businesses lose relative market share, as they are often allowed to do, they will end up as DOGS and be of limited value.

The top right box holds QUESTION MARKS (sometimes called wildcats): low RMS positions but in high growth markets. In this case 'question mark' is a very good description of the business, since it has an uncertain future, and the decision on whether to invest in the business is both important and difficult. If a question mark does not improve its relative market share – that is, if it remains a follower – it will end life as a DOG. On the other hand, if the volatility that market growth bestows is used and investment is made in a question mark to drive it into a leadership position, the business will migrate to being a star (profitable) and ends its days as a cash cow (very profitable and very cash positive). The problem is that question mark businesses very often turn into CASH TRAPS, as money can be invested without any guarantee (and in some cases much chance) of attaining a leadership position. A business that is invested in heavily without ever attaining market leadership (like much of the British computer industry up to the 1980s) will simply be an investment in failure and a gross waste of money.

The bottom right box is the dog kennel. Dogs are low relative market share positions in low growth businesses. The theory therefore says that they should not be very profitable and should not be able to gain share to migrate into cash cows. Given that the majority of most firm's businesses may be in this box, this is not a very cheerful notion.

In fact, the greatest weakness in the BCG theory relates to dogs, largely because of this fatalism. The entry later on dogs puts the case for their defence and stresses the ways in which dogs can often be made valuable parts of a firm's business portfolio. Briefly, dogs *can* migrate into cash cows, by resegmenting the business or simply by having greater customer responsiveness than the market leader. Even if leadership is not possible, it is usually worthwhile to improve market share position within the dog category. A business with a relative market share of 0.7 × (70 per cent of the leader) may be quite profitable, highly cash positive, and quite different from a business with an RMS of only 0.3× (30 per cent of the leader).

Nevertheless, it may be true that there is limited room for manoeuvre with dog businesses, and they will generally be less attractive than stars or cash cows.

BCG superimposed on the Growth/share matrix a theory of cash management (sometimes confusingly called portfolio management) which is intriguing and makes some useful points, although it is also flawed. The theory looks at the cash characteristics of each of the quadrants (Illustration 4.23).

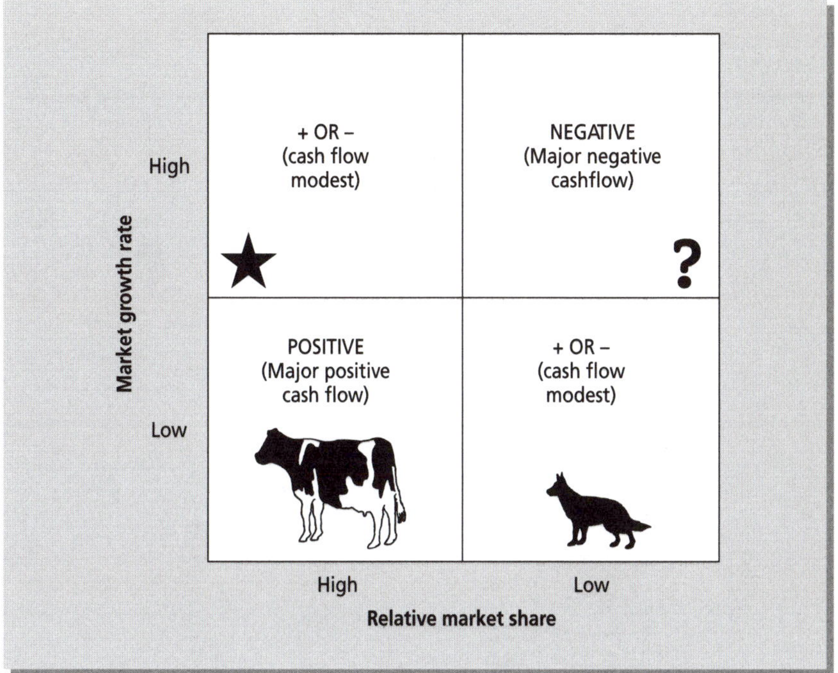

ILLUSTRATION 4.23 ◆ The Growth/share matrix cash characteristics

BCG's theory then came up with a hierarchy of uses of cash, numbered from 1 to 4 in their order of priority (Illustration 4.24).

1 The best use of cash, we can agree, is to defend cash cows. They should not need to use cash very often, but if investment in a new factory or technology is required, it should be made unstintingly.

2 We can also agree that the next call on cash should normally be in stars. These will need a great deal of investment to hold (or gain) relative market share.

3 The trouble begins here, with BCG's third priority, to take money from cash cows and invest in question marks. The bastardised version of the theory stressed this cash flow in particular. BCG countered by stressing that investment in question marks should be selective, confined to those cases where there was a real chance of attaining market leadership. With this qualification, BCG's point is sensible.

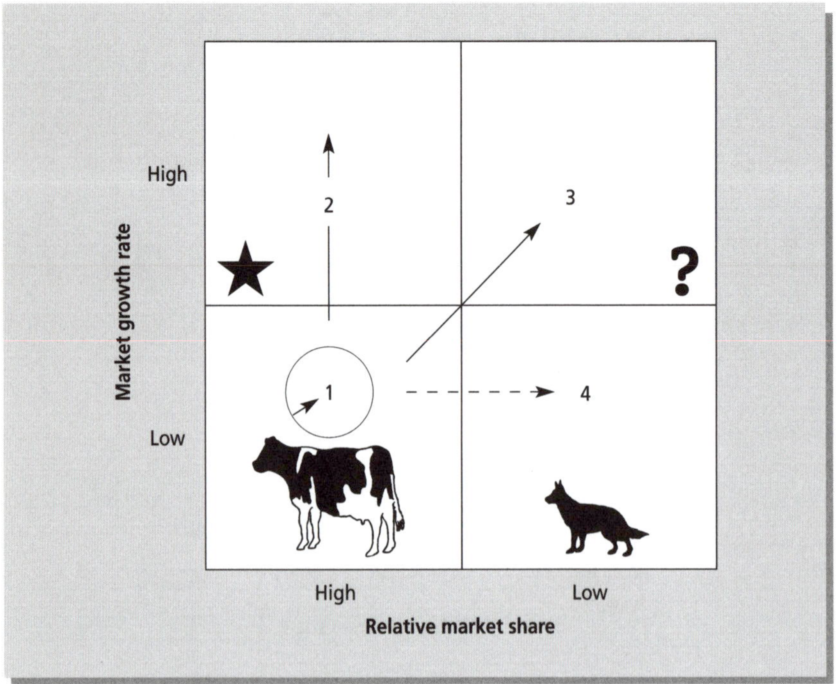

ILLUSTRATION 4.24 ◆ How to use the cash

4 The lowest priority was investment in dogs, which BCG said should be minimal or even negative, if they were run for cash. This may be a sensible prescription, but the problem is that the dog kennel may contain a large range of breeds with different qualities, and a differentiated cash strategy is generally required within the dog kennel.

One real weakness of the BCG cash management theory, however, as BCG came to realise, was the assumption that the portfolio had to be in balance in respect of cash on an annual or three-year basis. In fact, the cash invested in the overall business portfolio does *not* have to equal the cash generated. Surplus cash can be invested outside of the existing portfolio, either by acquiring new businesses, by entering them from scratch, or by reducing debt or giving cash back to the shareholders. Conversely, if a business needs to invest more cash (for example, in an important and cash-guzzling star) than the business portfolio is generating, it should go out and raise the cash from bankers and/or shareholders to fund the cash gap. The business portfolio should not be thought of as a closed system.

The second major weakness of BCG views on cash, and one not fully realised until much later, was the implicit assumption that *all* businesses should be managed from the centre in a cashbox-plus-strategic-control way. BCG's theory was immensely attractive to chairmen and chief executives seeking a sensible role for the Centre, and probably did a great deal more good than harm, but only a small minority of businesses are actually run in this way. Indeed, the recent work by GOOLD, CAMPBELL and ALEXANDER largely divides businesses into just two categories: those that are run by financial control on the one hand and those that follow either strategic control or strategic planning on the other. These are two very different approaches, the former decentralised, the latter more centralised, and it is difficult to combine the two styles, as BCG's approach assumed. Perhaps, in the future, someone will devise a method of control which does incorporate the strong points of both styles, but it will take much more than a two-by-two matrix to realise this vision.

The BCG MATRIX marked a major contribution to management thinking. From the mid to late 1970s BCG tended to retreat too much under the weight of critical comment, and the matrix is not much used today. It is well overdue for a revival. Anyone who tries to apply it thoughtfully to his or her business will learn a lot during the process.

HARVESTING

Deliberate or unintentional running down of a business and its market share position in order to extract short term profit: 'selling' market share. Harvesting can result from a number of policies: holding or raising prices higher than competitors, not reinvesting in marketing and selling effort or in new equipment, or by stopping advertising. Such steps could result in a short term increase in profits but the competitive position of the business will be weakened and with loss of market share it – will end up as a smaller business which may not even be viable in the medium term. Harvesting may happen without management being aware of it – reinvestment does not occur because it 'cannot be afforded', and market share is gradually lost – or if they do realise, without them connecting it to the failure to invest as much as competitors.

Harvesting as a deliberate strategy is not much practised, and for good reason: you cannot tell how fast market share will be lost, and the business can disappear into an irreversible DOOM LOOP much faster than expected. Harvesting can be a very rewarding tactic, however, if it is intended to sell a business within a year or so. The final year's profits can be significantly boosted, and the buyer may apply a normal PE Ratio to buy the business without realising that it is losing market share and that the profits are not sustainable.

Harvesting, like so many other concepts, was the invention of the Boston Consulting Group. See BCG MATRIX.

HEARTLAND BUSINESSES

Businesses within a multibusiness corporation where the Centre can add a great deal of value. Heartland businesses have opportunities to improve that the Centre knows how to address, and they have critical success factors that the Centre fully appreciates.

ILE (INTER-LINKED ECONOMY)

Kenichi OHMAE's phrase for the 'borderless' economy comprising the US, Europe and Japan (the triad), and increasingly taking in aggressive, outward-looking economies such as Korea, Taiwan, Hong Kong and Singapore. The economy embraces much more than trade, being a complex network of corporate inter-dependencies led by the world's largest companies (which used to be called multinationals but are now more accurately described as multilocals). The ILE comprises one billion people, mainly affluent consumers, and most of the world's wealth is created and consumed in the ILE. See OHMAE, GLOBALISATION and GLOBAL LOCALISATION.

INSIDERISATION

1 Kenichi OHMAE's term for the process of replicating or recreating a home-country business system in a new national market, adapting the system to the new market's unique characteristics. The classic example is Coca-Cola's innovation in Japan when confronted with the multi-

layered distribution system for soft drinks. Coke organised local bottlers to create a national network of Coke vans distributing bottles and collecting empties, driven by a new Coke national sales force. The company thus became a fully paid-up 'insider', and was able to use its distribution network to sell a variety of soft drinks as well as Coke. Insiderisation means taking the trouble to understand and develop a local market rather than imposing a model based on 'home' market characteristics; it is an important method of GLOBAL LOCALISATION.

2 The process of making outsiders to an organisation in some sense insiders, by sharing information with them and encouraging them to identify with the firm.

JUST-IN-TIME (JIT)

Valuable system developed first in Japan for production management aimed at minimising stock by having materials and work-in-progress delivered to the right place at the right time. As well as lowering costs, JIT can have other major benefits: the systematic identification of operational problems and their resolution by technology-based tools; higher levels of customer service and speeding up the time to market; higher quality standards by being RIGHT FIRST TIME; and higher standards of COMPETENCE in the production function generally. To be most effective, JIT should be introduced as part of TQM (Total Quality Management), and it should be recognised at the outset that JIT is not just a technique but a way of changing behaviour. A full JIT programme such as that introduced by Toyota or Matsushita may take years to complete. But companies without JIT which compete against those with JIT will have a major handicap.

Properly conceived, JIT should be seen as a synchronising way of life: jobs must be completed quickly, but even more important is that they be completed just in time to fit in with the next step in the dance. This is a radically different concept from traditional assembly line thinking, which is sequential rather than synchronising. Charles HAMPDEN-TURNER and Fons TROMPENAARS point out that culturally, the US, UK, Sweden and Holland are disposed towards trying to speed things up sequentially, whereas Japan, Germany and France are more geared towards synchronisation. This means that when installing JIT and other synchronising techniques in 'Anglo-Saxon' and similar countries, it should be realised that JIT can go against the cultural grain, so people need to be retrained to think and act in a synchronised way.

KEIRETSU

Literally, a 'headless combine', and one of the most important secret weapons of Japanese industry. An economic grouping of many firms organised around trading companies and/or banks. These groups originated from the Zaibatsu, the large and in many cases centuries-old groups of industrial and financial holding companies. Keiretsu are their descendants, and involve intricate cross-holdings of shares, where a bank will hold shares in all commercial companies, and the latter will own shares in each other. Examples include Dai Ichi Kangyo, Fuyo, Mitsui, Mitsubishi, Sanwa and the Sumitomo group.

Keiretsu are organised on the basis of common loyalty, reciprocity and complementarity. They collaborate to help members maximise their market shares, particularly in the case of 'front line' companies competing on a global scale. They help procure cheap raw materials, share technology, raise and enforce quality standards, share market intelligence, and provide mutual financial support. They can pool resources to help the front line company win – Chrysler competes not with Mazda, but with the combined might of the Sumitomo group, which is willing to forego short term profit for market share gain. Technology sharing is perhaps the most important single benefit.

Not all Japanese firms belong to keiretsu: Canon, Sony and Toyota do not, for example. Even in these cases, however, the mentality of the keiretsu is evident – they collaborate with partners inside and outside Japan to develop new technologies and improve quality standards.

KEY FACTORS FOR SUCCESS (KFS)

The reasons why some firms are more successful than others in particular products or industries. Should be based on an in-depth understanding of why consumers buy the products concerned, as a spur to resegmentation and/or innovation. See SEGMENTATION.

KNOWLEDGE MANAGEMENT STRUCTURE (KMS)

Concept put forward by Tom PETERS as a development of the LEARNING ORGANISATION. The 'new' firm must destroy bureaucracy but needs to nurture knowledge and skill, building expertise in ways that enhance the power of market-scale units, and that encourage those units to contribute knowledge for the benefit of the firm as a whole. This is a matter of shared values, feeling part of a family, and big travel budgets! McKinsey and Goldman Sachs are examples of firms operating KMSs, but the concept is applicable to all corporations, not just professional service firms.

LEADING INDICATOR

Early signal that something is about to happen. Noah's dove was a leading indicator that the flood was over. Market share gains can be a leading indicator of higher profits, even if these are currently depressed by the investments to gain market share.

LEAKAGES

Customers or customer segments that leak away from particular suppliers because the right product or service is not being provided; loss of revenue as a result. Very often a firm tries to find new customers without applying the same energy to the even more important task of retaining existing customers. See CUSTOMER RETENTION.

LEAN ENTERPRISE

Catch-phrase describing re-engineered companies that have five attributes:

1 They embrace a cluster of cross-functional processes.

2 They include close relationships with suppliers, distributors and customers to enhance value continually – the 'extended enterprise'.

3 They have a core of defined expertise.

4 Functional areas such as design, engineering, marketing, procurement, personnel and accounting should still exist, but be schools of learning and skill-bases that different teams in the firm can draw on.

5 Careers should alternate between membership of multi-functional teams and time spent building up skill within particular functions or departments. Honda has used this alternating approach successfully both in Japan and the US.

LEARNING ORGANISATION

Term originated by Chris Argyris to highlight the importance of collective learning within the corporation: it learns as an entity, a whole, over and above the individual learning of executives. As Arie De Geus says: 'Institutional learning is the process whereby management teams change their shared mental models of their company, their markets, and their competitors.' See also KNOWLEDGE MANAGEMENT STRUCTURE in this section, and the entries on ARGYRIS, DE GEUS, QUINN and SENGE in Part Three.

LEVERAGE

Means many things, including financial gearing, and the way in which influence is effectively exerted to produce a pronounced result. The sense in which it is most interesting to us, however, is as the third of the Ashridge Strategic Management Centre's five generic strategies for the Centre to add value. In this sense it means leveraging corporate assets or skills – such as brands, licences, patents, know-how, or relationships with collaborators or regulators – across a number of businesses. Virgin's use of its brand is a good example.

LINK

The fourth of the five strategies for the Centre to add value in the Ashridge model. 'Link' implies the effective use of cross-business synergies, where the Centre acts as a catalyst. For link propositions to be real rather than well-intentioned but value-subtracting mirages, there must be a good reason why the operating businesses are blocked from realising the synergies on their own. Examples of 'link' propositions include Unilever's sharing of consumer marketing expertise; banking and insurance where channels of distribution and access to customers is key; and industries where buying power is critical.

LOGICAL INCREMENTALISM

The process by which the leaders of a corporation evolve strategy in a loose way, allowing internal decisions and external events to flow together, so that the corporation learns and political support is built inside the company for the emergent strategy. See QUINN in Part Three.

LOYALTY

The term used by Fred REICHHELD to describe how to create competitive advantage and lasting value for a company through increasing the loyalty of customers and employees. 'Loyalty' means keeping existing valuable customers and employees for a very long time. Key customers and employees cost a lot to recruit and 'train' and so their defection is very costly, forcing the firm to constantly churn its pool of people. Successful firms such as Toyota, John Deere, MBNA, State Farm insurance, the Leo Burnett advertising agency, and the Pick 'n Pay supermarket chain in South Africa use the principles of loyalty to increase customer and employee retention and hence attain above-average profits. See REICHHELD and CUSTOMER RETENTION.

MAKE OR BUY DECISION

1 The decision on whether to make components or any other part of the product or service in-house, or whether to use outside suppliers (the latter being called outsourcing). 'Make or buy' has long been a topic of debate, but it is becoming increasingly important. It can now determine relative profitability in an industry, as in computers.
2 Igor ANSOFF used 'make or buy' to mean organic expansion versus expansion by acquisition.

Charles Coates, an expert on manufacturing strategy, believes that a key condition of competitive advantage is that firms focus only on those activities that are critical to their proposition and where they have distinctive COMPETENCIES, and outsource all other components and activities. In practice this means a great deal more outsourcing than most firms currently use. The reason outsourcing is so valuable is that the COSTS OF

COMPLEXITY are crippling for a firm engaged in many activities. In some cases this complexity is not avoidable, but in most it is – via outsourcing.

Coates says that make/buy policy should follow three rules:

1 Divide all components into 'critical' and 'non-critical'. Critical components are those that are key to the firm's competitive advantage, where it can undertake them to a quality standard and cost that is second to none. 'Critical components are those upon which delivery of the key attributes of the firm's proposition depend. They may include components which incur a high proportion of total cost, those that require specialised skills, high quality levels or quick response that outside suppliers could not match, or those that have proprietary technology that the firm must protect.' All critical components must be made in-house. It does not follow, however, that all non-critical components should be outsourced: a further rule is required.
2 Outsource all non-critical components where suppliers have an advantage through greater focus and lower cost.
3 For non-critical components where suppliers do not have an advantage, make them but manage the production of critical and non-critical components separately, and be ready to switch to outsourcing the latter if a low cost specialist emerges.

In the computer industry, make/buy decisions are now the most important in determining success. Coates showed that in 1991 there was a clear correlation between higher profits and higher outsourcing (Illustration 4.25).

Major established suppliers such as IBM make many of their parts, including disk drives and processors. Recent entrants such as Dell assemble products in leased factories and outsource all their parts. IBM's investment went into production, Dell's into an effective purchasing network and into sales and service training, focusing particularly on the quality and productivity of its telesales people.

MANAGERIALISM, THE MANAGEMENT THEORY OF THE FIRM, THE MANAGERIAL HERESY

Very important view that given absentee landlords in the form of institutional investors, power in corporations falls to the senior managers, who may advance their own interests rather than those of the owners.

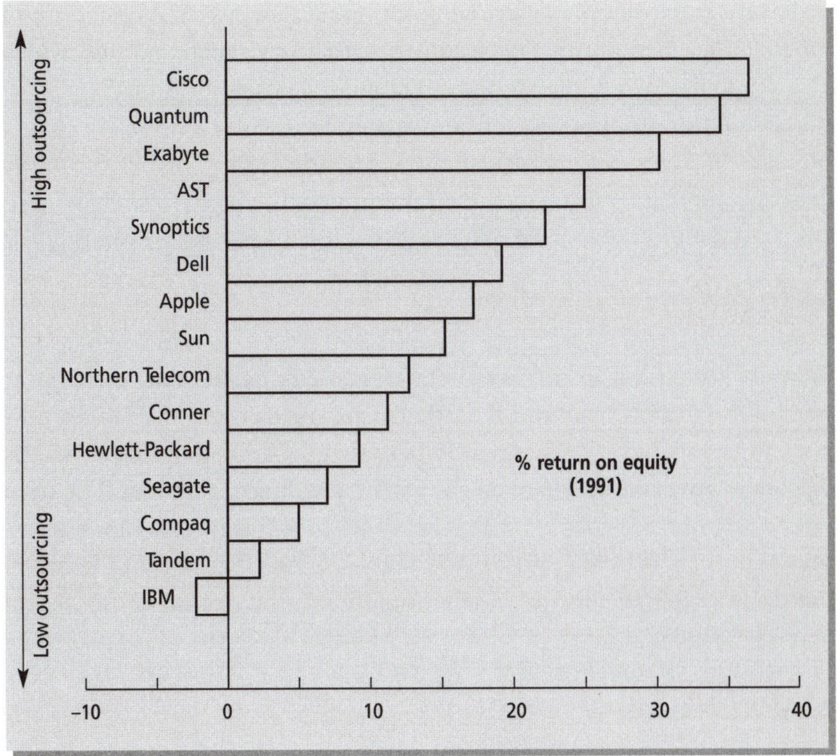

ILLUSTRATION 4.25 ◆ Profitability in the computer industry (1991)

Evidence that the managerial theory has a strong element of truth can be seen in any or all of the following: valuing turnover growth even without profit growth; reluctance to sell non-core companies or demerge, leaving a smaller company; reluctance to outsource to the proper extent; a preference for acquisition rather than disposal, or than being acquired; large perquisites for executives, so that you would need a massive income to have an equivalent lifestyle outside the firm and paying tax; executive jets, chartered planes, or, if times are hard and you have to slum it by flying on a commercial airline, first class travel, which almost nobody could afford if required to pay for oneself; retreats in expensive hotels; hospitality trips (at which the British excel) to Ascot, Wimbledon, Henley, Cheltenham, Glyndebourne, Covent Garden, and all the other delights of the season; paying top executives a very high multiple of average employee or lowest employee pay; increasing top executive pay above the rate of inflation, or when profits fall; granting oneself large share options, which give a free ride when the stock market goes up, regardless of the performance of the company itself; and generally ensuring that one has a pleasant lifestyle and interesting work, regardless of what the corporate priorities are. None of these activities advances the interest of shareholders, or of the firm as a whole. Who says that the managerial heresy is dead?

MARKET CHALLENGER

STRONG FOLLOWER in market share terms: companies that are not far behind the market leader in a particular product or service. The term is not wholly satisfactory because it implies that the second or third player is gaining relative market share on the leader and challenging him. The term strong follower does not carry this implication, and is reserved for a RELATIVE MARKET SHARE of at least 0.7×, that is, at least 70 per cent the size of the leader. Neither term is widely used, hence the neglect of DOGS that may have potential.

MARKETISING

The process of turning cost centres into profit centres, making them respond to an internal or external market.

MAVERICK

An unconventional competitor, often a newcomer to the market, who does not respect the rules of the game, but writes his own rules. Excellent examples are Apple (revolutionising the computer business by developing very powerful PCs) and IKEA (the Swedish furniture retailer that made this a business susceptible to international scale and a new division of labour between customer and supplier: see DELIVERY SYSTEM for more on IKEA). It is very difficult for established competitors to cope with mavericks: all the familiar levers for dealing with competitors do no good. When considering market entry, a good question would be: is there scope for being a maverick here? If not, enter another market, unless there is very high sharing of cost or know-how in the new market.

M-FORM ORGANISATION

Originally used by Oliver Williamson in *Markets and Hierarchies* (1975) to mean a multidivisional enterprise. More recently a book by Bill Ouchi called *The M-form Society* described Japanese corporations as forming multidivisional companies around a common central core of technology. M-form companies include Fujitsu, Honda, Hitachi, Matsushita, Mitsubishi, Nippon Electric, Toshiba, Sharp and Sony. For example, Matsushita has a common technological 'learning core' that feeds into six different divisions (consumer electronics, home appliances, lighting equipment, system/media products, business machines and electronic components).

There are examples of M-forms in the West, including IBM, ICI, Apple, DEC and Philips, but in general there is a greater proportion of technology located in the divisions than in the Japanese M-form, and technological know-how tends to ooze around the divisions rather less luxuriantly. The West also has far more pure conglomerates, where there is common ownership but few or no operating links between the divisions or companies. The M-form is clearly superior at utilising technology.

MISSION

What a company is for; why it exists; its role in the world. This is an enormously important issue. A large number of US and UK companies have formal mission statements, but a big distinction must be made between such documents and the company having a real mission, or 'sense of mission'. Most companies that have mission statements do not have a sense of mission: the document is propaganda, or at best, well intended 'motherhood', but not what most people in the organisation believe. Yet some firms such as Marks & Spencer that clearly have a sense of mission do not have mission statements.

A sense of mission is essential if employees are to believe in their company. They have to think that the company is there to achieve something.

The concept of mission and 'sense of mission' covers all aspects of the firm's sense of direction and the way in which its members behave: there must be a consistent pattern that runs through all aspects of the firm's personality. The most useful way of thinking about this is the Ashridge Mission Model, which describes four parameters of mission: purpose, values, strategy and behaviour standards, as shown in Illustration 4.26.

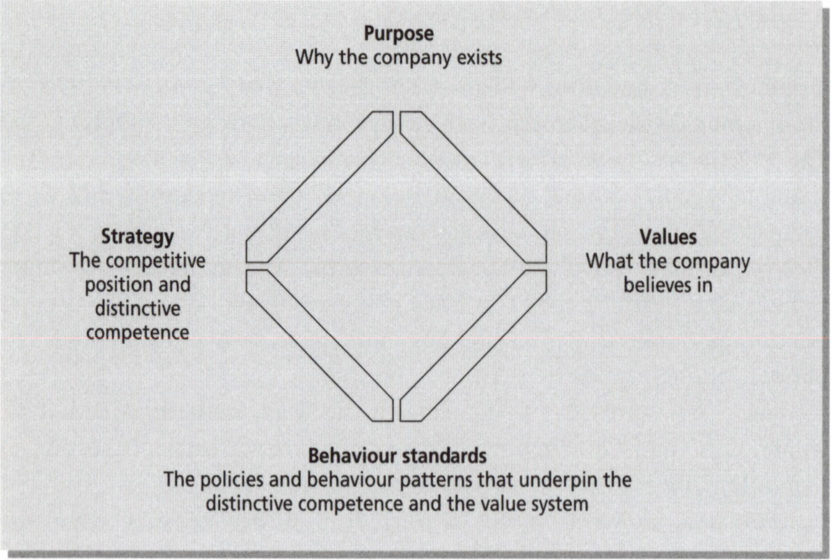

ILLUSTRATION 4.26 ◆ The Ashridge Mission Model

The model can be illustrated by two examples of very different companies and mission. First Hanson, which is highly unusual in actually believing in shareholder value, rather than just making motherhood statements about it (Illustration 4.27).

The second example is Hewlett-Packard, a decentralised corporation with very different values to Hanson, but a similarly consistent sense of mission (Illustration 4.28).

Why does it matter that employees believe in their company? Well, most would rather work for a company they can believe in. Such a company will attract the best recruits, and keep them. It will get the most out of its people, both as individuals and in teams. It will be respected by customers and investors. It will learn, renew itself, and become more powerful, while still having the ethic of service to others. It will gain market share, and have the best long term profitability, and the highest market rating.

All in all, it is quite important. Unfortunately, though most Western firms have mission statements, few have a sense of mission. Although precise data is not available, the best estimates are that 10 per cent of large UK firms, 20 per cent of those in the US, but 50 per cent of Japanese firms have a sense of mission. Clearly there is a great deal of need for TRANSFORMATION.

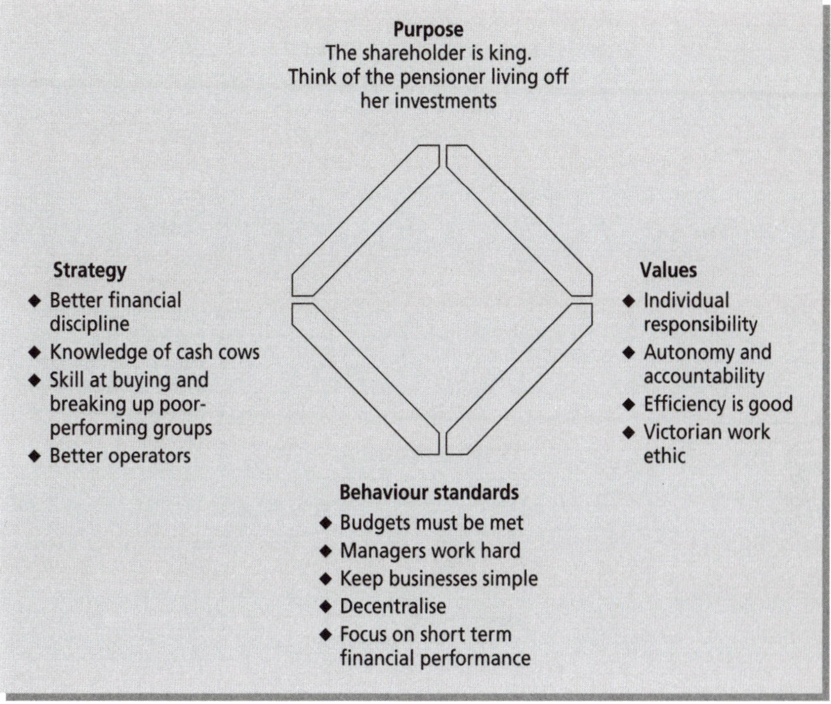

ILLUSTRATION 4.27 ◆ A summary of Hanson's Mission

MOP UP STRATEGY

Consolidating an industry by gaining market share at the expense of smaller competitors and/or buying them up, usually in a so-called declining industry. Almost always a good strategy.

NAVIGATOR, NAVIGATION

A recent idea from the Boston Consulting Group. The navigator is the company in a value chain that controls navigation, which itself is defined as 'the activities shaping how customers search, compare, and decide what to buy'. The navigator positions itself as the 'customer's friend', bringing her more information, wide choice, and the ability to tailor products and services to her particular wants.

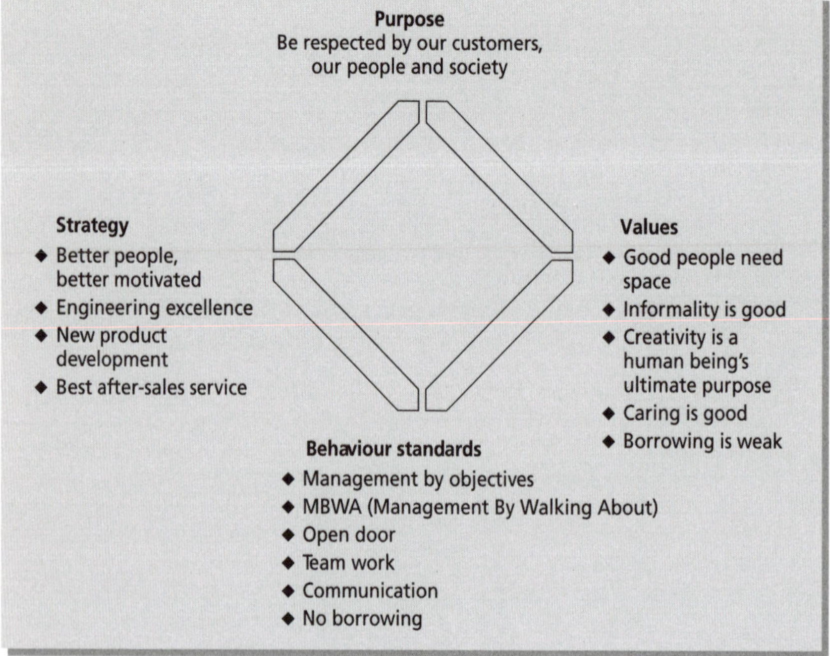

ILLUSTRATION 4.28 ◆ Hewlett-Packard's Mission

Although the word is new, navigators have been around for more than a century. Department stores were once the new navigators of their era; mail order companies had their time too; more recently, 'category killers' with edge-of-town specialist mega-retail outlets, such as Toys 'Я' Us, have been navigators. Increasingly, however, the new frontier of navigation is the Internet. See towards the end of Part Five.

OPPORTUNITY/VULNERABILITY MATRIX

An interesting outgrowth from the BCG MATRIX, although not developed until the late 1970s/early 1980s (mainly by Bain & Company) and refined later that decade by The LEK Partnership, another strategy boutique. BCG had posited that high relative market share businesses (leaders) should be extremely profitable, and the logic of the experience curve certainly suggested that the higher the market share, the higher the profitability (unless the firm was not using its potential advantages or pricing to penetrate the market still further). It followed that it should be possible to construct a 'normative curve' to describe the profitability of the average BUSINESS SEGMENT in a particular industry, or, with a wider band, all industries, according to a normal expectation given the segment's relative market share. This normative band is shown on the matrix in Illustration 4.29.

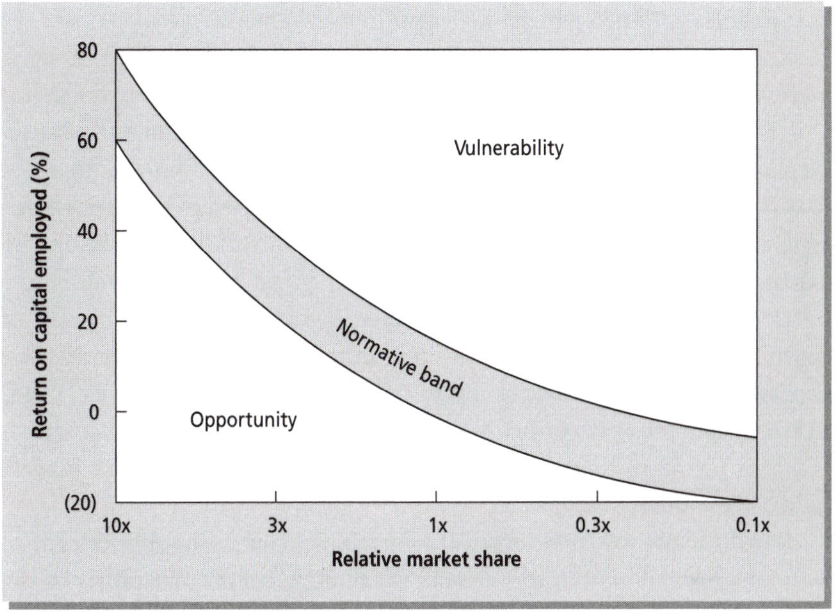

The parallel area between the two curved lines represents the normative curve: depending on the exact data used, perhaps 80 per cent of observations would fall between these broad limits, and it would be unusual (only 20 per cent of business segment positions) for businesses to fall outside the band. (The normative band can be constructed based on actual data of business segment positions and profitability, but only after correct segmentation: in practice such data can be obtained with any degree of confidence only after working within a client organisation, and building up an anonymous database of the relationships.) In fact, empirical data did enable the normative band to be built up in this way. The band used to be shown coloured in yellow, hence the chart became known as a 'bananagram'.

So what? Well, one implication is that high relative market share positions, correctly segmented, are as valuable as BCG said, whatever reservations one has about the experience curve. Managers should therefore strive to be in such businesses and cannot expect to have profitability above the required rate of return of investors unless a majority of their sales are in leaders or strong followers (at least .7× Relative Market Share, that is, at least 70 per cent as the leader in the segment).

Another implication, not really made clearly by BCG, and in some ways obscured by the doctrine of the BCG matrix about DOGS, was that it was useful to improve relative market share in a business segment *whatever the starting position*: useful to take a .3× RMS business and move it to a .6× RMS position, to take a .5× position and take it to 1.0×, to take a 2× position and move it to 4×, and so on. Illustration 4.29 enables one to calculate roughly what equilibrium profitability can be expected from any particular position, so that it is possible to state roughly the benefit of moving any particular segment position in this way and compare it to the expected short term cost of doing so (by extra marketing or service, product development or lower prices). In this way it can be seen (a) whether it is worth trying to raise RMS, and (b) which segments give the biggest bang for the buck.

But the most valuable use of the matrix lies not in the 80 per cent of positions that fall within the banana (normative curve), but rather in the 20 per cent that fall outside. Two examples of possible such positions are given in Illustration 4.30.

Business A is earning (say) 45 per cent Return on Capital Employed, a good return, but is in a weak Relative Market Share position (say .5×, or only half the size of the segment leader). The theory and empirical data from the matrix suggest that the combination of these two positions is at best anomalous, and probably unsustainable. Business A is therefore in the 'VULNERABILITY' part of the matrix. The expectation must be that in the medium term, either the business must improve its Relative Market Share position to sustain its profitability (the dotted arrow moving left), or that it will decline in profitability (to about breakeven). Why should this happen? Well, the banana indicates that the market leader in this business may well be earning 40 per cent or even more ROCE in the segment (the beauty of the method is that this can be investigated empirically). What may be happening is that the leader is holding a price umbrella over the

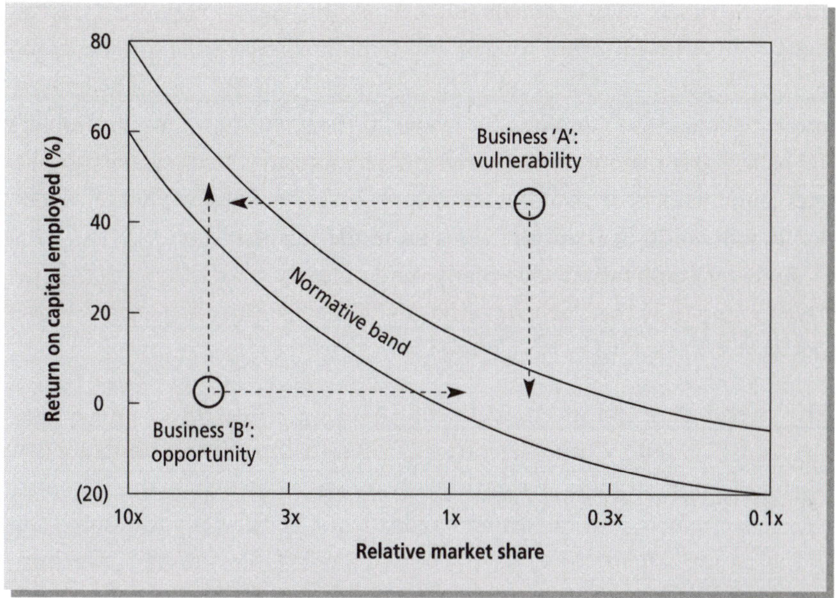

ILLUSTRATION 4.30 ◆ Opportunity/Vulnerability matrix – illustrative positions of business outside the banana

market: that is, is pricing unsustainably high, so that even the competitors with weak market share are protected from normal competitive rainfall. What happens if the market leader suddenly cuts prices by 20 per cent? He will still earn a good return, but the weaker competitors will not. (The leader may not cut prices, but instead provide extra product benefits or service or other features, but the effect would still be a margin cut.) It is as well to know that business A is vulnerable. If relative market share cannot be improved, it is sensible to sell it before the profitability declines.

Now let's look at Business B. This is a business in a strong relative market share position: the leader in its segment, four times larger than its nearest rival. It is earning 2 per cent ROCE. This is a wonderful business to find. The theory and practical data suggest that such a business should be making 50 per cent ROCE, not 2 per cent. Nine times out of ten when such businesses are found, it is possible to make them *very* much more profitable, usually by radical cost reduction (often involving BPR), but sometimes through radical improvement of the service and product offering to the customer at low extra cost to the supplier, but enabling a large price hike to be made. Managements of particular businesses very often become complacent with historical returns and think it is impossible to raise profits in a step function to three, four or five times their current level. The bananagram challenges that thinking for leadership segment positions, and usually the bananagram is proved right. After all, high relative market share implies huge potential advantages; but these must be earned and exploited, as they do not automatically disgorge huge profits. OUTSOURCING see CONTRACTING OUT and MAKE OR BUY DECISION.

PARENTING ADVANTAGE

The useful concept invented by the Ashridge Strategic Management Centre which is to Corporate Strategy what 'competitive advantage' is to Business Unit Strategy. Parenting advantage exists when the parent or Centre is the best possible owner of a business, because it adds more value to the business than any other potential parent. Unless there is parenting advantage for any business under the parent's control, the business should be divested.

PIMS (PROFIT IMPACT OF MARKET STRATEGY)

A co-operative database originating from research by GE in the US that collects data from member firms about market share, profitability and a variety of other variables (such as R&D spend) that might be expected to influence profits. The data are confidential but aggregate results are fed back to members so that they can see how to raise profits. Some of the research has been published and has demonstrated beyond reasonable doubt that high market share correlates with high profits, though there are significant industry variations. Two problems with the approach are that it accepts the firm's own segment definitions, which may not correctly describe business segmentation or be sufficiently disaggregated; and it pays insufficient attention to relative market share. See RMS and OPPORTUNITY/VULNERABILITY MATRIX.

PORTER'S FIVE COMPETITIVE FORCES

Michael Porter was an innovator in structural analysis of markets, which previously, even with BCG, tended to focus largely on direct competition in the industry, without looking systematically at the context in other stages of the industry VALUE CHAIN. Porter's five forces to analyse are:

1 Threat from potential new entrants.
2 Threat from substitutes using different technology.
3 Bargaining power of customers.
4 Bargaining power of suppliers.
5 Competition among existing suppliers.

The interactions between the five forces are shown in Illustration 4.31.

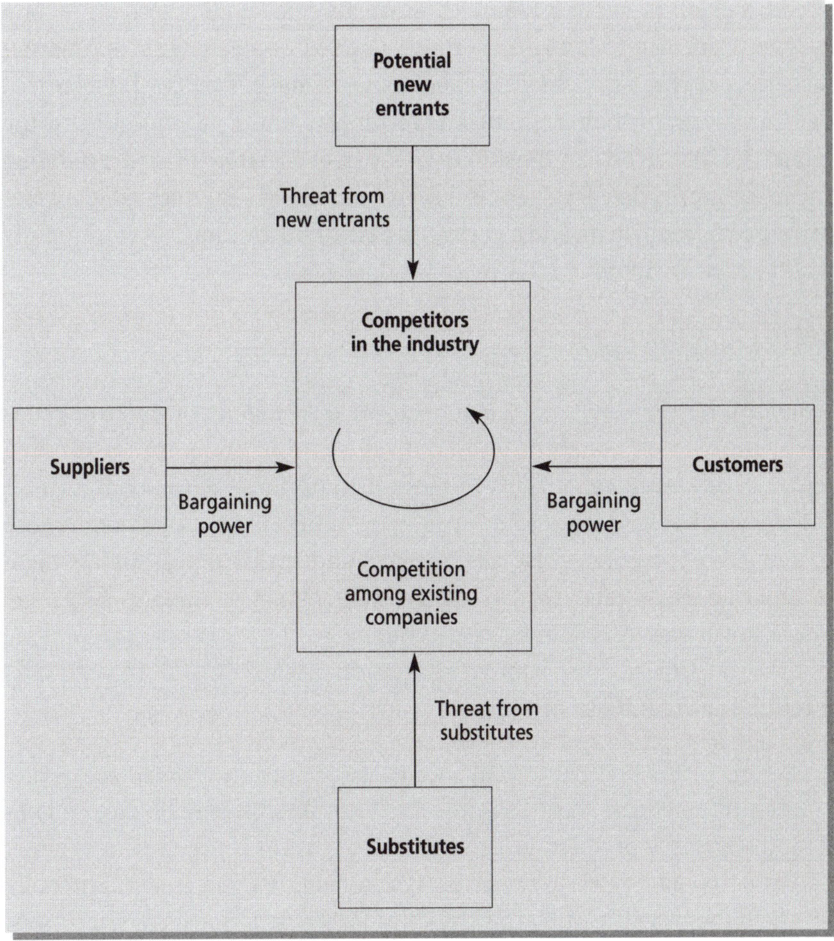

ILLUSTRATION 4.31 ◆ Porter's Five Competitive Forces

From this Porter builds a useful model of industry attractiveness and how this might change over time, both because of objective economic changes and also because of the ambitions of the players themselves.

POSITIONING

Finding a marketing position for a product or a company that differentiates it from competitors and occupies a 'slot in the brain'. This may be entirely emotional and subjective rather than defined by product or verifiable criteria. For example, British Airways was repositioned as 'the world's favourite airline' to let travellers know that the cabin crew no longer bit their heads off or ignored them. An interesting positioning technique for a new entrant or a follower is to draw a veiled contrast with the market leader, as in Avis's successful slogan 'We're Number Two. We Try Harder', or 'Carlsberg, probably the best lager in the world', as opposed to the biggest or the strongest. Positioning is partly a matter of understanding the most appropriate battleground for a product, but it is also a highly creative process of identifying vacant ground and finding an emotionally warm pitch. Positioning is far more art than science.

PRICE UMBRELLA

Colourful term meaning a high general price level in an industry or product, held over all competitors to stop the rain of competition spoiling anyone's day. Although it leads to short term profits, it is usually a mistake for the market leader to hold out a price umbrella, as it prevents more marginal competitors exiting the business and makes it possible for them to build up experience and lower their costs, thus becoming more viable. See OPPORTUNITY/VULNERABILITY MATRIX.

PRICING STRATEGY

1 Setting prices in order to gain a long term competitive advantage, rather than to maximise short term profits. There are three main rules: (1) in introducing a product, price at or below cost in order to gain volume, cut costs, and deter competitors; (2) in fighting competition, especially when the market is still growing, consider sudden, startlingly short price

cuts, so that the price is immediately perceived as low by the consumer, and as too low to be matched by competitors; and (3) ensure that the true costs of all products are known, including all overhead costs, and that the more complex, special products are not under-priced and the standard, high-volume products under-priced. See EXPERIENCE CURVE, AVERAGE COSTING, AVERAGE PRICING and BCG MATRIX.

2 More broadly, the major decisions made on pricing.

PRODUCT LINE PROFITABILITY

Much neglected, highly useful analysis of how much money a firm makes (fully costed) on each of its products or services. Usually throws up results that surprise managers, often showing that a majority of products lose money on a fully costed basis, and 100 per cent or more than 100 per cent of the profits are made by a small proportion of exceptional money spinners. No-one has yet standardised a universally applicable way of conducting this analysis. Traditional accounting systems make it very difficult, and accurate product line profitability is usually supplied by outside consultants.

QUESTION MARK

A firm's position in a business segment where the market is growing fast (expected future volume growth of 10 per cent or more per annum) but the firm is a follower, that is, has a RELATIVE MARKET SHARE of less than 1.0×. One of the four positions on the BCG MATRIX. Unlike two of the others, very well named: there is a real question about such businesses that must be faced up to. Should the corporation invest a lot of cash and management talent to try to drive that business to a leading position, hence becoming a STAR (high market growth, high relative market share) and eventually a much bigger and highly positive CASH COW? Or should the business be sold for a high price earnings ratio, because people pay highly for 'growth' businesses without usually thinking too hard about the relative market share position? There is another option, which is usually taken, and usually wrong: putting *some* cash into the business but not enough to drive it to a leading position. The BCG theory and observation both lead to the conclusion that this will tend to give a poor return on the cash invested: the business will eventually become a DOG, and though it may throw off rather more cash in this state than the original BCG theory, it is unlikely to show a very good return (IRR) on the cash invested.

So is it to be investment to drive to leadership, or a quick and lucrative sale? It depends, of course, on the sums of cash involved, but particularly on whether you think leadership is attainable at acceptable cost. And then it depends on the reaction of the current leader, who has the STAR position: he ought to defend it to the death, but may not. Getting into this kind of battle is unpredictable and like playing poker: once started, you have to keep upping the ante to persuade your opponent that you will win in the end; and if you are to cut your losses at any stage, you had better do it early. What is the size of your pot of cash compared to his? The strength of your hand versus his is also very important. Do you have the knack of satisfying customers better, or higher quality, or better people or better technology, or just greater will power and commitment, or preferably all of the above?

STAR positions are enormously valuable once obtained and defended. But most attempts to back question marks fail to turn them into stars. Unless you are determined to win and have a greater than evens chance, sale is usually the option that will better enhance shareholder wealth. As a shareholder you should hope that the latter consideration weighs more heavily with the management than wanting to stay in a glamorous growth business.

RARE GAMES

Rarely, a market or ECOSYSTEM can be so attractive, for a time, that even mediocre competitors make high returns – and maybe all competitors do so. Andrew CAMPBELL and Robert Park call these 'rare games'. They happen when a new market opens up and supply can't keep up with demand. Sometimes rare games occur because competitors – either traditional or new – price so high that new entrants can come in and reap good returns. In the eyeglass market at the time of writing, for example, traditional opticians (optometrists) price very high, both to make high profits and to cover the cost of eye-testing. Direct suppliers of glasses, using the phone and Internet, can price much lower (when no eye test is necessary), offer customers great apparent value, and yet make very high profits because they can source the products at very low cost. There are low barriers to entry in this market, and yet currently all direct competitors are growing fast and very profitable.

The normal rules of strategy are suspended for rare games – anyone can enter such an easy environment without special skills or assets and make good money. But only for a time. Within a few years, only competitors with some advantage will still be very profitable. The best sources of competitive advantage in rare games are early entry, creating a new brand that becomes synonymous with the new ecosystem, and becoming the largest, so that there are economies of scale in marketing.

The characteristics of 'rare games' are:

- High market growth
- Every player has high return on capital
- Customer value high relative to producers' cost
- Business model allows high margins
- Market can be entered without high cash exposure
- Risks easy to control and mainly under control of each player
- No clear current leader – market leadership available.

RCP (RELATIVE COST POSITION)

The cost position of a firm in a product relative to that of a competitor. For example, if it costs Heinz 20¢ to manufacture a can of beans, and it costs Crosse & Blackwell 22¢ for the same can, Heinz has an RCP advantage of about 10 per cent, or an RCP of 91 (C&B = 100). Classical economics assumes that firms in an industry will come to have the same cost position, but in the real world this is almost never true. RCP can be quite difficult to establish (usually requiring the use of specialist consultants) but it is often not what managers imagined, and the differences between competitors usually emerge as much greater than previously thought. It is necessary to look at RCP at each stage of the VALUE CHAIN: for example, X may have a 30 per cent cost advantage in production but have an inefficient salesforce, and be at a 10 per cent cost disadvantage in selling. Relative cost advantage is often, but by no means always, related to scale or experience advantages (expressed in Relative Market Share).

RCP analysis is not invalidated by differences in quality, or the fact that one supplier may have a better brand. The cost position can be looked at with the price realisation of each supplier indexed at 100, so that if Heinz receives 24¢ for its can of beans and C&B only 20¢, Heinz's total and sub-divided costs can be looked at relative to the 24¢, and C&B's

relative to the 20¢ that it receives. On this basis, Heinz would have a total cost of 83 (10/12) and C&B a total cost of 110 (11/10): Heinz would be making a profit margin of 17 per cent but C&B would be losing 10 per cent. The real cost difference between the two firms (adjusted for price realisation) would be 27 per cent (110 minus 83). Heinz might be spending more on marketing, to help capture the extra price realisation, but the analysis would show this as well.

RCP analysis is expensive and worth doing only when there is a lot of turnover in the products being compared and there is a good chance that it will reveal things that can be acted upon, or help to set a competitive strategy in a battle worth winning. RCP analysis can lead to cost savings through imitation – for example, a competitor may miss out a process step altogether that the firm can also eliminate – or lead to a dramatic redesign of production to take out perhaps 30 per cent of cost.

RCP is little practised but where it has been used it has generally been extremely insightful and effective, saving tens of millions of pounds and giving a return of about 20–50 times the amount paid for the analysis (which will be several hundred thousand pounds). RCP cannot be conducted vis-à-vis most Japanese competitors because it is impossible to discover their real costs, partly because of deliberate obfuscation, and partly because of the KEIRETSU system. See also RPP (Relative Price Position) and RMS.

RCR (RELATIVE CUSTOMER RETENTION)

How well a firm retains its customers relative to its competitors. A key influence on relative profitability. See CUSTOMER RETENTION.

RECOMPETE

To change the basis of competition in an industry, to change the rules of the game, to find a new and more effective way of competing, to invent a different way of doing business that gives a new competitor a place in the sun and superior profitability.

One early example of recompeting was Georg Siemens's invention in 1870 of the first universal bank (Deutsche Bank) with a mission to unite and industrialise Germany. In the same decade, Mitsubishi was established as the first important Japanese multinational, on the principle we now know as the M-FORM ORGANISATION. Another early example was Henry Ford's invention, at the start of the twentieth century, of the mass-produced automobile.

After the first world war, Marks & Spencer changed the nature of clothes retailing by (1) intervening to design and commission clothes rather than just buy them, and (2) creating a mass-market that spanned previously inviolate class barriers. In the early 1950s, IBM replaced Univac as leader of the emergent computer industry by changing the rules of the game, manufacturing (rather than hand-crafting) multi-purpose machines. In the past 20 years, Apple has recompeted by basing itself purely on Personal Computers, developing a symbiotic relationship with emergent software suppliers such as Lotus and Microsoft.

Other recent examples include Direct Line insurance, First Direct banking (and other telephone- and computer-based banks without a branch network), Kwik-fit and Midas car service centres, and IKEA (in furniture retailing).

See section 10 of Part One.

RIGHT FIRST TIME

The idea that goods should not need to be inspected for quality because the objective should be to build quality in and ensure that all product is of high quality the first (and only) time round.

RMS (RELATIVE MARKET SHARE)

The share of a firm in a BUSINESS SEGMENT divided by the share of the firm's largest competitor. Much more important than market share as an absolute number. For example, if Sony's nearest competitor in making Walkman-type products is one tenth the size, Sony will have an RMS of 10 times (written as 10×, or 10.0×, or sometimes simply 10). The competitor, on the other hand, will have an RMS that is the reciprocal of this: it will have an RMS of 0.1×. One more example will suffice: if Coca-Cola in one national market has a market share of 60 per cent, and Pepsi-Cola 30 per cent, then Coke has an RMS of 2×, and Pepsi 0.5×.

Relative market share should correlate with profitability. If it does not, one (or more) of five things is happening. Either:

1 The business segment has been defined incorrectly.

2 The smaller competitor is much cleverer than the bigger. The leader is not using his potential advantage properly, and/or the follower has found a nifty way to lower costs or raise prices that has overcome the advantages of scale and experience.

3 The leader is deliberately forfeiting profit by expense reinvestment that will compound his advantage in the future, and lead to much higher profits.

4 There is over-capacity in the industry so that the key concern is capacity utilisation, and the bigger competitors may simply have too much of the excess.

5 It is a business not susceptible to normal scale, status and experience effects.

Let us take each of these in turn. (1) *Incorrect business definition*: more often than not, this is the reason. In most cases, the segment will not have been defined in a sufficiently disaggregated way. (2) *A clever follower*: this does happen, and is usually manifest in a refusal to play by the usual rules of the game. See MAVERICK and DELIVERY SYSTEM. (3) *Long term compounding strategy by the leader*: may be true if it is Japanese or Korean, almost certainly not otherwise. (4) *Excess capacity*: yes, sometimes. (5) *Industry and business not susceptible to scale, experience or status*: very rare. Even service businesses generally are skewed in favour of the bigger players, who have greater advantages in terms of branding, reputation, lower marketing and selling costs, and greater expertise and ability to attract the best recruits.

One of the most useful charts to draw for any business, if the data can be collected, is shown in Illustration 4.32, which looks at the profitability (in terms of ROS or ROCE) of different competitors in a business segment. It shows a typical pattern, but the beauty of the method is that empirical data can be displayed to see whether and how far the expected pattern applies. If there is deviance from the normal pattern, the reasons given in (1) to (5) above can be systematically investigated.

The chart stops at 2× (two times) RMS only because in this case the leader was here. In other examples the relationship has been observed to continue working over whatever range of RMS applies. Businesses with a 10× RMS really do make very high ROCE – normally in the 60–90 per cent range.

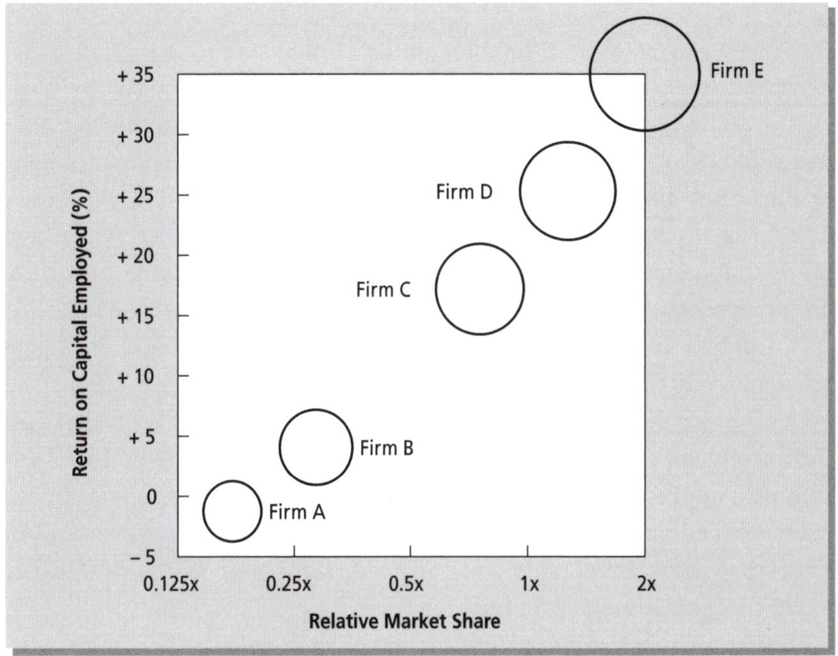

ILLUSTRATION 4.32 ◆ Typical pattern of profitability by RMS

Observation of this relationship led to the development of a very useful tool – the OPPORTUNITY/VULNERABILITY MATRIX. See this entry for the action implications of RMS and profit relationships. See also RCP.

RPP (RELATIVE PRICE POSITION)

A complement to RCP (Relative Cost Position). RPP looks at the price realisation for two or more competitors in the same product or service. If two identical packets of chips are sold in the same outlet, one under the KP brand and one under a retailer's private label, and the former is 40¢ and the latter 36¢, the KP RPP is 40/36 = 111 and the RPP of the retailer's brand is 36/40 = 90. RPP shows how far there is a brand, quality or distribution advantage. See also RCP.

SAPLINGS

Term invented by Andrew CAMPBELL and Robert Park to describe businesses within a company that are neglected but have strong management and could be a jumping-off point for growth. Saplings are operating units in a firm that already exist and are often unloved or ignored. Their attraction for canny strategists is that the firm does not need to learn anything more about saplings and they have very able managers, who may have insight into how to grow the activity profitably.

Campbell and Park quote the example of Hewlett-Packard's largely accidental and unplanned move into computers. In the 1960s HP started making processors for its instruments business to avoid dependence on third-party suppliers. In the 1970s the unit began to sell computers for technical applications. For many years the unit's excellent management team lobbied to enter the market for commercial applications, and in 1980 they were grudgingly allowed to do so. Today HP is one of the world's biggest computer makers.

People are more important than markets, and may even be more important than conventional strategic principles. Back your strongest managers.

SBU (STRATEGIC BUSINESS UNIT)

A profit centre within a firm that is organised as an autonomous unit and that corresponds roughly to one particular market. SBUs originated in the 1970s and have proved popular since then. The story of how they came about is interesting. SBUs began in 1970 when Fred Borch, head of the American GE, decided to decentralise, abolish or curtail staff functions, and reorganise on the basis of stand-alone SBUs. GE set up the following criteria required for a group to be a pukka SBU:

- An SBU must have an external, rather than an internal, market: must have a set of external customers.
- It should have a clear set of external competitors it is trying to beat.
- It should have control over its own destiny – decide what products to offer, how to obtain supplies, and whether or not to use shared corporate resources such as R&D.
- It must be a profit centre, with performance measured by its profits.

The move to SBUs in GE and in Western countries has on the whole been positive. The drawback with an SBU structure is that it does not encourage full use of the common skill base and technology that a corporation may have, although it does not prevent it either. The SBU structure is not well equipped to deal with the challenge of Japanese companies which not only draw fully on common internal skills derived from and serving a variety of products, but also benefit from each other's skills in an interlocking way. See M-FORM ORGANISATION and KEIRETSU.

S-CURVE

The growth pattern resembling an S: slow to pick up, followed by a period of maximum growth, then a point of inflection leading to gradually slower growth. Study of the 1665 Plague in England led to the conclusion that the spread of disease followed a mathematically predictable path, and the same methodology has been used with some success to predict the rate at which a new product will penetrate into any given population, given the early experience. If, for example, you knew that the penetration of dishwashers into Korea was 1 per cent in the first year, 2 per cent in the second year and 4.5 per cent in the third year, you could calculate a prediction for future years.

The formula to be used to calculate each year's observation is f/1 – f, where:

f = the penetration (expressed as a fraction: e.g. 1 per cent = 0.01), and

1 – f = one minus the penetration fraction (e.g. 1 – 0.01 = 0.99)

f/1 – f = 0.0101 in this case, or for the 2 per cent observation

= 0.02/0.98

= 0.0204.

If the observations are plotted on semi-log paper or using appropriate software and a straight line is drawn through the observations, predictions for future years emerge in the form of the 'answer' above (e.g. 0.0204), which can then be converted by algebra into the percentage prediction. A simple computer program will perform the calculations without the need to resort to plotting on semi-log paper.

The same procedure can be used in modified form where you know that there will be a saturation level at a given point. In dishwashers in Korea, for example, you may know from similar cases that no-one below a certain income level will ever own a dishwasher. Let us assume that this cuts out 40 per cent of the population: the saturation level is therefore 60 per cent. Instead of using 1.0 as the maximum point, therefore, we would use 0.6, the saturation point(s). The calculation would then be f/s – f, and the first observation (at 1 per cent) would become:

$$0.01/.6 - 0.01 = 0.1695.$$

Many people are sceptical of the power of this methodology until they actually use it. It is not, of course, a magic predictor, but it does enable you to calculate what the answer will be if the current momentum persists. It will work out when the growth will slow because there is a diminishing pool of people to be 'converted' to the new product.

SEGMENTATION

Most usefully, the process of analysing customers, costs and competitors in order to decide where and how to wage the competitive battle; or a description of the competitive map according to the contours of the business segments. Sadly, segmentation is often used to describe a more limited (and often misleading) exercise in dividing up customer groups. See BUSINESS SEGMENT. Proper segmentation takes place only at the level of identifying the business segments: this is at the root of any firm's business strategy. Segmentation in this most useful sense is what is discussed below.

It is crucial for any firm to know which segments it is operating in, to know its relative market share in those segments, and to focus on those segments where it has or can build a leadership position. A segment is a competitive system, or arena, where it is possible to build barriers against other firms, by having lower costs or customer-satisfying differentiation (which will be expressed in higher prices, and/or in higher customer volume which itself will lead to lower costs). A segment can be a particular product, or a particular customer group being sold a standard product, or a particular customer group being sold a special product or provided with a special service, or a particular distribution channel or region, or any combination of the above. What matters is that the following conditions for a genuine segment are *all* satisfied:

1 The segment must be capable of clear distinction, so that there is no doubt which customers and products fall inside and outside the segment.

2 The segment must have a clear and limited set of competitors that serve it.

3 It must be possible to organise supply of a product or service to the segment in a way that represents some specialisation, and is differentiated from supply to another or other segments.

4 The segment must have purchase criteria that are different in important ways from other segments.

5 The segment must be one where competitors specialise, and where there is a characteristic market share ranking that can be described.

6 The segment must be capable of giving at least one competitor a profitability advantage, either by having lower costs, or higher prices, than other competitors, or both.

7 It must be possible to build barriers around the segment to deter new entrants.

Segmentation may change over time. To take the example of the motor car, Henry Ford created his own segment around the black Model T Ford: the mass produced, standard automobile. Initially, he had 100 per cent of this segment, and it satisfied all of the rules above. Then it became possible to provide other colours at relatively low cost, and General Motors changed the mass automobile market to include any colour, standard car: the 'black car' segment ceased to exist and became part of a wider competitive arena. Subsequently new segments emerged, based on sports/high performance criteria, and later on 'compact' low fuel consumption cars.

Geography is a fascinating and changing dimension of segmentation. Most products and services start out by having a very limited geographical reach: one region or one country. The UK crisp (what Americans call potato chips) market is an interesting example. At one time the market was dominated by Smiths, then by Golden Wonder (which led the way in introducing a range of flavours), both national competitors. Then, gradually, a new regional competitor, Walkers, emerged, based on superior quality. Initially Walkers' segment boundaries were restricted around the Midlands where the company was based. Within these regions the national segmentation did not rule: Walkers was the number one supplier by a long way, although nationally very small. Gradually, with greater production and improved distribution, Walkers became a national competitor, and for a time market leader, again causing the segmentation to revert to a national level.

An increasing number of markets are global: the battle between Pepsi and Coke, for instance, is fought beyond the boundaries of individual countries. Nevertheless, segment RELATIVE MARKET SHARE positions often vary significantly in different countries: if Pepsi outsells Coke in one national market, against the global trend, that national market is today a separate segment. If, on the other hand, relative market shares around the world converge, the whole world can become one segment for cola drinks. Economics comes into this as well. To take one far-fetched example, assume that Coke came to have a two to one advantage over Pepsi everywhere in the world except New Zealand, where Pepsi was by far the leader. Then it would be correct to speak of New Zealand as a separate segment, but the rest of the world would be one segment and the marketing scale advantage enjoyed by Coke everywhere else would make New Zealand a barely tenable separate segment for Pepsi. At some point, the most interesting segmentation would have become global, even if national segment enclaves temporarily continued to exist.

Similarly, segments can be carved out or relinquished within a product range. At one time, British motorcycles were the market leaders throughout the world whatever type or power of bike was being considered – motorcycles were one global segment. Then the Japanese began to develop bikes, based around the low powered vehicles for which there was greatest domestic demand. First this low c.c. market became a separate segment in Japan because the market leaders (Honda and Yamaha) were different from the leaders in the rest of the world market (and in Japan in mid and high performance bikes). Then the Japanese companies, by trial and error, managed to develop a market for these low c.c. bikes in America, and then throughout the world, so that low c.c. bikes became a separate global segment. Later, using modular designs and high cost sharing, the Japanese suppliers entered mid-size bikes and became the market leaders, thus changing the segmentation around the world by annexing the mid market, so that there were two global segments: the low to mid segment (dominated by the Japanese), and the high performance segment, still then dominated by Norton and BSA. Then, in the early 1970s, the Japanese began to edge their way into the high performance segment, and BMW created a separate high-comfort, high-safety segment, so that the world motorcycle market had two major segments: the 'BMW' segment, and the rest (the majority) of the market, served largely by Japanese competitors.

In diagnosing what segments you are in today – whether the market is one big segment or several small ones – the best way is to set up hypotheses that X market is a separate segment from Y market, and then test according to the following rules. To get the correct answer 95 per cent of the time, ask just two questions:

1 Are there separate competitors, with significant market share, in segment X that do not participate in segment Y? If so, it is a separate segment.

2 Are the relative market share positions in market X different from those in market Y, even if the same competitors compete? If so, it is a separate segment. For example, Heinz and HP compete in both the red sauce (ketchup) and thick brown sauce markets in the UK, but in the first Heinz is miles ahead of HP, and in the latter HP is way ahead – so they are separate segments.

To be absolutely sure, ask these additional questions:

3 Is your firm's profitability different in market X than in market Y? If so, even if it is the same product being supplied to different customers, it may be a separate segment.

4 Are the COST STRUCTURES different in the two markets?

5 Are there technological barriers between the two markets that only some competitors can surmount?

6 Are prices different (for the same product or service) in the different markets?

7 Is it possible to gain an economic advantage by specialising in one of the markets, by gaining lower costs or higher prices in that market?

Because segmentation changes over time, it is interesting to look both at the empirical segmentation today, which is defined particularly by the first two questions above, and also at potential segmentation based on the economics of the business: what is called economic segmentation.

Economic segmentation applies questions (3) to (7) above to ask not just whether the segmentation is distinct today but whether it could be distinct. Economic segmentation can be used as a technique to resegment a market, either by creating a new, smaller segment out of an existing segment (as with the initial Japanese move to create a below-250 c.c. motorcycle segment), or to merge two segments (as with the later annexation of first the mid and then the high performance motorcycle segments) in order to realise ECONOMIES OF SCALE. Economic segmentation asks: could we obtain lower costs or higher prices or both by redefining the segment and changing the rules of the game?

SEGMENT RETREAT

Policy of retiring from a particular market segment, conceding it to competitors, and focusing on other segments. Tends to be a continuous, sad process. One classic example is the UK motorcycle industry in the early 1970s which, faced with the onslaught of Japanese competition, retreated first of all from the small bikes segment, then the mid-bikes segment, so that it was left at the 'high end' of large and super-bikes. The problem was that the Japanese advanced just as the British retreated, and, given the high shared component cost between the segments, Japanese dominance in the lower end product eventually fed dominance in all segments. If pursuing a strategy of segment retreat, it is essential to build solid barriers against the advance, or the retreat will turn into a rout.

SELF-ORGANISING SYSTEMS

A system common in nature and society where the whole is different from the parts and organises itself spontaneously into the whole. Examples are diseases, cities, embryos, brains, storms and corporations. See COMPLEXITY THEORY.

SEVEN Ss, 7S FRAMEWORK

A framework for thinking about a firm's personality; a diagnostic tool for describing any company, developed by Peters and Waterman and their colleagues in McKinsey around 1980. Seven elements of an organisation, all beginning with S – strategy, structure, systems, style, skills, staff and shared values – can be used as a checklist. Do the Ss fit well together, or are they inconsistent or unclear? When the Ss fit well together and reinforce each other, the organisation is likely to be moving forward purposefully; where the Ss are in conflict, it is likely to lack unity and momentum. The Seven Ss are shown in Illustration 4.33.

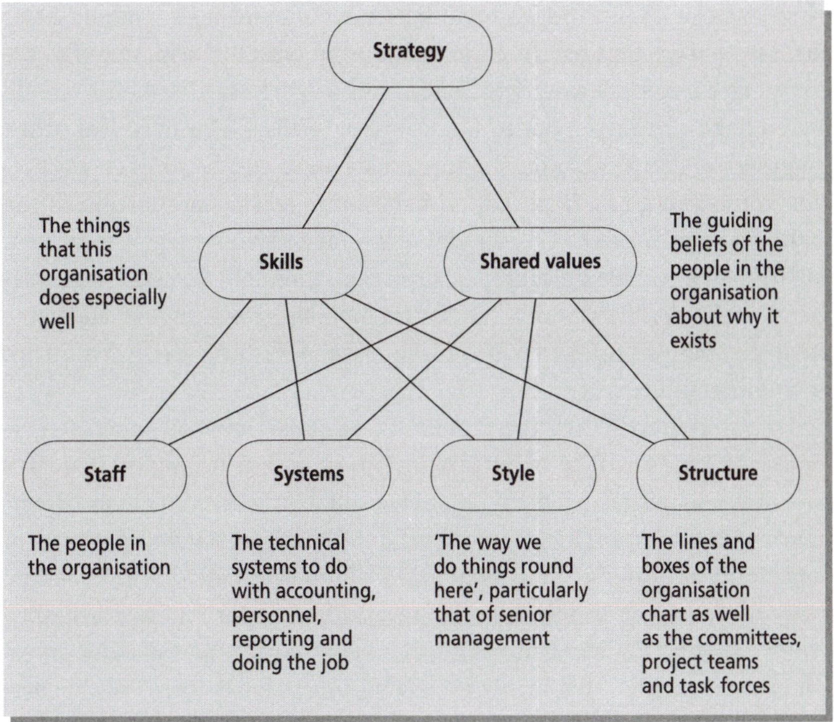

ILLUSTRATION 4.33 ◆ The Seven Ss

Note, however, that an organisation with seven consistent Ss will be much harder to change than one where the Ss are visibly in disarray.

SHAMROCK, SHAMROCK ORGANISATION

A form of organisation described by Charles HANDY using the Irish national emblem, a three-leaved clover. According to Handy, today's organisation is increasingly like a shamrock, made up of three distinct but interlocking parts. The first leaf represents the CORE WORKERS or professional core, the people who hold the knowledge of the organisation and are essential to its success. The core must be looked after and treated as partners, but this is expensive, so the answer is to have a much more selective and smaller core, and rely increasingly for less essential input on the other two 'leaves' of the shamrock. The second leaf is the contractual fringe: specialists outside the organisation who are experts in a particular part of the work and have a close relationship with the firm, but who are not on its payroll. All work which need not be performed in-house should therefore be contracted out to lower cost specialists. The third leaf of the shamrock is the flexible labour force, part-time and temporary workers who come and go as required, and are an increasing proportion of the total. Many of this third group will not want full-time employment, and will be young, female or 'retired'. The organisation may invest in some elements of the flexible labour force, for example by giving training and some privileges, but this third tranche of labour will never have the commitment or ambition of the core.

Handy believes that the shamrock organisation has increased, is increasing, and ought to be further increased, with a realisation that each part of the shamrock needs to be treated differently. Eventually the dominance of the shamrock organisation could change accepted patterns of behaviour, abolishing traditional views about work and career, leading many more people to take a portfolio of different sorts of work, significantly reducing the incidence of wasteful commuting, and making only a minority of people – the highly motivated professional core – really committed to their companies. This last group, however, must truly believe in what the organisation does and be zealots for it.

There is no doubt that this is the wave of the future.

SHAREHOLDER VALUE, SHAREHOLDER WEALTH

Phrase often used to mean what is in shareholders' interests, as in 'create shareholder value'. Often means 'get the share price as high as sustainably possible', and includes a sense of medium and long term value creation rather than short term share price maximisation (or manipulation). Generally not a neutral term: the users tend to imply that the main or exclusive responsibility of top management is to maximise shareholder value rather than worry about the interests of other stakeholders (e.g. customers or employees). Most US firms and many UK ones claim that shareholder value is their main objective; few mean it.

SPINOFF

When a multibusiness corporation splits itself up into two or more new businesses. Spinoff is both the process and the name for a new business spun off from the original one. See BREAKUP and UNBUNDLING OF CONGLOMERATES.

STAR

The most exciting of the four positions on the BCG MATRIX. A star is a business which is the market leader (has the highest relative market share) in a high growth business (generally over ten per cent per annum anticipated volume growth rate in the next three to five years). The star business is immensely valuable if it keeps its leadership position because the market growth will make it much bigger and because it should be very profitable, having higher prices or lower costs than lower market share competitors. The star business may not yet be very cash positive, in fact the usual expectation is that it will be broadly cash neutral, since although it earns a lot of profits it will require reinvestment in new facilities and working capital to continue to grow. But when the market growth slows, if the leadership position has been successfully defended, the business will become a large CASH COW and provide a high proportion of cash for the whole business portfolio.

It is said that there are three policy rules for looking after stars: 'invest, invest and invest.' Almost no investment is too great; whatever the financial projections say, any investment is likely to show an excellent return. The worst possible thing to happen to stars is that they lose their leadership position to someone else's QUESTION MARK (which then becomes the new star, relegating the erstwhile star to the position of a question mark and eventually, as growth slows, a DOG). If leadership is lost, the cash previously invested in building up the (former) star may never be recovered, and for all the glamour the business would have proved a cash trap. Hence the necessity to invest to hold the star's leadership position, and if possible further extend it, so that competitors can never catch up. This may require very rapid growth, perhaps up to 40–50 per cent per annum, which requires skilful management and possibly large amounts of cash.

Star businesses are very rare. But star businesses that are well managed and that keep their leadership positions are even rarer. The Model T Ford was once a star but lost its leadership position, became a question mark and eventually a dog. The Xerox range of photocopiers, Kodak cameras, TI (US) semiconductor chips, Du Pont synthetic fibres, Gestetner office machines, and Hilton hotels are all examples of one-time stars that became dogs, and never yielded the anticipated returns to investors. On the other hand, McDonald's hamburger restaurants, the Sony Walkman, and Coca-Cola are all examples of former stars that held their star status until the market growth slowed, and have since become enormous cash cows and given fantastic returns to shareholders. Filofax is an example of a business that lost its star position in personal organisers (outside the US), but then recovered it again. It is interesting that in all these cases the stock market fortunes of the companies reflected what BCG said would happen, with a time lag. All of these businesses were highly valued by the stock market when they were stars, often on PEs of 50 or over. Those businesses that lost share and ended up as dogs were over-valued and never fulfilled the implied promise; those that held on to leadership amply justified the confidence of investors.

STRATEGIC ALLIANCE

A mutual commitment by two or more independent companies to co-operate for specific commercial objectives, usually because the cost of development is too high for a single company, and/or because the companies have complementary technologies or competencies. A strategic alliance is different from a joint venture in that no legal entity is set up, and the scope of co-operation can be both broader and deeper, despite (or perhaps because of) the absence of tight contractual definitions of the partners' obligations. Strategic alliances can take place between competitors in the same business, as with that of Grundig and Philips to join their video and cordless phone businesses, or between Honda and Rover (but see below); between particular suppliers and their customers (Marks &

Spencer has informal strategic alliances with many of its textile and food suppliers, which date from long before strategic alliances were fashionable, and supplier/customer links are hugely important in Japan: see KEIRETSU); or between different firms that are not competitors but can each use a particular technology in their respective markets, as in the case of the alliance between France Telecom and Deutsche Telecom.

Strategic alliances are already important and will become one of the major global competitive weapons in the twenty-first century, and could conceivably lead to a new form of corporate organisation. But strategic alliances require a long term orientation and appropriate behaviour, the developing and cementing of trust, and above all the will from the top and middle of the partners to make them work. An example of where a strategic alliance fell down was between Honda and Rover, where the alliance had been working extremely well and to enormous benefit for both parties. Then, in early 1994, British Aerospace, the owner of Rover, decided that it wanted to sell its majority stake in Rover (Honda held 20 per cent). Honda was not prepared to buy the whole of Rover, so British Aerospace sold its stake to give control to BMW. Honda executives were furious and could not believe that their trust would be violated in this way; the top brass at British Aerospace were surprised at the reaction, and believed that they had served their shareholders well. Two mutually uncomprehending cultures collided.

Two things are clear: one, that Honda would never have behaved in a comparable way with a strategic partner; and two, that it will be much more difficult in the future for Japanese companies to trust British firms enough to enter strategic alliances with them. Strategic alliances are a passport to success, but the ability to receive passports from Japanese firms may be restricted for British firms.

In the late 1990s, strategic alliances became more important, more numerous, and faster growing than acquisitions. Strategic alliances can bring most of the advantages, and few of the drawbacks, of acquisitions, and at a fraction of the cost.

STRATEGIC DEGREES OF FREEDOM (SDF)

The dimensions along which a strategy can be radically reworked. Kenichi Ohmae insists that the dimensions of product improvement, for example, should not be viewed too narrowly or imitatively. If General Electric has brought out a coffee percolator that makes coffee in ten minutes, its competitors should not aim to bring out one that takes seven minutes. People drink coffee for the taste, but the taste depends most of all on water quality. The strategic degree of freedom here is finding ways to improve the taste via the water quality: and this leads straight to the conclusion that the percolator had to have a de-chlorinating function. See also OHMAE and SEGMENTATION.

STRATEGIC INTENT

The overall medium to long term strategic objective of a company. Like a CAUSE, often expressed in a snappy form, such as Henry Ford's aim in 1909 to 'democratise the automobile', Coke's objective of having its drink 'within arm's length of every consumer in the world', or Honda's desire to 'smash Yamaha'; but strategic intent usually has a timeframe of at least ten years, whereas a cause should be attainable within two to four years.

STRETCH

The fifth of the Ashridge options for the Centre to add value in multibusiness corporations. Here the Centre knows, for example, that a particular type of business can make a return on sales of 10–20 per cent and may spot a company of this type making only 5 per cent. The Centre may therefore acquire the under performing business and then organise the process by which the returns are increased. ABB and Emerson are often quoted as good examples of the Stretch proposition.

The Ashridge school stresses that the Centre should try only one (or at the most two) of its five generic strategies – to try to do a bit of each is a recipe for failure. The Stretch proposition is my favourite – because I have often seen it in action and because it is verifiable: the influence of the Centre is put to the test, and if found wanting, the Corporate Strategy or structure can be changed.

STRETCH AND LEVERAGE

Phrase used by Gary HAMEL. In his terms, it is what 'rule-breakers' – revolutionary new contenders in an industry – have to do. STRETCH is defined as 'misfit between resources and aspirations'. But STRETCH GOALS are not enough; they must be allied to skill in leveraging limited resources, by focus and by doing things differently. See HAMEL in Part Three.

STRETCH GOALS

Goals that are extremely demanding. Can be a useful supplement to normal budgeting and planning procedures. Can also be dangerous if they lead companies to increase expenses in order to reach unattainable goals. Use sparingly, unless you can use 'for free'.

STRONG FOLLOWER

Business that is between 70 per cent and 99 per cent the size of the segment leader. See MARKET CHALLENGER.

SUSTAINABLE GROWTH RATE (SGR)

Concept invented by BCG in the early 1970s to measure and demonstrate the effects of leverage and the proportion of earnings retained on the rate at which a company could grow. The point was that a firm could be constrained from growing (in the absence of new equity) if it had too little debt or retained too low a proportion of its earnings (that is, if dividends were too high a proportion of earnings). Since BCG believed (correctly) that the successful firm should aim to grow market share in its major markets, it tended to use the SGR to urge firms to become high debt, low dividend corporations, channelling as much money as possible back into investment. For the algebraicly inclined, the SGR formula is:

$$\text{SGR} = \text{D/E}\,(R - i)p + Rp$$

where:

D/E = Debt/Equity
R = return on assets, after tax
i = interest rate, after tax
p = percentage of earnings retained.

The SGR is more an interesting curiosity than a useful management tool, except where firms are competing pretty much head to head in a single segment business. The flaw in the thinking is that very few firms are that: there are usually a very large number of businesses and funds for one can come from one or more other businesses, or from the sale of one or more businesses. It is rarely the case that financial policy constrains growth.

SWOT MODEL

The classic Harvard Business School strategy model of a corporation's Strengths, Weaknesses, Opportunities and Threats. See Kenneth ANDREWS in Part Three.

SYNERGY

2 + 2 = 5 (or more) rather than 4, or 3 (negative synergy). Usually used in the context of an acquisition: if there is no synergy expected, it is difficult to justify paying a premium for an acquisition; and even if it is a merger with no premium, why bother unless there is some synergy? There is often a great deal of cynicism about the reality of claimed synergies, and the word is certainly overused, but it is a key concept.

There are really two different types of synergy: (1) structural synergy, where the synergy derives from combining resources to lower costs or raise revenues; and (2) management synergy, where the improvement is due to better management, without structural change. Some people use synergy only in the structural sense. Examples are when two sales forces can be combined, saving costs; or when one company's products can be sold through the other's distribution network, both raising revenues and lowering the unit cost of sales. Structural synergy is clearly greatest where two firms are engaged in the same or adjacent products and markets, but where they have different in-going configurations. It is not unusual to see cost reductions in the order of 15–25 per cent or revenue gains of 20–30 per cent as a result of acquisitions pregnant with such structural synergy.

Management synergy exists when an acquirer runs a company better than the previous management, as when a new financial control system is put in to raise returns, when managers are given greater responsibility and compulsion to meet budgets, when unnecessary costs are cut (without structural synergy), or when non-core businesses are sold to someone else who will pay more than their value to the seller. Management synergy can produce large cost reductions, though more rarely significant revenue increases.

Synergy can also exist independently of acquisitions, for example in joint ventures, in strategic alliances, in closer relationships with suppliers, from realising synergies within an existing group of companies, by getting managers to help each other. Such synergies could be called 'cheap synergies' because they do not involve paying an acquisition premium: they should be looked at before acquisitions. Synergy is any unrealised potential open to a group from a better mixing and matching of resources.

TIME-BASED COMPETITION

Concept invented by BCG which holds that the time it takes a firm to get a product from conception to the customer, or to complete its tasks and provide goods or services to market, can be the key to COMPETITIVE ADVANTAGE. Time is a crucial factor in the internal and external chain of customers and suppliers. At each internal or external customer/supplier interface there is not just a risk but a near-certainty that time will be wasted. And time really is money, as well as being service. The total time taken through the chain – throughput time – not only determines the firm's costs but is a litmus test of the firm's responsiveness to customers. Concentration of time to market therefore kills two birds with one concept: service and cost. If quality is free, reducing the time to market has negative costs as well as customer benefits. Notwithstanding its importance, time-based competition is basically a package of earlier discoveries, and it in turn has been repackaged as just a part of BPR (BUSINESS PROCESS RE-ENGINEERING).

It has been long realised that most of the time taken to make a product or provide a service is generally not 'productive' time but the gaps between different stages of the process. An example is given in the entry on BPR of IBM Credit, which at one time took seven days to process a credit application for a would-be computer buyer, yet the actual work involved took only 90 minutes. By cutting out the gaps and giving responsibility to one person, costs can be cut, customer satisfaction and retention increased, and profits dramatically increased. Another example, this time quoted in the 'bible' of time-based competition (*Competing Against Time: How time-based competition is reshaping global markets*, by George Stalk, Jr. and Thomas M. Hout), is the 'H-Y War' in the early 1980s between Honda and Yamaha. This revolved around the speed with which new motorcycles could be produced. Honda won the war by producing first 60 new motorcycle models in a year, and then another 113 new models in 18 months, speed that Yamaha could not match.

Most organisations, even well run ones like Yamaha, soak up time like a sponge. Stalk and Hout invented the '0.5 to 5 rule', which says that most products are receiving value for between one-half of one per cent and five per cent of the time that they are in the value delivery system of the firm. In other words, more than 95 per cent of the time products spend in their companies is wasted; eliminate the wasted time, and time to market can be increased between 20 and 200 times!

The time to market of a product can be calculated and compared to that of several competitors; the idea behind time-based competition is to become the shortest time-to-market competitor. It is worth stopping to think through the implications for your business.

TIME ELASTICITY OF PROFITABILITY

BCG's term for the relationship between a supplier's profit and the speed with which the product is supplied (the elapsed time between the customer's decision to buy and his receipt of the product or service). Short elapsed time equals high profit; long elapsed time equals low profit. This is because the customer will pay top whack if he can obtain the product at once, but if he has to wait he will shop around and may lower the price he will pay. Customers made to wait may also cancel their orders.

The firm's value-delivery system therefore needs to be changed to speed up time to market. Any extra costs will be more than compensated for by higher prices and greater market share.

TRAFFIC LIGHTS

Andrew Campbell and Robert Park have devised a very useful tool called Traffic Lights to go alongside five insights they have developed about whether firms should try to expand into new areas.

Campbell and Park use their five insights (A to E) to derive four tests (Value Advantage; the Profit Pool; Leadership and Sponsorship; and Impact on Existing Core Business) for any proposed new business. Each test results in a red (negative), yellow (neutral), or green (go) signal. One green signal, as long as there are no red ones, can be enough to approve the idea. Any red signal should stop it. Here's a very brief summary of the Traffic Lights.

Test 1: Value Advantage

Do we have a value advantage?

- *Green*: Significant advantage
- *Yellow*: Small or uncertain advantage
- *Red*: Disadvantage.

Insight A:

Managers rarely consider the tradability of their unique value

In thinking about new businesses to enter, managers correctly consider the unique value that they bring to the new business. For example, the brand may be useful in enhancing acceptance of a new product or may raise the price at which it can be sold.

But managers do not normally consider the tradability of their unique assets when assessing whether to enter a new business. They may be right that an asset such as the brand is useful. But it may be possible to use that asset without entering the new business themselves. They might be able to license the brand to a third party in the new business. If so, they could capture some of the benefit without using their own capital or risking entry to the new business.

Therefore, in assessing whether to enter a new business, only the extra value brought by the company *that cannot be traded* should be taken into account. Since many types of unique value can be licensed or 'cashed' through a joint venture, deducting this from the business case put forward often tips the balance of assessment from positive to negative.

Insight B:

Managers rarely assess the cost of learning a new business

Entering new businesses requires new learning, both for the business unit managers and for the corporate managers at the centre. The more different the new business, the greater the learning required. Yet, because learning costs are hard to quantify, they are usually ignored. As a result, firms often make costly mistakes. In the first few years learning costs are rarely less than 10 per cent of profits and can be more than 50 per cent.

When Shell entered the aluminium business, it encouraged the managers to vertically integrate, a strategy that had worked well in oil – but led to large losses in aluminium.

The Value Advantage is:

- the value of the firm's unique contribution to the new business
- minus the amount of that contribution that could be traded without entering the new business
- minus the unique contribution of competitors
- minus the cost of learning the new business.

Test 2: The Profit Pool

How attractive is the profit pool?

- *Green*: It's a 'rare game'
- *Yellow*: Average (80–90 per cent of cases)
- *Red*: It's a dog

Insight C:

Most market analysis is unnecessary for making a go/no go decision

Managers pay too much attention to the potential of the market they are thinking of entering. Generally, a company will only earn above-average returns, whatever the market, if it has competitive advantage. It is only in exceptional circumstances, perhaps 10–20 per cent of the time, that the market is so bad or good as to make all the difference. The first thing to do, therefore, is work out whether the market is exceptionally good or bad. If it is neither, gathering information about the market doesn't help to make the go/no go decision.

Campbell and Park focus attention on what they call RARE GAMES, those few markets which are so good that almost anyone entering at the right time would be likely to make high returns. The private equity business in the 1960s was a rare game, as was Internet service provision in the 1990s.

Test 3: Leadership and Sponsorship

Do we have strong leaders and the right sponsors?

- *Green*: Clearly superior leaders to the industry average and the right level and type of sponsor at the Centre
- *Yellow*: Team similar to industry average
- *Red*: Leaders less strong than in a competitor and/or sponsor is not the CEO or head of a main division

Insight D:

People are the most important predictor of success – and managers do not pay enough attention to new business leadership issues

Managers in large companies believe that they have plenty of managerial talent or that it can be hired in. But who leads the new business, and to whom it reports to, are critical issues.

People are more important than market opportunities. More than two thirds of Campbell and Park's success stories involved unusually strong management teams. Unless the new team is *markedly and obviously better* than competitors' teams, this is a warning signal.

The person to whom the business reports, at the corporate centre, is even more vital. This person (the sponsor) should:

- *Be a line manager, ideally the group CEO, or head of a division or region*. In Campbell and Park's sample, 90 per cent of the successes reported to the CEO or head of a main division. No other single factor came close in terms of predicting success
- Give the new business resources and support it through setbacks
- Understand and influence the business, challenge and coach its leaders, and share in critical decisions.

Test 4: Impact on Existing Core Business

Would entering the new business be likely to help or hurt the core business?

- *Green*: It would help significantly
- *Yellow*: Neutral
- *Red*: Strong possibility it would hurt the core

Insight E:

Focus on the new project can harm the core business

Managers often underestimate the harm to the core business when attention shifts to a new business and some of the best managers are seconded to it. The cost to existing businesses can be many times the benefit derived from the new business, even when successful.

Between 1999 and 2005, Mercedes slumped from being number 3 in the JD Power ranking of industry reliability to number 28 (out of 37). In 2004 Mercedes' profits slumped 60 per cent. The *Financial Times* said the reason was 'the seconding of many of its engineers to work on Chrysler's problems', following Mercedes' acquisition of Chrysler.

When firms invest in new businesses, executives often start underestimating the growth opportunities in the core business and competitor threats to it.

The probability of serious damage, the research indicated, depends on two factors:

1 the degree to which the base business has serious issues demanding scarce management and cash

2 the extent to which the new business will compete for these scarce resources.

TRANSFORMATION

Changing an organisation's culture and behaviour, so that it ascends to a new level of financial and market performance. Not surprisingly, transformation is difficult: 75 per cent of attempts fail. There do seem, however, to be six conditions which are always present in successful transformations:

1 They are driven by demanding and inspiring leaders, and one person embodies the transformation ethic.

2 The top team (those who really run the company) are emotionally united – they are on the same side and want to help each other personally, as well as the firm.

3 There is a slogan used as a rallying cry – either a medium term cause or a longer term statement of STRATEGIC INTENT.

4 Baronies are absent or destroyed.

5 The change process focuses on real business issues, changing attitudes on the back of commercial success. There are simple performance measures so that everyone knows what is expected.

6 The firm has or builds at least one world class COMPETENCY: a skill where it is as good as or better than any competitor.

TYPE 1, TYPE ONE EXECUTIVE

A very useful typology of people into three types (1, 2 and 3), invented by Harold LEAVITT. Type ones are *Visionaries*: bold, charismatic, original, often eccentric, brilliant and uncompromising, the type of person who offers a clean break with the past and a new heaven and earth. Historical examples include Jesus Christ, Churchill, Garibaldi, Ghandi, Gladstone, Hitler, John F. Kennedy, the Ayatollah Khomeini, Martin Luther King and Margaret Thatcher. Type ones have insights and inspire followers, they follow their instincts, led by heart more than head, and they can see the destination so clearly that they are often impractical about the obstacles *en route*. They can be extremely impractical and bad at getting things done.

Understanding whether you (or close colleagues) are type 1, 2 or 3 can be of practical value, for two reasons. First, you should aim to move your job in the direction where the skills of your particular type can be deployed most fully and effectively. Second, you should aim to team up with and rely on close colleagues who exemplify the two types different from your own in order to provide a balanced ticket and the skills you lack. See also TYPE 2 and TYPE 3.

TYPE 2, TYPE TWO EXECUTIVE

See TYPE 1. Type 2 executives are *Analysts*. They deal with numbers and facts, not opinions; they are rationalists, calculators and controllers. They deal in black and white, not grey: there is always a right answer. The analyst par excellence uses numbers and accounting to control a vast empire – to run a financial control company. Examples include Clement Attlee and Sir Owen Green, Robert Macnamara, [Lord] Arnold Weinstock, Harold Geneen and from further back in history, Pitt the Younger and Sir Robert Peel. Type 2 are great systematisers and control system users. See also TYPE 3.

TYPE 3, TYPE THREE EXECUTIVE

See TYPE 1 and TYPE 2. Type 3 are *Doers*, successful men (and women) of action, implementers, fixers, pragmatists. Generally unencumbered by either vision or analysis, the type 3 leader revels in arm-twisting, lining people up to do his will, leading troops into battle, and all the hurly-burly of business. Historical type threes include Noah, Attila the Hun, Alexander the Great, Julius Caesar, Louis XIV, Napoleon, Bismarck, Lloyd George, Lenin, Stalin, Eisenhower, James Callaghan and Lyndon Johnson. Type 3 need a programme or vision from a type 1 and the calculation of a type 2 as supplements to increase their own effectiveness.

UNBUNDLING

1 When a firm (especially after a takeover) decides to sell off non-core businesses and focus on just one or two core businesses. Sometimes less politely called asset stripping.

2 Process of segmentation whereby customers are offered the chance to buy individual parts or modules of a product, rather than having to buy everything together. For example, investors used to buy a bundled service from stockbrokers, comprising advice and execution; now, execution-only services exist for those who do not need advice. Every supplier should ask whether there is an opportunity or threat from unbundling. See BUSINESS SEGMENT.

UNBUNDLING OF CONGLOMERATES

Expression used mainly in South Africa to mean the same as the American term SPINOFF and the British term DEMERGER. In South Africa, it is generally associated with conglomerates 'unbundling' particular businesses, whereas elsewhere BREAKUP (the generic term) is often associated with non-conglomerate splitting, as for example when Marriott split itself into a hotel operating company and a hotel property-owning company.

UNIVERSAL PRODUCT

One that is sold in the same form throughout the world, like the original ModelT Ford, or Coca-Cola, the Mars bar or the Big Mac, or indeed, the Apple Mac computer. In many ways this is the American dream: a standard product, made up of defined and highly controlled parts (thus the servant of analysis), high quality and low cost, capable of being rolled out around the world for ever. The two keys are the widest possible product appeal, based on the insight that people around the world may be different, but consumers are the same; and standardised manufacture, so that the product can be produced cheaply and to the same standards anywhere around the world. In a way the whole concept of business strategy à la BCG or PORTER is a vision of a Universal Product, batting against the cultural peculiarities of different nations. Note that the idea of a Universal Product could never have originated in France or Germany, and these countries have a poor record in producing Universal Products.

VALUE CHAIN

A firm's co-ordinated set of activities to satisfy customer needs, starting with relationships with suppliers and procurement, going through production, selling and marketing, and delivery to the customer. Each stage of the value chain is linked with the next stage, and looks forward to the customer's needs, and backwards from the customer too. Each link in the value chain must seek COMPETITIVE ADVANTAGE: it must either be lower cost than the corresponding link in competing firms, or add more value by superior quality or differentiated features. The basic idea behind the value chain has been around ever since the concept of value added and COST

STRUCTURES, but was first made explicit by Michael PORTER in 1980. See also COMPETITIVE ADVANTAGE and PORTER.

VALUE DESTRUCTION

When the Centre of a multibusiness corporation destroys value, often in opaque or invisible ways, in the businesses it owns. It is easy to measure the value that a Centre adds to its operating businesses, but more difficult to detect or admit the value destruction. Probably, most multibusiness corporations destroy more value than they add. They should therefore break themselves up. See BREAKUP.

VALUE INNOVATION

The term invented by W. Chan Kim and Renée Mauborgne of INSEAD business school to describe the creation of a new ECOSYSTEM by splitting an existing business category into two, focusing on the needs of a subset of customers. Value Innovation, which is also called BLUE OCEAN STRATEGY, is perhaps the most important component of Corporate Strategy and is described in detail in section 5 of Part Two.

VIRTUOUS CIRCLE

The opposite of a DOOM LOOP: when a firm is able to continuously reinforce a strong position. Illustration 4.34 shows how a virtuous circle can operate.

VISION

An inspiring view of what a company could become, a dream about its future shape and success, a picture of a potential future for a firm, a glimpse into its Promised Land. A vision is the long term aspiration of a leader for his or her firm, that can be described to colleagues and that will urge them on through the desert.

The word vision is often used as a synonym for mission, particularly in non-English speaking countries, where 'mission' is difficult to translate. But the two concepts are different. Mission is why a firm exists, its role in life. Vision is a view of what the firm could become, imagining a desired future.

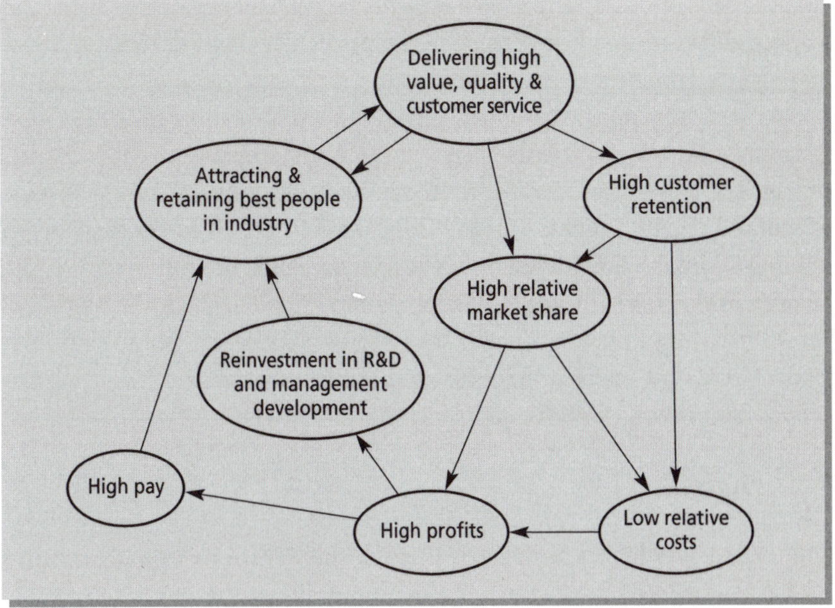

ILLUSTRATION 4.34 ◆ Illustration of a Virtuous Circle

Vision may be thought of as reaching a future goal. A good example of a vision that was fulfilled was President Kennedy's preposterous pledge in 1961 of 'achieving the goal, before this decade is out, of landing a man on the moon and returning him safely to Earth'. An industrial equivalent may be the number 26 in the world league table of drugs companies aiming to reach the top five within the next 5–10 years. Another popular vision is for a regional (say, European) company to become 'truly global', where this is defined as having at least 25 per cent of sales and profits in each triad of the world (North America, Asia and Europe). Or for a small company to become larger than its largest competitor. Or for a derided airline to become 'the world's favourite'.

It was Marvin Bower's vision in the 1940s to think that McKinsey, a small, regional US consultancy, could become a huge firm with offices all around the world and with a reputation for developing professional management. Likewise, it was Henry Ford's vision in 1909 to 'democratise the automobile'. Steve Jobs' vision at Apple was to change work habits by making PCs user friendly to normal executives. The vision at IKEA was to change for ever the structure of the furniture market, become the first and leading global competitor in an industry previously dominated by separate national leaders. And so on.

Many writers imply that a new leader should have a ready-made vision from the start or in the early stages of the transformation process. This is wrong. The best visions evolve from experience during the first five years of a transformation process. In the early stages it is best to concentrate on making a break with the past, developing a cadre of supporters of the change process, modifying values, and obtaining early commercial successes with the new approach. Once real progress has been made, the leader should lift up his or her eyes, and identify the vision.

See also TYPE 1, MISSION and VALUES.

VULNERABILITY

The extent to which a firm faces threats; the degree to which sales and profits may come under attack. Vulnerability is not the opposite of profitability; rather, it is its soft underbelly. Many very profitable firms are highly vulnerable.

Vulnerability exists when any of the following conditions apply:

- When high profitability (measured by ROS or ROCE) co-exists with a poor relative market share position.
- When a firm is more profitable than competitors yet has lower productivity per employee.
- When RMS is being lost to at least one more aggressive competitor.
- When depreciation exceeds new capital investment over a sustained period.
- When the rate of investment in new capacity is lower than that of one or more competitors.
- When expense investment in R&D, marketing and management development is lower than that of competitors.
- When competitors have access to greater cost sharing, shared technological development, a superior supplier network, or better distribution.
- When some of the best people have been leaving, for whatever reasons.

- When it is difficult to recruit the best people in the industry into the firm.
- When the firm is locked into SEGMENT RETREAT, conceding more and more markets and focusing on a narrower customer base.
- When competitors can bring out new products faster.
- When competitors have owners that will accept a lower rate of investment return or lower dividends.

Vulnerability exists, in short, when a business has been HARVESTING its position, preferring short term profits to long term reinvestment, or, conversely, when a competitor has been doing the reverse, investing for the future, to a greater extent. Systematic identification of when companies are vulnerable, or the opposite (what we may perhaps call latent opportunity), is the key to identifying shifts in relative market share and is a leading indicator of future swings in shareholder value. See OPPORTUNITY/VULNERABILITY MATRIX.

ZEUS

One of Charles HANDY's four GODS OF MANAGEMENT. A Zeus culture is a club based around one leader, so that the organisation can best be depicted not as a normal hierarchy (as on a pyramid-like organisation chart) but as a series of lines running into the centre, where the leader (Zeus) sits; or as a web radiating out from this centre. The concentric lines closest to the centre represent the greatest power (apart from Zeus himself); power and influence are measured by the amount of time that Zeus spends with each executive and the regard in which Zeus holds him or her.

The culture is the norm in young, entrepreneurial firms, and also in investment banks, boutiques of all sorts, small and medium-sized brokers, small professional service firms, in politics, sport and the performing arts.

The great advantages of the Zeus culture are:

1 speed of decision taking
2 empathy, trust and emotional commitment ('what would Zeus do in this circumstance?')
3 lean and economical structure and absence of bureaucracy (no memos, committees or corporate politics).

Zeus organisations can be amateur, blinkered, inequitable, cruel and riddled with courtiers rather than good professional managers. But equally, with high quality people, Zeus organisations can exhibit great flair, unleash enormous energy and commitment, and change the world. Microsoft is a Zeus organisation; so too are (or were) The Body Shop (with the more dominant Zeus being female), Egon Zehnder, GEC, Filofax, Hanson, LL Bean, Mars, Maxwell Communications Corporation, McKinsey, Polly Peck and Virgin. Lonrho was a Zeus organisation before Tiny Rowland ceded power to Dieter Beck. Succession is always a major issue.

Zeus organisations flout all the laws of scientific management and most of the classic management principles that we still implicitly believe in. Zeus organisations are the wave of the past but also the wave of the future. See also ATHENA, APOLLO and DIONYSUS.

PART 5

Strategic shifts in the twenty-first century

The impact of increasing returns, networks and the net

During the past quarter century, there has been a cumulative process of important change in the economy and corresponding changes in the nature of competitive advantage. The dynamics of competition have become much richer. Although the rules of strategy have not been overturned, they certainly need to be supplemented.[1]

Four shifts in the economy

The significant changes in the economy itself are:

- the increasing importance of networks
- the Internet and the separation of information flows from physical flows
- the deconstruction of the economy and its value chains into a greater number of separable layers, some of which are 'sweet spots' of much greater value than other layers
- the prominence of 'increasing returns' and 'winner takes most' economics, as opposed to the traditional view that markets and companies are subject to 'diminishing returns'.

Networks

Networks make up an increasingly important part of the economy, and they have their own intense economic characteristics. One phone or fax is no use. Two is of some value. Ten is much more valuable than five times two, because the number of people in the network expands much more than five-fold. In 1980, Bob Metcalfe promulgated his law: the value of a network equals $n \times n$ (*n squared*), where n is the number of people in the network. So a ten-person network is worth 100, but a 20-person network is worth 400: double the membership and you quadruple the value.

Networks have always been an important part of the economy. In the late nineteenth century, for example, the connection of cities by the railway network had an exponential effect in cutting journey times and creating whole new industries such as the mass production and distribution of processed foods. The invention of gas and electricity, and the mass production of cars in the early twentieth century, had similar effects in transforming the economy and society.

Still, the recent development of many networks, including the fax, PC operating systems, the FedEx courier system and, most importantly of all, the Internet, means that networks have become a very important part of the total economy. And networks exhibit the clearest form of 'increasing returns' in the economy, both for all members of the network and for leading suppliers to the network. An expanding network becomes a self-reinforcing virtuous circle, as everyone in the network has an incentive to recruit other users.

One interesting aspect of networks is that monopoly or something approaching it becomes desirable *from the consumers' viewpoint*. Who wants three competing PC operating systems? Who wants different standards?

Also, with networks, openness and proliferation become virtues. In traditional economics, value comes from scarcity and having a proprietary system. With networks, things are turned on their head. Cash machines are more useful if they take as many cards as possible. Open architecture for PC operating systems is the way to enlarge the market. What is lost in the exclusivity of value capture is more than made up in the value creation from dramatically enlarging the network.

Hence Paul Krugman comments:

> ***'In the network economy, supply curves slope down instead of up and demand curves slope up instead of down. The more you have, the more you want. The more we make, the cheaper and easier it becomes to make more. If networks ally with other networks, they become*** **much** ***more valuable.'***

Networks are wonderful. They are deflationary because they lower prices continuously. And they are expansionary because more useful things are created and used much more frequently.

The Internet: separating information flows from physical flows

There is a revolution in the economics of information. Information was the glue that encouraged and supported vertical integration. The cost of rich information used to be very high, and its value very great, if you had a propriety information system and your own assets. Traditionally, information flows and physical flows had to be part of the same system.

No more. Take the case of a retail store – it is both a physical entity, a warehouse taking stock from the manufacturer and supplying it to the shopper, and a source of information: what is on the shelves is what is available. But what amazon.com does, for instance, is to separate the physical flows from the information flows. Amazon originally provided the latter without having to get involved with the former. In doing so, it could have infinite stock with zero inventory. It could perform the Houdini miracle: escape the inescapable tradeoff between cost and choice.

Wherever the Internet can be used to do business, wherever physical flows can be separated from information flows, wherever customer choice can be maximised by a supplier at no cost to that supplier, whenever these things happen, vertical integration becomes unnecessary. More than that, it becomes undesirable. One supplier is able to create the most value in the system, while avoiding the expense of owning the rest of the value chain. Great for that supplier and for the consumer. Less so for everyone else.

Deconstruction of the value chain and emergence of 'sweet spots'

This follows from the separation of physical flows from information flows. Many more self-contained segments are formed at different levels of the value chain – what BCG calls 'layers' of the chain. Whether the different layers contain integrated or non-integrated competitors, the key arena within which competition takes place is each specific layer.

Book retailing via the net becomes a separate layer, as does the holding of inventory and its physical distribution. The 'integrated' book store business really becomes two businesses: the shop front and information bulletin board to customers, and the holding of inventory. In the first business it is competing against amazon, and in the second business it is competing against wholesalers and distributors.

What is particularly important is that *some layers of the value chain become much more valuable than others*. Some layers are very scale sensitive – market share has tremendous value, and the value of dominance in these 'sweet spots' is extraordinarily high – while other layers are naturally fragmented and it is difficult for anyone to make high profits there. BCG calls those who control the sweet spots the 'orchestrators' of the value chain. The new battle for competitive advantage in these sorts of 'deconstructed' markets is the battle to the orchestrator rather than the orchestrated. Successful orchestrators use their customer contacts, brands, technology or other key assets and skills to appropriate most of the value in the chain, while keeping their own operations and capital base to a small part of the chain. Successful orchestrators can therefore earn high returns on capital, while the orchestrated can't.

Nike, Hewlett-Packard and Sara Lee are all trying to leverage their brands to orchestrate their value chains. Nike manages to dominate the trainer (athletic shoe) market; directly, it just designs and markets, which are not capital intensive activities, while controlling an offshore network of low-cost suppliers which it does not own. Dell Computer dominates the supply of PCs to businesses; Dell is a direct retailer but also the orchestrator of a fragmented supply chain of made-to-order PCs.

The classic example of dominating a key business layer is the example of Microsoft in PC operating systems. In 1980, IBM gave Microsoft an exclusive deal to write the software for the IBM PC. Once DOS (Microsoft's operating system) and IBM had established a clear lead, it was bound to go further ahead because of the cost to switch between systems (this is the network effect). But the 'open architecture' adopted to increase the network size meant that Microsoft benefited far more than IBM – when IBM clones are sold, IBM derives no benefit but Microsoft does. Microsoft is creaming off a huge amount of the value in the whole chain, despite having costs associated with only one part of the chain.

The existence of common standards in software creates a big market, leading to more investment by software application engineers, and by the makers of the chips that go in the PCs. As a result, Windows has indirectly but dramatically reduced the cost of the PCs themselves. Microsoft's near-monopoly of the PC cost structure – in which Windows is only about 2 per cent – makes the production of PCs – comprising about 75 per cent of the cost structure – fiercely competitive. The result is that the market expands even more. Great for the consumer, great for Microsoft, and not so great for IBM and its competitors. Yet IBM propelled Microsoft to its pre-eminent position in what has become the sweet spot of the value chain!

Increasing returns and 'winner takes most' economics

Both the existence of networks and of sweet spots within value chains means that returns for the leading competitor in the sweet spots can be extremely high – and increasing! Even where there are no networks or sweet spots in the value chain, returns may increase dramatically where there are high up-front costs, especially in R&D rather than production. (This was also true in the case of Microsoft. The first Windows sold cost $50m to make; the second, just three dollars!) The same is true when 'customer groove-in' and the barriers to switching from one supplier to another are important: again, this is true for most software, and for the majority of other high-tech products sold to ordinary consumers.

Whereas some economists claim that 'increasing returns' are a new phenomenon – they would say that, because micro-economics is predicated on diminishing returns – experience in business suggests that returns have generally always increased with market share. As BCG stressed back in the 1960s and 1970s, the value of a business is maximised not by restricting supply and taking high prices but by gaining the long term advantages of high market share: lower costs than competitors. In the BCG model, which reflects the real world much better than the opposite classical micro-economists' model, returns for the leading competitor *must* increase if margins increase or capital can be used more intensively by the leading competitor; in other words, if there are any significant scale effects.

The economists touting increasing returns talk about the 'new economy'. This is misleading. The new economy is really just the old economy in a more intensified form. But the new economy – of networks (especially the Internet), deconstructed value chains, sweet spots within value chains, and increasing returns, especially for dominant competitors who can orchestrate a whole value chain from a small part of it, and/or who can take possession of information flows while leaving physical flows to others – somewhat redefines what constitutes competitive advantage.

Changes in the nature of competitive advantage

Of greatest importance are:

- the identification of sweet spots in the value chain
- the race to establish dominance in a sweet spot
- the establishment of dominant standards
- the development of skills in orchestration
- the struggle with rival orchestrators
- the struggle with the orchestrated
- increased danger that competitive advantage is temporary
- the need to find the next frontier of customer value creation
- the emergence of a new type of player: the 'navigator'.

Identification of sweet spots in the value chain

Sweet spots have the following characteristics:

- They have the greatest value to customers, and especially, in fast moving consumer goods, to the end-consumer.
- They benefit from network effects to a greater extent than other parts of the value chain.
- Competitors in this layer must be few in number and/or suffer some kind of competitive advantage, or be capable of being relegated to an inferior competitive position – their brands, technology, reputation, service, financial muscle or other key factors for success in the layer must be inferior.
- They are good positions from which to orchestrate others: there are many competing players in the other layers of the value chain, eager for business and with relatively poor bargaining power.

Clearly, you have an advantage if others don't recognise the sweet spots. But if they do, it's a race. If you don't have the resources to win the race alone, form an alliance with the firm which can do most to propel you to the sweet spot, even if you have to give up some of the value to that firm.

Establish dominant standards

This is a means to dominating the sweet spot. As Todd Hixon of BCG puts it:[2]

> ***'Today, failure to compete means not so much a failure to drive costs and prices down as a failure to unlock customer value. Doing so is less a race for cost advantage than a race to establish a dominant standard in an emerging layer business with winner-takes-all dynamics.'***

Developing orchestration skills

Orchestration is difficult. It requires skills in managing across the boundaries of your company, using leverage assuredly but without the control mechanisms possible within the corporation. And as Lenin said, a chain is as strong as its weakest link. The chances are that your corporation has never before attempted such complex orchestration, so you have to learn to do it as you go along. Make too many mistakes along the way, and your brand and reputation may become irretrievably tarnished.

On the other hand, no firm likes being orchestrated. Sometimes, the orchestrated bite back. The best example is Microsoft which, remember, started off being orchestrated by IBM when it first outsourced its PC operating system software design to Microsoft. Later, the balance of power shifted decisively because Microsoft's market size and value increased faster than IBM's. This, in turn,was because IBM committed to open architecture without thinking through how the balance of power in the industry might evolve.

The orchestrated can only fight back if they have special skills and potential scale in their own layer that are denied to others in the layer. Keep the orchestrated down by fragmenting your supply base and cross-fertilising quickly any special skills developed by any individual supplier.

The struggle with rival orchestrators

The bane of orchestrators' lives is imitation. Orchestrators need a supplier base and they specify exact standards. So before long, a whole industry exists where supply is standardised and transparent. The suppliers can therefore offer their services to rival orchestrators.

Nike faces this problem. There are imitators, rival brands and excess supply of product. It's not apparent that Nike has an answer to imitation – although it still has high profits, its growth has stalled.

Competitive advantage may become more temporary

This follows from the desire of rival orchestrators to share the sweet spot and from the desire of the orchestrated to escape their lot. If the battle shifts from low cost position to the need to establish dominant standards, you may be sure that others will be trying to find the *next standard* that will hand them dominance. A low cost position is usually easier for the leader to defend than a dominant standard which can be changed by ingenuity in delivering extra value to the customers – and the arena in which this is found may be quite different from the arena dominated by the current leader.

Microsoft cannot rest on its laurels. Netscape and its collaborators are promoting '*network computing*', in which *any* PC operating system (including Windows) becomes subordinated to a new high-value strategic layer controlled by a Java-enabled browser. There are many other attempts to find the next sweet spot in the computing value chain, any of which, if successful, could undermine Microsoft's position and profits without in any way challenging its dominance of the current sweet spot.

It follows that competitive advantage in sweet spots, though hugely valuable, may be temporary. The only true defence for the leader is to find the next standard before anyone else does, or else to take extraordinary steps to overtake an incipient leader while the new standard is still emerging.

Finding the next frontier of customer value

This becomes the only true defence of a dominant position. The new value layer must be incorporated into the system and standard that is currently dominant. This is why Microsoft scrambled to incorporate browser technology into its operating system, risking the ire of the anti-trust authorities, but managing to head off this particular challenge from Netscape. Now Microsoft has to worry about the *subsequent* new frontiers. There is no rest for the dominant.

The emergence of the 'navigator'

BCG has defined navigation as 'the activities shaping how customers search, compare, and decide what to buy'. A navigator is a firm that positions itself as the customer's friend in improving her choice and information. Schwab OneSource gives data on the performance and charges of more than 3,000 mutual funds. Chemdex lists and evaluates the specialty chemicals from more than 100 suppliers for the benefit of industrial users.

Earlier navigators included retail outlets of all kinds, especially those which championed the interests of consumers and provided wide choice and low prices. Today, most new navigators use the Internet.

Navigators appropriate a chunk of industry value added and are thus a threat to suppliers, increasing the power of customers at the expense of suppliers. Navigators hog space between the supplier and the customer, often purloining valuable information in the process, and decrease the information value of suppliers' brands, perhaps even substituting their own.

Being a leading navigator, especially where there is plenty of value added to appropriate, is a great idea. But for suppliers, the best counter to new navigators is to provide the navigation tool oneself, or to provide extra value to customers that the navigator cannot match. This process may involve the supplier 'deconstructing' its own channels – removing the intermediaries between itself and customers, wherever feasible – before anyone else gets the chance to do so.

Conclusion

The number and diversity of competitive segments is increasing. More layers now comprise discrete competitive systems in their own right, rather than being part of a wider, integrated competitive system. Competitive advantage in each segment and each layer used to be desirable; now it is essential.

Dominance still offers very high profits, higher, in fact, than ever. But the part of the value chain that a firm dominates has become much more vital. A small part of the value chain may offer the lion's share of total profits. And the majority of those returns may go to just one dominant player.

The price of extraordinary returns is eternal innovation. The sweetest spot in the value chain may keep changing. Only the most nimble competitor – the one who sets the standards that are most attractive to the customer, and then sets the next key standard, and the one after that – will be able to maintain competitive advantage and the bonanza it brings. There will always be hope for innovators, however tenuous their position. But most innovations will end up trapping talent and cash.

As always, the winners will be those with the best products, the best services, the greatest appeal to customers – and the best strategies. The essentials of strategy have become a little richer and even more exciting than they used to be. But they are still pretty simple. That's just as well, because the other ingredients of success look more demanding than ever.

Notes

Part 2: The joy of Corporate Strategy

Note 1

Throughout Part Two, I use 'product' to mean 'product and/or service'.

Note 2

See the entry on Porter in Part Three.

Note 3

See the entries on HAMEL and PRAHALAD in Part Three, and on CORE COMPETENCE in Part Four.

Note 4

Michel Robert (1993) *Strategy Pure and Simple: How Winning CEOs Outthink Their Competition*, McGraw Hill, New York.

Note 5

In speaking of 'ecosystems' I am following Peter Johnson. An 'ecosystem' is a business segment as defined in Part One, but 'ecosystem' captures the living, human and dynamic qualities much better than 'segment'. The ecosystem is organic, comprising customers whose needs, views of the firm, and bargaining power vary from time to time and from place to place. The firm serving the ecosystem, and the firm's competitors, are comprised of people, who influence the ecosystem and are influenced by it.

Note 6

R. H. MacArthur (1958) 'Popular ecology of some warblers of northeastern coniferous forests', *Ecology* 39, pp. 599–619.

Note 7

Philip Selznick (1957) *Leadership in Administration*, Harper and Row, New York, pp. 135–9.

Note 8

Note that single-status firms often describe themselves as egalitarian, yet can also be hierarchical and have highly differential rewards for employees. The Mars companies are cases in point.

Note 9

These trends were identified presciently in Michael Goold and Andrew Campbell (1987) *Strategies and Styles: The Role of the Centre in Managing Diversified Corporations*, Basil Blackwell, Oxford.

Note 10

This thought is derived from Parenting theory – see section 'Become the best possible parent' on pages 121–5.

Note 11

Chris Zook and James Allen (2001) *Profit from the Core*, Harvard Business School Press, Cambridge, MA.

Note 12

See the entry on PORTER's Five Competitive Forces in Part Four.

Note 13

Michael Goold, Andrew Campbell and Marcus Alexander (1994) *Corporate-Level Strategy: Creating Value in the Mulitbusiness Company*, John Wiley, New York.

Note 14

This section draws heavily on the excellent new book: Andrew Campbell and Robert Park (2005) *The Growth Gamble: When Leaders Should Bet Big on New Businesses and How to Avoid Expensive Failures*, Nicholas Brealey, London.

Note 15

The different brands had widely different prices, of course, because they were positioned above and below each other in terms of quality and purse, but each division followed the same cost-plus formula to arrive at their prices. This prevented any division from pursuing an 'experience curve' strategy of bringing down costs and compounding volume, which would have benefited customers and shareholders alike.

Note 16

Michael E. Porter (1987) 'Competitive Advantage to Corporate Strategy', *Harvard Business Review*, May–June, pp. 43–59.

Note 17

See David Sadtler, Andrew Campbell and Richard Koch (1998) *Breakup! When Large Companies Are Worth More Dead Than Alive*, Capstone, Oxford.

Note 18

It is too early to tell whether this will be the case. I say it 'should' be purely on the basis of the economic value destroyed by MBCs. But, just as we have known for more than a decade that most big-company mergers and acquisitions destroy value, yet the M&A market continues pretty much unabated, so too it may be that MBCs persist for the simple reason that the executives who control them prefer it that way. Top managers prefer to run very big companies rather than very profitable ones.

Note 19

In 1979, the *Fortune 500* companies accounted for almost 60 per cent of US GNP. Within 12 years, this proportion had plummeted to 40 per cent – almost a third down.

Note 20

See W. Chan Kim and Renée Mauborgne (1997) 'Value Innovation: the strategic logic of high growth', *Harvard Business Review*, January–February, pp. 103–12, and their new book, *Blue Ocean Strategy: How to Create Uncontested Market Space and Make the Competition Irrelevant* (2005), Harvard Business School Press, Boston. Both are excellent and well worth reading. The account of value innovation given above is my own, but it rests heavily on their concepts.

Note 21

Al and Laura Ries (2004) *The Origin of Brands: Discover the Natural Laws of Product Innovation and Business Survival*, HarperCollins, New York.

Note 22

See the essays on SEGMENTATION and SEGMENT RETREAT in Part Four.

Part 3: Strategic thinkers

Note 1

Andrew Campbell and Robert Park (2005) *The Growth Gamble*, Nicholas Brealey, London.

Note 2

Gary Hamel (2000) *Leading the Revolution*, Harvard Business School Press, Boston.

Note 3

Charles Handy (2001) *The Elephant and the Flea: Looking Backwards to the Future*, Hutchinson, London.

Note 4

Richard Koch (1997) *The 80/20 Principle: The Secret of Achieving More With Less*, Nicholas Brealey, London/Currency Doubleday, New York.

Note 5

Frederick F. Reichheld (1996) *The Loyalty Effect: The Hidden Force Behind Growth, Profits, and Lasting Value*, Harvard Business School Press, Boston.

Note 6

Al Ries and Laura Ries (2004) *The Origin of Brands: Discover the Natural Laws of Product Innovation and Business Survival*, HarperBusiness, New York.

Note 7

Chris Zook and James Allen (2001) *Profit from the Core: Growth Strategy in an Era of Turbulence*, Harvard Business School Press, Boston.

Note 8

Chris Zook (2003) *Beyond the Core: Expand Your Markets Without Abandoning Your Roots*, Harvard Business School Press, Boston.

Part 5: Strategic shifts

Note 1

As always, the Boston Consulting Group is on top of the change. The account that follows incorporates some of the points made by BCG in an excellent series of *Perspectives* on the subject of what it calls 'the Deconstruction of Value Chains'.

Note 2

Todd Hixon (1999) *Failure to Compete – Revisited*, The Boston Consulting Group, Boston.

Index